VOICES
FROM THE
CAMPS

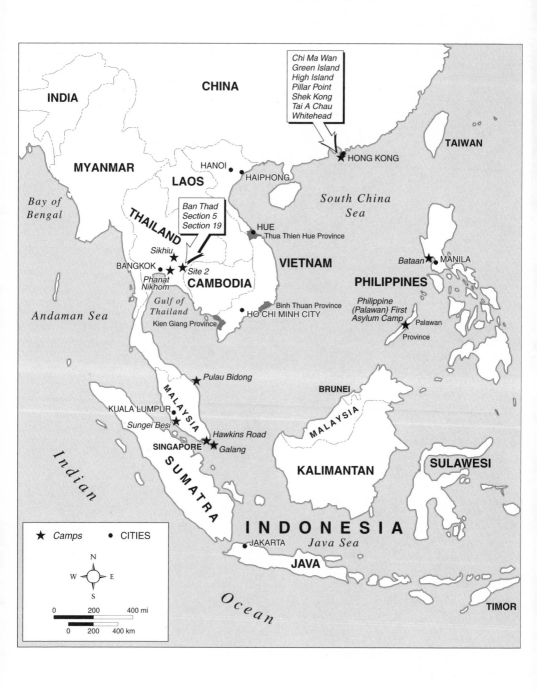

CHINA

INDIA

Chi Ma Wan
Green Island
High Island
Pillar Point
Shek Kong
Tai A Chau
Whitehead

TAIWAN

MYANMAR

HANOI
HAIPHONG

LAOS

★ HONG KONG

Bay of
Bengal

THAILAND

Ban Thad
Section 5
Section 19

South China
Sea

Sikhiu ★

HUE
Thua Thien Hue Province

BANGKOK ★ ★

VIETNAM

Bataan ★ MANILA

★ Site 2

Phanat
Nikhom

CAMBODIA

PHILIPPINES

Andaman Sea

Gulf of
Thailand

Binh Thuan Province

Kien Giang Province

HO CHI MINH CITY

Philippine
(Palawan) First
Asylum Camp

★ Palawan
Province

★ Pulau Bidong

MALAYSIA

BRUNEI

KUALA LUMPUR ★

MALAYSIA

Sungei Besi

Hawkins Road

SINGAPORE ★ ★ Galang

KALIMANTAN

SULAWESI

Indian

SUMATRA

I N D O N E S I A

★ Camps   • CITIES

N
W ✦ E
S

0   200   400 mi

0   200   400 km

JAKARTA

Java Sea

JAVA

O c e a n

TIMOR

James M. Freeman and Nguyễn Đình Hữu

VOICES
FROM THE
CAMPS

VIETNAMESE CHILDREN SEEKING ASYLUM

University of Washington Press
Seattle and London

This publication was supported in part by the
Donald R. Ellegood International Publications Endowment.

Cataloging-in-Publication Data

Freeman, James M.
Voices from the camps : Vietnamese children seeking asylum /
James M. Freeman and Nguyen Dinh Huu.
p.   cm.
Includes bibliographical references and index.
ISBN 0-295-98313-2 (alk. paper)
1. Refugee children—Vietnam.   I. Nguyen, Dinh Huu.   II. Title
HV640.5. V5F74   2003
325'.2597'082—dc21   2003040227

The protection and welfare of children seeking asylum should be the first priority of those persons and agencies entrusted with their care.

CONTENTS

PREFACE

THEY ARE GAUNT, UNDERSIZED, and ragged. Their responses to questions range from open defiance to words spoken softly while bowing their heads and averting their eyes. Some have been shattered by the experiences they have endured, others distrust and openly resist authority, while still others vainly hope for a miracle that will rescue them from their present hell. Their views of the events and people affecting them are often partial and distorted. These are the voices of unaccompanied children who fled Vietnam. This book describes their treatment in first asylum camps and what happened to them when they were resettled in the United States or repatriated to Vietnam.

Different countries refer to these first asylum camps in a variety of ways, such as refugee camp, detention center, and first asylum center. At various times, these camps have housed people seeking refugee status, denied refugee status, or given refugee status.

When we began our project, our intention was to provide assistance and advocate for Vietnamese unaccompanied minors in detention camps in Hong Kong and Southeast Asia. The book that finally developed is the result of a collaborative effort between a social worker and an anthropologist. Nguyen Dinh Huu, who came to the United States in 1975 as a refugee, is a U.S.-educated social worker with a specialty in child welfare and protection. He has spent many years providing direct services to children in America, including Vietnamese-American unaccompanied minors needing foster care. James M. Freeman has spent many years as a professor of anthropology and has published two books about Vietnamese refugees.

In the early 1980s, we collected the life histories of Vietnamese refugees. The resulting publication, *Hearts of Sorrow: Vietnamese-American Lives*, conveyed the actual experiences of a people from their own points of view.[1] In 1983–1984, we teamed up to run a federally funded English-language and job-training program for Highland Laotian refugees in Santa Clara County, California. The program was both practical and culturally sensitive. We administered that program as unpaid volunteers while we continued in our regular social services and university employment.[2]

In the middle 1980s, Vietnamese unaccompanied minors coming from refugee camps to the United States were woefully unprepared to cope with life in America. This contrasted sharply with earlier arrivals from these camps. In 1987, Nguyen visited several Southeast Asian refugee camps to observe the living conditions of the unaccompanied minors. He found situations of extreme neglect and abuse. When he returned, he informed Freeman of the terrible conditions and the two of us founded a nonprofit organization of unpaid volunteers called Aid to Refugee Children Without Parents, Inc. (now Aid to Children Without Parents).

Between 1987 and 1995, we visited eighteen camps that housed Vietnamese people in Southeast Asia and Hong Kong (every camp then in existence in Southeast Asia and 75 percent of the Hong Kong camps). Over 62,000 people were in these camps; about half of them were children, and over 5,000 were unaccompanied minors. Each year, one or both of us, and other members of our organization, visited the camps at our own expense. We raised funds from a variety of sources, including private donations, concerts, and Vietnamese students associations in high schools and colleges throughout the United States. For over a decade, Vietnamese students at the University of California, Davis, sponsored an annual bike-athon and donated a large portion of their proceeds to our organization. With these funds, we provided assistance to the unaccompanied minors in the camps and collected information on their needs and how we could best help them. Our activities included financing education (books, supplies, and salaries of teachers), building schools, building a bread-baking facility, and financing Christmas, Mid-Autumn Festival, and Vietnamese New Year (Tet) celebrations, and other cultural activities. We did not seek funding from government or international organizations, since we did not wish to be dependent on them.

The people who joined our organization were idealistic students and young professionals, mostly Vietnamese Americans, who were willing to donate time, energy, and often money to help the children. Seven volunteers spent a year each in Philippine First Asylum Camp (PFAC), Palawan, which housed about 9,000 people. Our volunteers provided counseling and educational services for the children. Another three volunteers provided similar services in Vietnam.

Because we returned several times to the same camps, we were able to build a sense of continuity associated with our visits and assistance. Officials accepted us enough to give us access to every camp we asked to visit. Children, though initially wary, agreed to talk with us, and many came to trust us. We worked cooperatively with many nonprofit agencies and government organizations. Although we were critical of some of their policies and actions, the Office of the United Nations High Commissioner for Refugees (UNHCR) invited our organization to visit Vietnam in 1991 to assess the situation of repatriated unaccompanied minors, and in 1995 we extended our assistance to these children in Vietnam, financing a children's shelter in Hue, along with educational services and work training. We were concerned that the children would continue to need assistance for a few years after they returned, and we vowed to help them. UNHCR in Hong Kong asked us to keep them informed about our project helping repatriated children in central Vietnam, and we did so. In 1996, the Philippines let Vietnamese asylum seekers remain indefinitely in their country, though without permanent resident status (by 2002, their legal status was unchanged). Our organization coordinated fund-raising in Northern California, collecting over $336,000 to contribute to the construction of the "Viet Village," a Vietnamese community in Puerto Princesa City, Palawan, the Philippines. We ran Aid to Children Without Parents until 1999, when we felt we had completed our mission. In that year, central Vietnam was hit by the worst floods in 500 years. We founded another nonprofit organization, Friends of Hue Foundation, and opened an office in Hue to provide long-term assistance to the victims of this natural disaster and other impoverished families. We turned over the administration of Aid to Children Without Parents to other volunteers.

Although we have academic and professional backgrounds, we approached the writing of this book less as scholars formulating a distant theoretical problem than as persons involved first-hand with the practical concern of protecting children who were being neglected and harmed. The methods of data collection, the topics we cover, and the expertise we draw on flow from that concern. In the Southeast Asian and Hong Kong camps, we found that unaccompanied minors needed protection but little or none was given. Camp guards and adult detainees abused the children physically and sexually. Officials removed children from their own adult relatives and put them in foster care or group living situations. In some camps, officials abruptly moved detainees to other camps or camp areas, disrupting their daily routines. During the later years of the camps, under the recommendation of UNHCR, camp officials closed many of the educational facilities and reduced food rations. Both UNHCR and officials in most countries of first asylum intended to make life in the camps so unpleasant that detainees recommended for repatriation would have "no feeling of permanence" and would decide instead to return to their homeland.

Drawing on our fields of expertise, we set about to call attention to and correct these situations in a practical and feasible manner. We emphasized the context in which events occur, the varieties of Vietnamese cultural patterns, children's alternatives to official points of view, and a comparative outlook. This enabled us to see past the rationalizations bureaucrats used (their actions are in the best interests of the child) to justify their often harmful decisions regarding the treatment of unaccompanied minors, and to suggest alternatives to conventional official views. We wrote this book to show what went wrong and what steps could be taken to ensure that it never happens again.

The critical stance of this book is a result of interviews with more than 200 unaccompanied minors in the camps, in the United States, and in Vietnam. In the camps, we collected their life stories, to hear their concerns in their own words so that we could help them and advocate for their protection. Our primary aim was to discover gaps in the treatment and protection of the children and then to correct these. For example, in Malaysia's Sungei Besi Camp, authorities withdrew funding of schooling to discourage children from remaining in the camp and to encourage them to return to Vietnam. We felt that this was harmful to the children, so we helped to keep the school open; we conducted our interviews while providing this assistance. We sought leads to find those children who were the most vulnerable. The children knew of our organization and its activities, and many of them approached us to tell their stories. They would recommend other children who they knew were experiencing difficulties. Many of those who sought us out were boys. Female social workers helped us to locate and interview girls in addition to those who initially volunteered. We interviewed and observed the activities of unaccompanied minors for periods from a couple of hours to several days in a variety of settings, including dwellings, schoolrooms, offices, health clinics, and jails. Some of these children kept in touch with us by mail, either directly or through the assistance of adults in the camp.

When we collected life narratives of children in the refugee camps, the children often spoke not in a linear, chronological fashion, but helter-skelter, jumbling dates, events, and thoughts. The narratives in their original form are difficult to follow, sometimes confused and contradictory, and often elliptical. Yet the children spoke to us in ways that were more formal than they would if they were speaking among themselves.

These interviews were conducted under less than ideal conditions. The refugee camps were basically prison camps. Our interviews had to be hurried to ensure that we would be able to collect basic information in limited time. We used a set of interview questions, to which the children responded. This affected their responses and probably limited variation in their accounts. Many of the children had been traumatized or were desperately lonely and frightened. Some told their stories in a flat, unemotional way; others burst into tears. Because we were outsiders, the children were initially very cautious in their responses. They did not know if what they said would affect their chances of being resettled. For some of these children, we were among the first outsiders they had spoken with, and they often did not know how to respond. They had no familiarity with telling their life stories or even knowing what a life story meant. At the same time, by living in the camps, the children had learned some stock phrases that camp detainees had told them people wanted to hear, for instance, that they had escaped Vietnam to get a better life, and that they were fleeing Communism. In summary, these were traumatized, frightened, and depressed children who did not know what was going to happen to them next, and their narratives reflect both uncertainty and the disarray of their lives.

Because this is not a linguistic text, we do not present the narratives verbatim. To make sense of them, we have arranged events of the narratives in chronological order and emphasize the central concerns that the children express. While not literary, their stories are affecting and sad. They are also a testimony to the human spirit, to endurance, hope, and dreams in the face of insurmountable odds.

We also interviewed dozens of adult refugees, camp officials, international relief organization workers, UNHCR officials, and officials of the countries in which the children were detained. Frequently, people who worked directly with the children would call our attention to problems in the treatment of children that otherwise we might have missed. For example, in the Thai camp of Sikhiu, a camp social worker, also a detainee, introduced us to a girl whose assistance from an international organization was about to cease. Her story appears in this book.

Between 1991 and 2000, we visited Vietnam (Nguyen nine times and Freeman three times) to examine the situation of repatriated unaccompanied minors and, as previously mentioned, starting in 1995 we provided direct assistance to children in central Vietnam. We discuss our activities in our chapter on interventions. Here, too, our interviews and observations were guided by our practical concerns in providing help to especially vulnerable returnees. While we focused our assistance on one particularly neglected region of Vietnam, our interviews of returnees included children from Haiphong in the north to those in the Mekong Delta in the south.

Our focus is on children without families. Although conditions in refugee and detention camps have received some attention, the narratives of children in these camps have not been widely publicized, and they differ significantly from official descriptions of refugee policies and programs. For one thing, the children tell partial and fragmented tales. They are repetitive, often relating similar experiences and concerns although coming from widely scattered camps throughout Southeast Asia. Most important, however, they convey the human impact of political decisions and refugee policies, in personal terms that are absent from official documents and reports.

Our book documents the history of one group of children who sought asylum. Some of these unaccompanied minors from Vietnam were orphans; others saw their parents killed during their flight; still others were separated from their parents or relatives during the escape. While their families remained in Vietnam, thousands of children were sent out alone. They became embroiled in conflicts resulting from historical events, national policies, and international tensions and agreements far removed from their personal experience. In tracing what happened to them, our book raises issues of child development and child abuse, children's rights, humane and intelligent policies for the treatment of children, appropriate interventions, and the development of support systems for children at risk. Much less has been reported about asylum seekers, especially children, who have been denied refugee status and forcibly returned to their homeland. We pay particular attention to this group because their situation has previously been invisible. The narratives of the children from the camps, Vietnam, and the United States are a mirror of the treatment of these children, which we can hold up not only to learn about them, but also about ourselves.

In these pages, Vietnamese children who fled to refugee camps and detention centers describe their own experiences, needs, and hopes. We contrast their views with those of the officials who were responsible for their care. We also ask how the condition of these children compares with those elsewhere who have suffered abuse from refugee flight and camp confinement, or from equivalent experiences. The issues raised by the treatment of the Vietnamese children of the camps apply to many other refugee and non-refugee communities in which children suffer traumatic experiences or abuse. We call attention to children's rights issues that otherwise might be overlooked and discuss ways to protect and improve the treatment of children who are in abusive environments.

To convey how these children have been affected by their flight from Vietnam and their subsequent repatriation or resettlement, this book covers a wide variety of topics. Complex motivations led families to send their children abroad on high-risk escapes, and heart-wrenching responsibilities and decisions were imposed on the children. We raise some of the social and ethical issues related to helping people and intervening in their lives, exploring the impacts of intervention both on the children and on ourselves. We discuss the meaning of childhood in the context of the disrupted lives of refugee children. We call into question conventional notions of family, culture, and group membership that typically are used to determine the fate of children who seek asylum, and we suggest alternatives that more accurately reflect the situation of the children.

The Vietnamese refugee camps are now closed, and all of the detainees have been resettled or repatriated. They constitute a small fraction of people worldwide who seek asylum. Lucia Ann McSpadden observes that the numbers and scope of uprooted people in the world depends on "who is counting and for what purpose." At the end of 1998, nearly 13.5 million people were counted as refugees, but perhaps another 30–35 million were internally displaced persons in refugee-like situations in their own countries.[3] By January 2001, UNHCR estimated that the number of persons of concern who fell under their mandate was 21,793,300.[4] In most refugee movements, at least half of those who seek asylum are children.

Of the unaccompanied minors who fled Vietnam since 1975, many are now in the United States, thousands deeply traumatized by their transit and detention camp experiences. Some of their voices appear in this book. While the events that create refugees and refugee camps vary widely in different countries, those who are the most vulnerable and deeply affected by war and social disruption are children, the victims of policies and decisions made by adults over which the children have no control. Repatriation, resettlement, and the widespread abuse of refugee children occur worldwide. Many countries and international agencies are concerned about the long-term effects of the abuse and neglect of children, including refugees, and they are seeking ways to improve their situation. In the United States, a growing issue is how to assist abused children who represent a diversity of cultural backgrounds and experiences.

It is easy to criticize the efforts of others involved in the care and protection of children seeking asylum. Many critics of the treatment of Vietnamese unaccompanied minors have called attention to discrepancies between principles and practice, failures to anticipate problems, abuse and neglect of detainees, and alleged corruption in the refugee determination process. More difficult is to demonstrate realistic alternatives to current approaches, but they do exist. We discuss some humane, practical, and cost-effective approaches for the protection and care of children at risk. While emphasizing flexibility in the treatment of individual cases, the basis of our approach is to put the protection and care of children first and foremost, rather than as an afterthought of other policies.

ACKNOWLEDGMENTS

WE THANK THE MACKINTOSH Foundation/US Bui Doi Committee, which granted us funds to initiate our project for repatriated unaccompanied minors and other children at risk in Thua Thien Hue, Vietnam. We are grateful to San Jose State University for granting James M. Freeman a sabbatical leave in 1998 to work on this book.

We wish to thank the following organizations and government agencies for their assistance and for granting us access to persons and sites that otherwise we could not have visited. We have been critical of some of these organizations; their magnanimous assistance to us in light of our differences is noteworthy. In 1991, the Office of the United Nations High Commissioner for Refugees (UNHCR) provided initial access for Nguyen Dinh Huu to visit repatriated unaccompanied minors in Vietnam and instructed its missions in Hong Kong, Vietnam, and the other Southeast Asian countries we visited to meet with us. Nordic Assistance to Repatriated Vietnamese (NARV) took us to visit repatriated unaccompanied minors in North and South Vietnam, opened their records for us, and discussed their projects with us at length. The United States Embassy in Bangkok, Thailand, and the U.S. Consulate General in Hong Kong responded to our several queries and allowed us to interview some of their officers concerned with refugee affairs. The Refugee Status Review Board, Hong Kong, granted us an extensive interview with their chairman.

Many other organizations worked with us in our projects and helped us with aspects of this book. We wish to thank Agency for Volunteer Services, Hong Kong; Caritas, Thailand; Catholic Office for Emergency Relief and Refugees, Thailand; Center for Assistance to Displaced Persons, Philippines; Community and Family Service International, Hong Kong and Philippines; International Social Services, Hong Kong Branch; Jesuit Refugee Service, Philippines; Joint

Voluntary Agency, Hong Kong; Red Crescent Society, Malaysia; Refugee Concern, Hong Kong.

The following countries kindly allowed us to visit their refugee and detention camps: Hong Kong, Thailand, Malaysia, Singapore, Indonesia, and the Philippines. We were given access to every camp we asked to visit. The camps are listed below.

We especially wish to thank Vietnamese officials in Vietnam, who allowed us to visit the repatriated minors and to establish a project for their assistance. In Vietnam, we were warmly welcomed and assisted by officials in the following agencies and organizations, listed alphabetically: Committee for Protection and Care of Children, Hanoi and Thua Thien Hue; offices of the Department of Labor, War Invalids, and Social Affairs (DELISA) in Thua Thien Hue and Binh Thuan Provinces; Institute for International Relations/Ministry of Foreign Affairs; Institute of Sociology/National Center for Social Sciences; Ministry of Labor, War Invalids, and Social Affairs (MOLISA); People's Aid Coordination Committee (PACCOM); People's Committee of Thua Thien Hue Province; People's Committee of Hue City; Vietnamese Fund for Children.

In this book, we use the real names of persons who are public figures, or who have identified themselves through their writings. We refer to all other people by their titles (Field Officer, Colonel, etc.), or, in the case of the children or adult narrators, by pseudonyms. We wish to thank the many persons who kindly granted us interviews or helped us in other ways. We list them in alphabetical order. Vietnamese persons are listed in the traditional way with their surnames first unless they use European names. Aziz Ahamed, Daniel Alberman, Ramon Arguelles, Jahanshah Asadi, Pam Baker, Kate Balian, Catherine Bertrand, Frances W. Blackwell, Joseph M. Bracken, Brian J. Bresnihan, Stenn Bronee, Christopher J. Carpenter, Pierre Ceyrac, Craig Clarke, John W. Crowley, Dao Huy Ngoc, Charles N. Darrah, Anne Dawson-Shepherd, J. A. English-Lueck, Peter Hansen, Luke Hardy, Alice Ho, Kathleen G. Howe, Brian Hurlock, Eugenia Janias, Kersten Karlen, Kirstie Laine, Le Van Anh, Veronique LeBlanc, Machiko Kondo, Carole McDonald, Anne McDonnell, Christie McKenzie, Carolyn McLure, Erik Bo Mikkelsen, Dan Miller, Morgan Morris, Irene Mortensen, Jacques Mouchet, Christine Mougne, Nghiem Xuan Tue, Nguyen H. Duyen, Nguyen Nhien, Paul Nguyen, Nguyen Thao, Nguyen Thiet, Naoko Obi, Jon Olson, Guy Ouellet, Adrielle Panares, Pascale Le Thi Triu, Pham Thi Hoa, Imran Riza, Goren Rosen, A. Shaharbi bin Shaari, Tove Skarstein, Sumaryo, Dan Tate, Bounlert Tharachatr, Tran Thi Hoang, Tuong Lai,

Adrie van Gelderen, Vo Van Hieu, Vuong Tuoc, Jane Warburton, Hans Willmann, Stephen Yau, James Yeo.

We also wish to express our gratitude to the unaccompanied minors whom we interviewed. We spoke with asylum seekers and more than 200 children and youths in the following locales: Hong Kong detention centers and transit camp (High Island, Green Island, Shek Kong, Whitehead, Chi Ma Wan, Tai A Chau, Pillar Point); Thailand (Ban Thad, Section 5, Section 19 Vietnamese Land Refugee Platform in Site 2, Sikhiu, Phanat Nikhom); Malaysia (Pulau Bidong, Sungei Besi); Indonesia (Galang); the Philippines (Palawan, Bataan); Singapore (Hawkins Road). In Vietnam, we spoke with unaccompanied minors in Hanoi Transit Center, Haiphong City, Thua Thien Hue Province, Ho Chi Minh City, Binh Thuan Province, and Kien Giang Province. In the United States, we spoke with children in several sites in California.

With the agreement of the University of Washington Press, a portion of Chapter 6 also appears in our chapter, "'Best Interests' and the Repatriation of Vietnamese Unaccompanied Minors," in *Ethnography in Unstable Places,* edited by Carol J. Greenhouse, Elizabeth Mertz, and Kay B. Warren, Duke University Press, 2002. A small section of Chapter 7 first appeared in James M. Freeman's *Changing Identities: Vietnamese Americans 1975–1995,* Allyn & Bacon, 1995, and is used with the permission of the publisher. The narrative of the Vietnamese refugee in Site 2, Thailand, found in Chapter 2, first appeared in our op-ed piece, "The Terror and Tragedy of Dong Rek," *San Jose Mercury News,* Perspective section, September 6, 1992.

Patricia Freeman read several drafts of this book, and we are grateful to her for her careful editing and comments.

VOICES
FROM THE
CAMPS

This boat started the perilous journey from Vietnam to the Philippines with
120 asylum seekers. All but one perished. The detainees of Palawan First Asylum
Camp displayed the boat as a reminder of what it meant to be a boat person.
Photo: James M. Freeman.

CHAPTER ONE

VICTIMS OF POLITICS

ON FEBRUARY 7, 2001, six Vietnamese refugees left Thailand for resettlement to France. The oldest of the group had been in Thailand 17 years, the youngest 9 years. Their departure heralded the end of the tragic and turbulent quarter-century saga of Indochinese refugees, people from Vietnam, Laos, and Cambodia, who escaped from their homelands seeking protection and asylum.[1]

The six Vietnamese who left for France were the last of more than two million people who fled Indochina after 1975, traveling overland through Cambodia and by boat to countries of first asylum, including China, Hong Kong, Taiwan, South Korea, Malaysia, Indonesia, Thailand, the Philippines, Singapore, Japan. At least 10 percent of those who fled overland or by sea perished.[2] They died from storms, thirst, and exposure; they were killed by Thai pirates, Vietnamese patrols, Khmer Rouge or other Cambodian soldiers, and Cambodian bandits.

But more than 1,600,000 refugees survived. Between 1975 and 1995, 1,438,719 Indochinese refugees arrived in other countries of first asylum. This included 839,228 Vietnamese: 796,310 boat people and 42,918 overland escapees. Nearly 60,000 were unaccompanied minors. In addition, over 250,000 people, mostly ethnic Chinese from Vietnam, fled to China, where they were accepted and resettled.[3]

In the 1970s and 1980s, almost all Vietnamese asylum seekers were automatically given refugee status and resettled. As thousands of Vietnamese continued to flee their homeland, countries became less willing to give temporary asylum or to resettle them. In 1988 in Hong Kong and at various dates in 1989 in other countries, refugee status determination procedures were established. Adults with their attached minors were screened. Because unaccompanied minors were considered unable to fully present their own case, a Special Committee used Special Procedures to determine their "best interests." People who were screened out (denied refugee status) were told to repatriate to Vietnam. By 1995, no country of first asylum would accept any new arrivals. In some countries, 75–80 percent or more of the post-cutoff date arrivals initially were screened out, and screening-in rates varied widely by country.

By 1996, except for a few thousand persons, all Vietnamese asylum seekers either had been resettled to third countries or repatriated to their homelands, and the camps that held them were closing. In the Philippines, nearly 1,600 people were allowed to remain indefinitely. They lived in a thriving community on Palawan Island.[4] The last camp in Hong Kong ceased operation on June 1, 2000, leaving Thailand as the last to close.[5] The Vietnamese refugee saga is over, but another story continues. The camps profoundly affected the children who were in them, whether they were repatriated to Vietnam or resettled in the United States or other countries.

Indochinese Asylum Seekers and the Definition of a Refugee

WHILE INDIVIDUAL countries have the sole authority to grant or deny refugee status to asylum seekers, they are influenced by UNHCR and its criteria for determining refugee status. The definition of refugee used in international law is based on the Protocol Relating to the Status of Refugees agreed upon by the United Nations in 1967, which is a revision of the old International Refugee Organization definition and the 1951 United Nations Convention Relating to the Status of Refugees. The Protocol states that the term refugee applies to any person "who is outside the country of his nationality . . . because he has or had well-founded fear of persecution by reason of his race, religion, nationality, membership of a particular social group or political opinion and is unable or, because of such fear, is unwilling to avail himself of the protection of the government of the country of his nationality."

If this definition is used to determine refugee status, many people who genuinely need refuge and assistance do not qualify, including those who flee because of deteriorating economic conditions. This suggests that "refugee" is a political term, the varying definitions and interpretations of which are of life and death importance for millions of asylum seekers.[6]

Indeed, over the past century, the definition and treatment of refugees have shifted as a consequence of global economic and political forces.[7] What started out as a concern for displaced peoples after World War I and World War II evolved into a focus on refugee crises occurring in the context of superpower rivalries and regional conflicts, and finally, with the end of the Cold War, the production of refugees resulting from internal conflicts involving ethnic identity, religion, and communal interests.

UNHCR was formed in 1950 as a successor to the International Refugee Organization, which resettled World War II refugees in Europe. UNHCR's mandate is to provide protection to refugees and to seek permanent solutions to their problems by means of voluntary repatriation or resettlement and assimilation in new national communities. The work of the High Commissioner is expected to be nonpolitical, humanitarian, and social, and to focus on groups and categories of refugees.[8] However, UNHCR's protection work often focuses on individuals, and states have not objected to this. Over the years, the United Nations General Assembly has given UNHCR wider powers and directives to deal with refugee crises not only in Europe but throughout the world.[9]

Several principles of UNHCR are intended to provide significant protection and assistance for refugees. The first is a broadened definition of a refugee to include persons from around the world.[10] Second, the phrase "well-founded fear of persecution" in the definition of a refugee recognizes both a subjective element in the attitude of the applicant and in the interpretation of "persecution," and an objective component in that the applicant must be able to demonstrate sufficient and plausible grounds for the claim of fear of persecution. Third, UNHCR can advocate for the protection of asylum seekers. This includes recommending that governments admit these people as refugees, concluding agreements to provide material assistance for refugees, and encouraging the integration of refugees in the countries to which they have fled. Fourth, UNHCR is expected to have a neutral outlook, advocating protection from humanitarian rather than political considerations. Fifth, UNHCR also advocates the principle of non-expulsion *(non-refoulement)* of refugees who fear for their safety. This ensures that refugees will not be repatriated against their will. Finally, the concept of durable solution provides, at least in theory, a humane and consistent principle for dealing with refugees.

The durable solutions advocated by UNHCR are, in order of preference, voluntary repatriation to the country from which a refugee has fled, integration in a country of first asylum, and, finally, resettlement in a third country. Robinson points out that from the start of the Indochinese exodus, UNHCR favored voluntary repatriation, even though the refugees and their countries of origin were against it.[11] The solution of voluntary repatriation is predicated on three principles: that it is safe for the refugee to return, that the refugee willingly chooses to return, and, given the first two, that repatriation to one's own country of origin and culture is always the best choice. If conditions are unfavorable for repatriation, then the next best choice is to integrate the refugee on the spot. To that end, assistance should be given to enable the refugee to become economically self-sufficient. If integration is not feasible or allowable, as has been the case with most Vietnamese refugees in countries of first asylum, the next best choice is resettlement elsewhere.

Regarding Vietnamese asylum seekers, people have disagreed about what does or should constitute refugee status. Vietnamese asylum seekers and their advocates have challenged the refusal to consider economic evidence of political persecution in defining who is a refugee.[12] Others have had different interpretations of who qualifies for refugee status even if they agree on the definition of a refugee. At what point do behaviors directed at someone become "persecution," qualifying that person to be considered a refugee, rather than "discrimination," which does not qualify a person for refugee status, and what stands up as evidence that persecution has occurred? What constitutes "best interests" for unaccompanied minors, how are they determined, and who is qualified to make this decision? The lives and destinies of unaccompanied minors rest on decisions about their status made in Geneva, countries of first asylum, and countries of resettlement.

The Indochinese Refugee Crisis

ALTHOUGH A sizable community of Vietnamese had lived in France for decades, and a few Vietnamese had come to the United States, the end of the war in Indochina in 1975 and the Communist takeover of that region marks the beginning of their massive migration.[13] The first-wave refugees were those who left at the fall of Saigon in 1975. They included many members of the South Vietnamese army and government, those who had worked for the Americans during the Vietnam war, and others who escaped in the confusion and panic of the final days and hours. South Vietnam had many people who had moved from the North in 1954, after the French-Vietnam war. Many of these people fled from the Communists a second time in 1975. About a hundred and thirty thousand of the people who escaped were resettled in the United States, while another sixty thousand were held in refugee camps in Hong Kong or Thailand. Some of the refugees were unaccompanied minors, often children who had become separated from parents or relatives during the escape.[14]

In Vietnam, the victorious North Vietnamese Communists did not initiate their socialist transformation immediately, and many South Vietnamese were lulled into believing that they would not be persecuted. As a result, once the first-wave refugees had left, only 378 people escaped from Vietnam in the remaining months of 1975.

A few weeks after the Communists gained control, they began to impose repressive economic and social policies that disrupted the fabric of South Vietnamese society. The new government sent several hundred thousand former South Vietnamese soldiers and government officials to harsh reeducation camps, where they were starved, forced to do hard physical labor, and subjected to political indoctrination for periods of a few months to fifteen years or more. Many of the children of these prisoners were refused admission to schools, especially higher grades, and others in the family were not permitted to hold jobs. The families of these prisoners were torn apart and impoverished. Over the next several years, the Communists relocated hundreds of thousands of people to uncleared forest lands (New Economic Zones) to do agricultural labor, nationalized major industries and businesses, attempted to nationalize agriculture, reduced the wages of people to below the minimum needed for survival, confiscated much private property, recalled old currency, and three times issued new currency. At the same time, Vietnam failed to bring in adequate foreign assistance, suffered the American economic embargo, and became embroiled in border clashes with China and the war with and decade-long military occupation of Cambodia, further draining Vietnam's already scarce resources. The consequences were disastrous: unemployment and poverty, massive food shortages, and numerous health crises, including extensive malnutrition, which, as late as the 1990s, afflicted over 40 percent of Vietnam's children.[15] The exodus of boat refugees began. Thousands of South Vietnamese families saw no future for their children in Vietnam and in desperation sent them out of the country.

As Vietnam's crises deepened, people left in increasing numbers. In 1976, the number of escapees jumped to 5,247. In 1977, 15,690 people escaped. In 1978 and 1979, the numbers skyrocketed to 85,213 and 185,826, respectively. In the 50 months between May 1975 and July 31, 1979, 292,315 Vietnamese successfully escaped by boat.[16] This is the first time in Vietnam's 4,000-year history that its people fled beyond Indochina.

In 1978, the ethnic Chinese, who had played an important role in urban commerce, fed the second wave of refugees. As tensions between China and Vietnam increased, the ethnic Chinese in Vietnam were told for security reasons to move to the countryside, away from cities and coastal areas. In early 1979, China and Vietnam fought a three-week border war. By that time, the

Vietnamese government was coercing ethnic Chinese to leave Vietnam and nationalizing their businesses. Some 230,000 ethnic Chinese, plus another 30,000 ethnic Vietnamese, most from North Vietnam, went to China, traveling overland and by boat. Hundreds of thousands of people from South Vietnam, mostly ethnic Chinese, fled to Southeast Asian countries.

Between 1978 and 1980, ethnic Chinese boat people reported that their wealth had been confiscated by authorities before they were allowed to leave. In some cases, Vietnamese officials connived with Chinese businessmen to bring about the departure of the ethnic Chinese in return for kickbacks. In two instances, widely reported at the time, refugees traveled on two large freighters containing fifteen hundred and twenty-five hundred persons. Most people, however, left in small fishing boats.[17]

The third wave of several hundred thousand refugees left by boat or overland between 1978 and 1982, at the height of Vietnam's economic crises and political repression. Their journeys were often perilous, as well as remarkable, such as the 5,000-mile journey of a small fishing boat, which eventually reached Australia. But others were not so fortunate. Thousands of people failed in their attempts to escape, missing rendezvous, being cheated by people who claimed to be organizing escapes, and being caught by security forces while trying to flee Vietnam. Since, according to Vietnamese law, leaving the country without permission was a crime, those who were caught were placed into crowded jails, women and children in one room, the men in another. They remained for months, usually until relatives or friends bribed "the right people" to secure their release.[18]

Despite failing, refugees made repeated attempts to escape. If they finally succeeded in eluding the shore guards and coastal patrols, they still faced the dangerous storms and swirling tides of the South China Sea. It has been estimated that at least 10 percent of the asylum seekers lost their lives while trying to escape, though some estimates are much higher; by 1987 the estimate was at least 100,000. Beyond that, the waters around Thailand and Malaysia were infested with Thai pirates who often worked in teams of boats to rape, pillage, and murder their hapless victims. Of boats surviving the South China Sea passages, one out of three was stopped and robbed by pirates; of those stopped, one out of three was also subjected to rape and murder. Pirates often attacked with the intention of killing everyone, sinking the boats, and leaving no evidence.[19] Some women were taken to Ko Kra Island and repeatedly raped over a period of days and weeks. Some of these women were rescued, but others were carried off to brothels in Thailand. Vietnamese patrols killed wantonly.[20]

Boat people who reached the refugee camps found primitive, crowded conditions in which they would have to remain for the six months to a year it would take to resettle them. In July 1978, Pulau Bidong was an uninhabited island 18 miles off the coast of peninsular Malaysia. Five months later, Das and Sacerdoti found that it was "swarming with 25,000 Vietnamese waiting for the outside world to determine their future." Despite severe crowding, insufficient materials to build temporary shelters, fears of contamination of the wells, the nearly total absence of medicine, and a food ration for each refugee of only one-half pint of rice per day and one tin of sardines every five days, the Vietnamese had organized the camp to make the best use of human and material resources. They allocated responsibilities for "supplies, security, construction, information and culture, social welfare (including health, water supply, and sanitation), interpreters, and administration."

Refugees continued to pour into Malaysia and were placed on the island. In the following year, Michael Grant described it as "a dangerously congested

Unaccompanied-minors building and sign in Pulau Bidong Camp, Malaysia. *Photo: Nguyen Dinh Huu.*

slum . . . a shantytown with a population of 42,000 confined to a living area of less than one square kilometer." Shanties, some three stories high, were constructed of timber beams with walls of cardboard, tin, or timber, with roofs of blue plastic sheeting or waterproof sugar sacks. "The beach was fouled with heaps of rubbish rotting in the heat and humidity . . . flies swarmed everywhere and the stench of human excrement was oppressive." Wells were polluted or dry, and the acute shortage of water led to long lines of people waiting to get a few drops. Tempers flared and fights were frequent. A refugee who spent nearly a year in Pulau Bidong said to Freeman that people were left for months, often lonely and with nothing to do but sit. "We had to stay too long in one place with no exercise," she said. "Life was monotonous. We had nothing to do."[21]

Some camps were far more brutal, especially those on the tense, unsettled border of Thailand and Cambodia. These housed over 360,000 Cambodians and a small number of Vietnamese, about 1,000 people, who had escaped from Vietnam through Cambodia. The most notorious incident occurred in 1978. To discourage the influx of Cambodian refugees streaming across their border, Thai authorities forced at gunpoint thousands of starving survivors of the Khmer Rouge holocaust to return to their homeland. They were made to walk down a mountain minefield into Cambodia; hundreds were blown up.[22]

International Response to the Refugee Crisis

AS HUNDREDS of thousands of refugees fled not only Vietnam, but also Laos and Cambodia, neighboring countries in Southeast Asia and Hong Kong found themselves unable or unwilling to absorb what seemed to be an endless stream that threatened to overwhelm them. Although China and Japan had done so, none of the Southeast Asian countries had signed the 1951 United Nations Convention Relating to the Status of Refugees and its 1967 Protocol, which provided guidelines for the protection of asylum seekers. (The Philippines ratified the Convention in 1981.) Of particular importance was the principle that people should not be returned against their will to a place where they fear persecution.[23]

Countries such as Thailand and Malaysia threatened to refuse to allow the boat people to land, claiming that the Indochina conflict that had produced these asylum seekers was not of their making, and that they were already housing refugees with no guarantee that they would subsequently be resettled elsewhere. In a number of well-publicized cases, Vietnamese refugee boats attempting to land in Thailand and Malaysia were towed back out to sea. In

Malaysia, some 40,000 Vietnamese were pushed back, though some simply landed further along the coast. While announcing a hard line, in practice Thailand and Malaysia allowed some boats to land and placed the new arrivals in temporary camps. Indonesia and the Philippines also allowed the Vietnamese boat people to land, even though they called them "illegal migrants" and "displaced persons," not refugees. Hong Kong, which received one-third to one-half of the asylum seekers, allowed them both to land and work outside the camps prior to their being resettled elsewhere. In the early days of the refugee exodus, Hong Kong's refugee policy was considered the most humane, though in later years it was to come under heavy criticism for its forcible repatriation of detainees, and the harsh living conditions and violence in its camps. Tiny Singapore, concerned that it might be inundated with refugees, refused to allow any landings. Singapore allowed a few persons rescued at sea to reside temporarily within their borders. The countries of the boats that picked them up were ultimately responsible for resolving their requests for asylum.

Although slow to respond at first to the Indochinese refugee crisis, in 1979 UNHCR took two actions. First, it convened a 1979 international conference in Geneva attended by 65 governments. Many of the industrialized nations of the world agreed to finance the protection and temporary housing of boat people in countries of first asylum, and to guarantee their resettlement outside of Southeast Asia. At the same time, UNHCR also asked Vietnam to stop the departures of large vessels of ethnic Chinese, which they claimed was not a refugee flow but an unacceptable mass expulsion. The evidence supporting this is considerable.[24]

Second, to prevent further escapes, which were "illegal" according to Vietnamese law, UNHCR negotiated with Vietnam the Orderly Departure Program (ODP). This would allow qualified persons to be resettled directly from Vietnam to countries such as the United States and Canada. Over the years more than 400,000 people came to the United States through ODP.

These people were processed either as refugees under the Refugee Act of 1980 or as immigrants under the Immigrant and Nationality Act. The Refugee Act of 1980 was passed to provide a means of regulating admissions into the United States. It widened the notion of refugee to include not only those fleeing communism, but also asylum seekers from other oppressive regimes.[25]

Under the ODP, Vietnamese could enter the United States if they had close relatives living there who applied to bring them over: spouses, sons, daughters, parents, grandparents, and unmarried grandchildren. Others who qualified were those persons and their close relatives who had been employed by Americans or American companies in Vietnam, officials, or soldiers. Those with other ties to America might qualify. These included students who had studied in the United States and Amerasians, people whose mothers were Vietnamese and fathers were American citizens. In 1987, the U.S. Congress passed the Amerasian Homecoming Act; it allowed 40,000 Amerasians and their relatives to come to America through 1994.

Political prisoners were excluded from the ODP until 1984, when the U.S. and Vietnam agreed to allow 10,000 former reeducation camp prisoners to emigrate to America. Vietnam only slowly released these people because they feared that they would mobilize in exile against the Vietnamese government. In 1988, under the Humanitarian Operation (HO) Program, the U.S. State Department pledged to secure the release and resettlement of the remaining 85,000 reeducation camp prisoners who had been incarcerated for at least three years; most of them had been brought to America by 1995.[26]

The Comprehensive Plan of Action

THE INTERNATIONAL community expected that, with each passing year, conditions would improve in Vietnam and fewer Vietnamese people would try to escape. For a while, the number did decline. Then, in 1986, a new flood of refugees appeared. Half of them were children, many without parents or relatives. Unlike their predecessors, who had come mainly from the south and the southern part of central Vietnam, many of these asylum seekers were from the north. They had been under Communist control since 1954 in the cities and as early as 1945 for people in the countryside. The younger escapees had known no other life. After relatively short and easy voyages, tens of thousands of these North Vietnamese arrived in nearby Hong Kong, which was reluctant to receive them. Officials and UNHCR asked why the North Vietnamese had not fled earlier. The answer, according to these officials, was that these people were not persecuted refugees at all, but "economic migrants" seeking a better life. The North Vietnamese had heard that the South Vietnamese had escaped and been resettled, and now they saw the opportunity to do the same. The officials said that the unaccompanied children were "economic anchors" who sought to be resettled and then bring out their parents from Vietnam. Increasingly, officials in other countries of first asylum made the same judgment.

The children we interviewed vigorously denied that they were economic anchors. Adult asylum seekers also rejected the economic migrant label, claiming that in Vietnam, "economics" could not be separated from "politics," since political decisions were the primary causes of their poverty. While this certainly applied to many South Vietnamese, who had been sent to reeducation camps and denied employment and education, and whose houses and businesses had been confiscated, it generally did not apply to the north, however desperately poor it was. But the continuing flood of escapees from the north changed the attitudes of UNHCR and officials of countries of first asylum about escapees from all regions of Vietnam.

By 1989, 160,000 asylum seekers were in Southeast Asian camps. Countries of first asylum and final resettlement no longer welcomed the new boat people as refugees. Officials in these countries talked of "compassion fatigue" and expressed concerns about how to stem the continuous flow of boat people.

As the Vietnamese exodus continued over the years, UNHCR actively strove to discourage further flight from Vietnam. Robinson cites a 1994 UNHCR report that blames the Indochinese asylum seekers themselves. Large numbers of mid-ranking and senior UNHCR staff who were assigned to work with Indochinese refugees during the first 15 years of their exodus saw themselves as "unwilling participants in an 'automatic resettlement machine.'" This led to a "widespread sense of disenchantment with the concept of resettlement." As a result, many of these staff "now seriously question the appropriateness of resettlement as a durable solution for refugees." The report concludes that their disenchantment with resettlement has interfered with UNHCR's capacity to resettle people effectively.[27]

The solution was the adoption of an agreement called the Comprehensive Plan of Action (CPA), signed in Geneva by 51 of the 77 attending nations, including Vietnam and the United States. Muntarbhorn describes it as "a package of measures interlinking the country of origin (Vietnam) with first-asylum countries and resettlement countries. The country of origin agreed to deter clandestine departures—for example, by means of a more extensive public information campaign—and to promote the Orderly Departure Program. The first-asylum countries undertook to guarantee temporary refuge to those arriving in the region." Specifically, the objectives of the CPA were to prevent organized clandestine departures from Vietnam, encourage and promote regular and legal emigration from Vietnam, maintain guarantees of first asylum, establish consistent refugee status determination procedures throughout the region of countries of first asylum, continue the resettlement of long-staying as well as newly determined Vietnamese refugees, and repatriate to Vietnam those asylum seekers who had been rejected as refugees.[28]

Different countries designated different CPA cutoff dates. Hong Kong stipulated June 16, 1988; the others followed nine months later: Malaysia and Thailand, March 14, 1989; Indonesia, March 17, 1989; the Philippines, March 21, 1989. Asylum seekers who arrived in these countries after their cutoff dates had to be screened to determine their refugee status, or, in the case of unaccompanied minors under 16, had to be evaluated by a Special Committee to determine whether repatriation or resettlement was in each child's "best interest."

In order to establish region-wide consistency in the refugee status determination procedure, the CPA stipulated that the status of an asylum seeker would be determined by a "qualified and competent national authority or body, in accordance with established refugee criteria and procedures." UNHCR would serve both as observer and advisor to ensure that the criteria and procedures were followed. UNHCR would advise each asylum seeker in writing about the procedure to be followed, the implications if they were rejected, and their rights to appeal the first-level rejection. The criteria for refugee status determination were those recognized in the 1951 Convention Relating to the Status of Refugees and the 1967 Protocol; the authoritative and interpretive guide for developing and applying the criteria would be the *Handbook on Procedures and Criteria for Determining Refugee Status* issued by UNHCR. The procedures would include, first, providing information to the asylum seekers about the procedures, the criteria that determine refugee status, and the presentation of their cases; second, prompt advice of the decision in writing within a prescribed period; third, a right of appeal against negative decisions and proper appeals procedures for this purpose based on the existing laws and procedures of the individual place of asylum. The asylum seeker would be entitled to advice, if required, to be provided under the auspices of UNHCR. In addition, UNHCR would institute, in cooperation with the governments of the area, a comprehensive regional training program for officials involved in the determination process, to ensure proper and consistent functioning of the procedures.

The CPA was put in place while pre-cutoff arrivals were still in the camps. These people were resettled, while the post-cutoff arrivals, 115,600 persons, were screened. Of this number, 32,300 were recognized as refugees and resettled, while 83,300 were denied refugee status and told to repatriate. This caused much resentment among the rejected, and over 45,000 of them refused to return.

The detainees said they were afraid to repatriate, since, as mentioned previously, Vietnam's criminal code stipulated that illegal emigration was a crime punishable by incarceration in jail. Provisions of two of the articles were especially worrisome. One was Article 88: "Illegally Organizing or Forcing others to flee to a foreign country or to remain abroad in a foreign country. (1) Whoever organizes or forces others to flee to a foreign country or remain abroad in a foreign country illegally . . . shall be sentenced to a prison term of 3 to 12 years." Article 89 provided jail terms even for those who did not "force" or "organize" others: "Illegal entry or exit on illegal stay overseas. (1) Whoever illegally exits from or enters Vietnam, or illegally stays abroad shall be subject to a warning or control up to one year, or imprisonment for a term of 3 months to 2 years."

The asylum seekers knew that those who escaped in 1975 but then chose to repatriate rather than resettle were immediately imprisoned. Many detainees in Southeast Asian and Hong Kong refugee camps had also been imprisoned in Vietnam for earlier unsuccessful attempts to escape. Even when Vietnam eased up on its persecution of individuals, announced that it would not retaliate against returnees (except for those who led the escapes), and backed down on enforcement of its illegal emigration law, thousands of escapees, distrustful of Vietnam's changing attitudes, still refused to repatriate.[29]

As incentives to repatriate, UNHCR offered each returnee, including unaccompanied minors, U.S. $360, assistance in reintegration, and free schooling or job training. Detainees who might qualify for ODP to the United States were required to return to Vietnam. They would not be allowed to emigrate from the camps.

Thousands of screened-out detainees still refused to repatriate. In March 1995, UNHCR, Vietnam, and the international community agreed to repatriate them against their will, and over the next year most of them were forcibly repatriated.[30] Under different rules, the forcible repatriation of unaccompanied minors began at the end of June 1993.[31] The detainees were told that they were economic migrants, not refugees, and Vietnam's economic situation had improved, offering them new opportunities.[32]

In April 1996 the United States started Resettlement Opportunities for Vietnamese Returnees (ROVR). Robinson observes that its aim was "to promote voluntary repatriation, avoid further violence in the camps and, at the same time, offer a last chance at resettlement for some screened-out groups of lingering US concern." If they returned from the camps to Vietnam by the end of June 1996, the date of the end of the CPA, they might be allowed to be interviewed in Vietnam by a United States INS officer. Some 9,000 people registered for this program.[33]

On July 17, 1996, agencies of the Philippine government and the Catholic Church signed a memorandum of understanding that allowed Vietnamese

President Fidel Ramos and Sister Pascale Le Thi Triu sign the memorandum of understanding between the Philippine government and the Catholic Church, allowing Vietnamese asylum seekers to remain indefinitely in the Philippines. *Photo: Center for Assistance to Displaced Persons.*

asylum seekers in the Philippines to remain there indefinitely. They could return to Vietnam any time they wished, but they would not be forced back. A total of 712 Vietnamese asylum seekers chose to repatriate; 1,589 registered for residence in the Philippines, including 350 who applied for temporary residence while waiting to be resettled with families elsewhere. Those who stayed were given the opportunity to build their own "Viet Village" and become self-sufficient residents of the Philippines. Donations to help build this community poured in from around the world.[34] On June 30, 1996, UNHCR withdrew from Palawan camp, ending the CPA in the Philippines.[35]

Prior to the CPA, countries of first asylum such as China and Malaysia had resettled some Vietnamese refugees. After the CPA was in force, the Philippines, the poorest of the countries of first asylum, was the only nation not to cave in to international pressure to forcibly repatriate the Vietnamese. They took this politically courageous step because it was the humane thing to do. All other countries sent back any asylum seekers Vietnam didn't refuse to accept.[36] Behind them, urging forced repatriation, were the United States, other countries of resettlement, and UNHCR.[37]

On September 30, 2000, the Center for Assistance to Displaced Persons (CADP), the Catholic agency that assisted the Vietnamese, closed its office in Manila, and the residents of the Viet Village took over all projects. CADP continues to provide legal assistance. The residents are still waiting for the decision on permanent resident status.[38]

Unaccompanied Minors: Vulnerable and Neglected

UNHCR ATTACHED to the CPA the "Note on Unaccompanied Minors," which recommended that, rather than being interviewed by an immigration officer, the child be interviewed by a Special Committee including social workers and lawyers familiar with children's issues. The Committee would determine the refugee status of the child and the durable solution in the child's best interests. For children 16 to 18 years of age, regular status determination procedures would be used, after which the Special Committee would consider their durable solution. Because they were considered especially vulnerable, unaccompanied children were supposed to be identified on arrival, documentation compiled within the first few days, and decisions implemented expeditiously "in the best interests of each unaccompanied minor."

What actually occurred provoked some of the most strident criticisms of the CPA. Countries of first asylum argued over the selection of Committee members and how to proceed, causing delays of 12 to 18 months after screening had started before they began the Special Procedure. In November 1990, 5,000 minors in the camps had not received their decision.[39] Minors in camps without their parents often were separated from other relatives who had accompanied them. The decisions of the Special Committee to repatriate unaccompanied minors in their best interests often contradicted the wishes of the parents who had sent the children out of Vietnam in the first place. Some critics claimed that the delays were deliberate, to persuade the children to voluntarily repatriate.[40]

Among the many critics of the Special Procedures is W. Courtland Robinson, whose research was facilitated by UNHCR. Robinson says that the Special Procedures "failed" to treat the vulnerable population of unaccompanied minors as "first among the first" of those who needed immediate attention. Because of the lengthy delays, the dangers of the camps, and the conflicting pressures on them to stay in the camps or to repatriate, the Special Procedures "did not appear to be in the best interests of the children they were intended to serve."[41]

Despite its flaws, the Comprehensive Plan of Action has achieved its primary goal: people now rarely attempt to escape from Vietnam, countries of first asylum refuse to receive them or let them remain, and those claiming asylum as refugees are required to document their claim on the basis of internationally accepted criteria.

CHAPTER TWO

A GUIDED TOUR OF MISERY

Behind Barbed Wire

THE SIGN at the gate was in English, Chinese, and Vietnamese.

> Royal Hong Kong Police, Shek Kong Vietnamese Boat People Detention Center. In Accordance with Immigration Vietnamese Boat People Detention Center Rule 1989 made under Section 13H of the Immigration Ordinance, Chapter 115, Law of Hong Kong. It is an offence to:
> 1. Enter a detention center without the permission of the commandant.
> 2. Bring into or carry out any unauthorized article without the permission of the commandant.
> 3. Aid the escape of any detainee.

To enter, we showed our permit to a guard. The massive steel gate creaked open, we stepped inside, and another guard immediately slammed it shut. A third guard led us along a corridor to the commandant's office, where we were given visitor's passes. The assistant commandant showed us the weapons that had been confiscated from detainees during searches of their quarters, a vast array of homemade daggers, clubs, and spears. We were then searched for weapons and other contraband but allowed to keep our cameras and film. In no other Hong Kong camp were we allowed to take unrestricted photos, but here the assistant commandant said, "You are welcome to go anywhere in the camp, talk to anyone, and take any photos you wish." He proudly announced that Shek Kong was well run and had few problems. He invited us to see this for ourselves.

We were visiting Shek Kong in December 1991 to inquire about the living conditions of the 1,015 unaccompanied minors and "aged out" youths (those over sixteen) in that camp, which at that time housed 9,909 detainees. On February 3, 1992, six weeks after our visit, the detainees of Shek Kong rioted, killing 24 people, including 10 children, and injuring more than 125 inmates. North Vietnamese locked their south Vietnamese victims inside their quarters, a Quonset hut, and set fire to it. Shek Kong was closed after an official inquiry and the detainees were dispersed to other detention centers.[1] The Shek Kong riot was one of dozens of violent clashes that rocked Vietnamese refugee camps from 1990 to 1995, not only in Hong Kong, but in other countries of first asylum throughout Southeast Asia. In Shek Kong, the riot occurred between north and south Vietnamese, who disliked each other. In other camps in later years, riots stemmed from protests over forced repatriation. Whatever the specific causes of the 1992 Shek Kong tragedy, the overall setting of extreme crowding, poor food, lack of organized and productive activities, and uncertainty and worry about forced repatriation to Vietnam provided a tinderbox for the explosion of violence that occurred. Rough treatment by guards also increased tensions. To break their will and coerce them to repatriate, guards would search and tear apart the living spaces of detainees, or would abruptly move them to another camp. This was to convey to the detainees that their stay in the camps was temporary.

Shek Kong, a bleak, treeless mass of concrete and steel, built on the runway of the Royal Air Force in the New Territories, was enclosed by two high barbed-wire perimeter fences separated by a wide corridor. The inner fences were built with eight-foot-high metal sheets from the ground up so detainees could not see out. Guard towers along the corridor loomed above the fences. Before entering the inner camp, we passed an enclosure containing several tents and a number of detainees. Those caught trying to escape were jailed here for a month or more on reduced food rations.

The grounds containing the living quarters were divided into six sections, each marked off by high fences and wide corridors to prevent contact between people of different sections. Guards patrolled the corridors between the sections and allowed only authorized personnel to pass from one section to another. Detainees were rarely allowed out of their section unless they had a medical emergency or were in school or job training, though much of this was subsequently terminated. In five of these sections, detainees lived in long metal Quonset huts with three tiers of bunks on each side. Each hut contained several hundred people. In the sixth section, some thirty-five hundred detainees lived in large tents, in which three people shared a sleeping space around five and a half by three and a half feet. The metal huts were too hot in the summer

Looking through the gate at Shek Kong Detention Center, Hong Kong, to another section of the camp. *Photo: James M. Freeman.*

and the tents were too cold in the winter. Flooding and poor drainage during the wet season added to the miseries of the detainees. Mosquito nets were available only to families of three; unaccompanied minors had no nets and were a mass of bites from the swarms of mosquitoes and flies that tormented them. The detainees received meager rations, enough to keep them alive but cooked so badly that many people recooked their meals. Later, the guards prohibited this. In theory, people with medical emergencies were treated, but minor ailments, rashes, and festering sores went untreated until they spread out of control.

While in the camp, we witnessed two weapons searches. Without warning, guards descended on a Quonset hut, locked in the inhabitants, including the children, and proceeded to tear apart the place, scattering people's few belongings everywhere. The small children, terrified, hid behind their relatives or, if they had no one to protect them, stood trembling, not knowing where to turn. Outside the hut, other detainees stood and waited sullenly until this latest disruption of their lives ended. The searches took forty-five minutes each.

Half of the camp population was comprised of children. For some toddlers, Shek Kong was the only world they had ever known, and the only color they saw came from the sky. The only relief was a brightly painted Quonset hut away from the living quarters that served as a school. The pictures of birds and trees, painted by adult detainees, contrasted with the nearby guard tower and the gray steel fences and barbed wire that surrounded the school. Children were allowed to leave their sections for a few hours to attend school. A thirty-by-one-hundred-foot vegetable garden adjacent to the school was the only area in the camp not covered by concrete.

Several agencies provided health care, schooling, and job training for the detainees. The employees of these agencies told us that Shek Kong was ready to explode. The people were hungry; they were depressed and scared because they did not know what the future held for them, and they particularly feared that they would be forced to repatriate to Vietnam against their will. The children showed the greatest effects; they were pale, undersized for their age, listless, and lethargic. They lived in a world of physical violence, drugs, prostitution, teenage pregnancies and sexual abuse, abortions, and depression. Most of them received little or no education or job training. They were lonely and anxious over an uncertain future. Most of the time they had no activities to keep them occupied. They lived in an emotionally starved environment with little or no parental or adult guidance. By far the most vulnerable were unaccompanied minors, who lacked protection from gangs in the camp. Adult detainees assigned to their foster care were often so depressed by camp conditions and their own lack of authority that they left the minors unattended.

As we walked through Shek Kong, and later through other camps in Hong Kong and elsewhere in Southeast Asia, children would cling to us. Many had been in camps for three or more years. Brutalized and devastated by their experience, they cried as they described their feelings and experiences to us. "I am afraid, but I do not know how to deal with my fear," said a 15–year-old girl. "I fear that I will be forced to return to Vietnam. I fear going out at night. I am alone; no one takes care of me." She was so upset that she was unable to study. In Palawan First Asylum Center in the Philippines, a fourteen-year-old boy said he was hungry. "We get bananas and mangoes, also one hundred grams of meat per day or two hundred grams of fish. But the fish is usually rotten and we cannot eat it. On Saturdays we get a can of fish. Three persons are supposed to use it for two meals, but it is not enough for one person at one meal. I eat two meals a day. I don't have breakfast. I am hungry in the morning, but there is nothing I can do about it."

In High Island Detention Center, detainees told us that the guards beat and kicked them. One person said, "Beatings are normal." A ten-year-old child told us he was hungry all the time and continually disturbed by mosquitoes

Interior of a Quonset hut, Shek Kong Detention Center, Hong Kong.
Photo: James M. Freeman.

Children play table tennis on a makeshift table, Shek Kong Detention Center,
Hong Kong. *Photo: James M. Freeman.*

and bedbugs, which he referred to as airplanes and submarines. "I'm sad. I cannot sleep. The mosquitoes and bedbugs make my life horrible. And the food distributed to an entire family is not enough for one person." A youngster with long, muscular arms, wearing a shirt with short sleeves rolled up to his armpits, said, "Not only mosquitoes, but scabies bothers us. When we are sick, it's very difficult to get treatment, and even then the doctor insults us and says, 'Go back to your hut.'"

Mai and Liem: Resistance and Capitulation

IN 1993, we met Mai, a seventeen-year-old from Haiphong, who had been in Whitehead Detention Center, Hong Kong for three years. This steel cage of ten sections teeming with nearly 25,000 detainees was difficult to control and security was hard to maintain. Mai, alone in the camp, was particularly vulnerable. With a forlorn expression, she said, "Life is unbearable here. There's lots of pressure. In the camp, I became a woman too early. There are lots of bad people here." This was her indirect way of saying she had been sexually abused, and that to survive, she had allowed an adult male to "protect" her. The disruption of her life went further. "UNHCR promised us a good life if

Whitehead Detention Center, Hong Kong. *Photo: Nguyen H. Duyen.*

we returned to Vietnam, but I don't believe them. The UNHCR [and Hong Kong government] policy to move us around constantly totally upsets our lives, our emotional life, and our education. Last year, we were moved four times, from Section 9 to Section 1, then to number 5, then to other sections and camps. When we move, we pack everything. We have to throw some things away. When we arrive in a new camp, there are not enough things to use for cooking and our things for sleeping are gone. Then we have to readjust to school. This disrupts our life. We have to throw things out and then we miss them. As soon as we are established, we have to prepare to move again."

Mai received this treatment because she refused to repatriate. She explained her decision. "It is very difficult to make decisions living like this and thinking about repatriation. UNHCR advised us to return. If we go now, we'll get repatriation allowances. If we go back later, we'll not receive anything. To return or not depends on the situation of the individual. If it's not appropriate, people don't return. If there was any benefit for me to return, I would have decided before UNHCR threatened me. Because I get no benefit, I won't return, even though they threaten. I'll stay here until the refugee problem is resolved. I have nothing to return to in Vietnam."

Liem, fourteen years of age, was so beaten down by the horrors of detention camp life that he gave up. He had been placed in Chi Ma Wan, Hong Kong, a gloomy camp hidden by trees and nestled behind a cove on the southeast coast of Lantau Island. Lower Chi Ma Wan housed about 1,500 detainees. Upper Chi Ma Wan, a higher-security facility holding less than 500 people, was reserved for those who committed criminal offenses including acts of violence, incited riots, or repeatedly tried to escape. Most of the detainees in Lower Chi Ma Wan came from north Vietnam, and they intimidated and abused the small minority from the south. In 1987, Liem had arrived in Hong Kong with an uncle and aunt, before the CPA began. Because they were adults who could be resettled, the uncle and aunt were removed to Pillar Point camp, which housed people designated as refugees, but because they were not his parents, Liem, a minor, was not allowed to accompany them. Since Liem had no parents in Vietnam, he was stuck in Chi Ma Wan. In four years, he had had only one year of schooling. "For two years, there was no teacher and no materials, pens, or texts." After that, he became discouraged. He said, "In the camp, I live with friends. We were assigned two to a bed, no choice. The bed is 1.2 by 1.5 meters. Not much space. But I have nothing, so I don't need any space to keep anything. I've volunteered to repatriate. I have no hope, so I better return home. I cannot bear life anymore. The surroundings, the atmosphere, the very disorder here. I don't want to return to Vietnam because I have no parents there, but I have no hope in the camp." We watched as the guards pushed people out of one of the huts Liem described, which housed 250–300 people in three-tiered bunks, and tore the place apart, looking for contraband. As in Shek Kong, the detainees looked sullen and forlorn.

Some children were so shattered by their experience that they contemplated or attempted suicide. In Palawan First Asylum Center, an American volunteer from our organization spoke with an unaccompanied minor who confided that it was against his faith to commit suicide, so he prayed to God that he would die in his sleep.[2] In Galang, Indonesia, a girl spoke with us of her hopes for resettlement. We were in her dormitory room, a shaky wooden structure with blue plastic tarps on the walls. She was one of nearly 1,800 unaccompanied minors out of about 20,000 detainees on that ten-square-mile island in 1992. Several weeks later she was informed that she would be resettled, but, shortly after, the decision was reversed. She set fire to herself and died.

Anh: "I Lost Control and I Beat Him Badly"

IN SOME camps, children became hardened and full of rage. Anh was a 17–year-old orphan, an illiterate ex-buffalo herder who had become a dissident leader and troublemaker in Chi Ma Wan Camp, Hong Kong. We interviewed him in 1991, two years after he had arrived in the camp. One time, he ran amok, badly beating another boy. He explained his actions. "It's so tense here. When I reacted, I didn't care; I lost control. I beat up somebody. The surroundings made me tense and angry. I had no parents to control me or give me advice. I lived wildly, just reacting at the moment. The person was older than I but he insulted me. I lost control and I beat him badly. I was sent to disciplinary camp in the north. You have to be over sixteen for this. I received prison rations, which meant less food, about half of the normal ration. There was no freedom. I stayed there for three months."

Anh's whole life had been a series of rejections by adults. By the age of five, he had been orphaned. Foster parents raised him for a while, but when they could no longer afford it, they left him with a priest. When the priest could not care for him, he sent the boy north. Alone and with no ties in Vietnam, Anh escaped to Hong Kong. He had neither memories of a nurturing family nor expectations that anyone cared what happened to him. His adjustment to this was to become tough, self-sufficient, and self-contained. But he couldn't keep it all in. After receiving his punishment, including reduction of already meager food rations, he realized that his behavior was self-destructive, and he changed his ways. His street-smart adjustments and uncompromising tough-mindedness in the harsh environment of the camp made him a youth leader.

Anh worked during the day, helping in the kitchen, for which he earned HK$90 a month. He used the money to buy monosodium glutamate "to sweeten the watery soup. The soup here is just water and grease." Anh viewed the camp in economic and class terms. "The cafeteria is only for those who can afford to buy food—imperial rolls, rice noodles with onion and grease. Here in the camp there is a difference between the haves and the have-nots. The haves are people who have relatives outside the camp in other countries who send them money. The have-nots like me are people with no relatives to send them money. We have no pocket money. And many minors with no money are too young to be employed but too old to be in school. They call them 'aged out.' This is a real problem; we see it more and more in the last year, with minors caught in the middle.

"Here in the camp," said Anh, "there is a lot of theft, extortion, violence, and running amok. I used to do that, but not now. I'm just starting training school and I'm paid to do it. And I help other unaccompanied minors now. When they have a problem, they come to me. I organized some soccer games and I contacted Social Services to see if they could give a prize. When I see a child who is sad or has emotional problems, I talk to them. Mostly they worry about repatriation."

Anh expressed no real hope for the future, no expectation of a better life, which was not surprising given the harsh life he had endured. "I've had a tough life. I hope some day to be taken out of Hell and have a better life . . . but I don't know what 'better life outside' means." Anh knew that such a view did not impress outsiders. Many camp children believed that they would have a better chance of being miraculously rescued if they said they wanted to be socially useful. So Anh, like many others whom we spoke with, said, "But I want to get out. I would look for a better opportunity to improve my life and become useful to society." The notion of being productive may be a widely held cultural value for Vietnamese youngsters, but, significantly, Anh had no idea what "becoming useful to society" might mean.

Hieu and Hoc: "I Had to Run Away"

IN CHI Ma Wan, we also interviewed two boys, fifteen and twelve years of age, who had been put in the camp jail for attempting to run away. We asked them about the conditions of their jail confinement and what we could do to help them. During our discussion, the older boy, Hieu, recounted many details of his life story. Hieu escaped with an aunt. She was accepted as a refugee, but since Hieu's parents were still in Vietnam, the Hong Kong authorities told him he would have to return to Vietnam. They separated Hieu from his aunt; she was resettled in Denmark, while Hieu remained alone in the barbed-wire confines of Chi Ma Wan, treated like a criminal, under the scrutiny of prison guards. "You hear that siren?" Hieu asked. "That's the second time today the people of the camp have been thrown out of their Quonset huts and made to wait while the guards search for weapons."

Hieu and his friend Hoc were given meager food rations; the standard food allowance left them hungry. They feared the guards, but also the adult inmates and the youth gangs who intimidated them and ran the camp in collusion with the guards. Each day was filled with dread; they were terrified that they would be called to an interrogation that they would not understand and then sent back to Vietnam. They were lonely, with no relatives in the camp. But they did not want to repatriate because they feared that the authorities would punish them for escaping. They did not attend school in the camp because they were too discouraged and depressed to study. They sat around doing nothing.

One day, the unaccompanied minors of the camp were taken on an excursion to another island. Hieu described what happened. "We went on an outing with other unaccompanied minors. My friend Hoc and I were wandering along the beach. We were curious to look at things and we got lost. By the time we got back, our boat had left. Suddenly we realized that we had a chance to escape from the prison and be free. We tried to get on a ferryboat but got caught. So the two of us are back here." They were punished with two months' confinement in jail, with half rations.

One of us observed, "There was nowhere for you to run. You were on an island."

Hieu smiled, acknowledging the futility of his attempted escape. "I'm in this room with bars because I *had* to run away."

Disregard of Humane Standards

UNACCOMPANIED MINORS were mistreated, not only in the Hong Kong camps, but in those of other countries as well. There are internationally accepted standards of child care and protection. While some people question the universality of some or all of these principles, they are, nevertheless, widely held up as minimum standards for the humane treatment of children. They are found in several documents. The best known is the United Nations Convention on the Rights of the Child. The others are "Refugee Children: Guidelines on Protection and Care," based largely on the Convention, and two documents specifically written regarding unaccompanied minors from Southeast Asia seeking asylum, the "Note on Unaccompanied Minors" of the Comprehensive Plan of Action, and the updated "Guidelines for Implementation of the Special Procedures."[3]

These documents state unequivocally that children have the right to adequate food, housing, health care, and conditions that promote mental health. Adequate provision must be made for their education and their cultural, social, and recreational needs. Officials could have protected the children according to these standards but they failed to do so. The reasons for this are the subject of this book.

Even in the best of the camps, the international standards were violated or disregarded; in the worst camps, the children were deeply scarred. Many writers have described the shocking details of the prison-like conditions of these camps. The Hong Kong detention centers such as Whitehead were the most widely visited, photographed, and written about. Norwegian anthropologist John Knudsen, who was involved in relief efforts for Vietnamese refugees, writes of his visit to Whitehead, "I felt dizzy, ridiculous, like a tourist on a guided tour of misery. We knew we could not help them."[4] Novelist Heather Stroud, who worked for six years in the detention centers, describes how, at the risk of severe punishment, detainees in Whitehead scaled the internal fences to meet people in other sections.[5] Diana Bui, a women's and children's advocate for an American voluntary organization, Indochina Resource Action Center, states, "This warehousing of people is part of a systematic process of dehumanization. People become numbers and, after a while, even refer to themselves by number."[6] Linda Hitchcox, in her book on Hong Kong detention camps, refers to this process as institutionalization, intended to mold detainees so that they would become dependent and compliant, according to the will of their jailers.[7]

Susan Comerford, Victoria Lee Armour-Hileman, and Sharon Rose Walker, writers for Refugee Concern Hong Kong, an activist legal rights organization, give a chilling account of the physical conditions of the Hong Kong camps and the social and psychological effects that these had on children. Arbitrary prison rules created an environment of "anguish, demoralization, and humiliation." They comment that with unstructured time, people had no relief from a tense and violent environment. Adults felt powerless to protect children, and the children in turn were deeply affected by being around adults who were violent

Detainees wait in line for health care, Whitehead Detention Center, Hong Kong. Subject to numerous regulations used to control them, the detainees must sit in a row behind the metal barrier. *Photo: Nguyen Dinh Huu.*

Children playing on a platform used as a sleeping space, Whitehead Detention Center, Hong Kong. *Photo: Nguyen H. Duyen.*

and who engaged in illicit activities, including prostitution, theft, and assault. The camp rules, including etiquette towards guards, were so numerous that no detainee could identify all of them, and no one had been given explanations of them. Detainees engaged in prohibited activities in order to survive or improve the quality of their lives. For example, they might recook their food (prohibited to break their spirit), or fashion knives both to protect themselves and for daily activities such as cutting an orange. The family, the central institution of Vietnamese culture, was under assault, replaced by fear, intimidation, lack of respect for powerless elders, loneliness, and the absence of both traditional discipline and nurturing found in the ideal Vietnamese family.

The authors interviewed twenty unaccompanied minors, average age fifteen-and-a-half. The minors said that their main fear was violence, and that they could not escape from it. All of the children interviewed had witnessed acts of violence, including murder. They feared that they would be harmed. Sixteen of them had been injured, and six had been hospitalized. A seventeen-year-old boy said, "I run, but there is nowhere to hide when people start fighting. I am scared."[8]

All the children interviewed said that their anxieties from living in the camp had affected their eating and sleeping habits. Eleven children said they were unable to concentrate or found it hard to do so, and twelve of the twenty were not attending school, even though all were of school age. They said they were too worried to be able to learn. The children began to exhibit behavioral problems in the camps, including withdrawal, various forms of aggression, and even self-mutilation. Some were afraid to leave their dwellings; they stayed indoors, thus failing to make contact with the world outside.[9] Unaccompanied minors, with no one to direct them, learned how to be street-smart survivors, without formal education, technical skills, or social etiquette that might prepare them for a life beyond the camps. The authors conclude that the lives of these children had been put on hold, interrupting their transition to becoming adults.[10]

In other countries, detention centers were also demoralizing prisons. An Australian Sister of Mercy, who worked in several camps, noted that the longer children remained in the camps, the more stressed they became. Boys were often drawn into gang activities; girls tended to withdraw. A Jesuit Brother, who was thrown out of Malaysia's Pulau Bidong Camp for complaining about the lack of sufficient food for unaccompanied minors, wrote to us that they were "kept like dogs on a short line." They were "living without spirit." They had been moved away from their friends and were lonely and depressed. No Special Committee had been formed, so the children waited in limbo. This camp worker alleged that the Malaysian Task Force authorities, the Malaysian Red Crescent Society, and UNHCR had lied to the children. They received detention of one to two months "for nothing," and then had to report to the Task Force every two hours for the next two to four weeks.[11]

At first glance, Galang, where we met the girl who later committed suicide, did not have a prison appearance. This luxuriant island, about one day's boat journey from Singapore, had ample space for people to walk around. But the temporary wooden dwellings swaying in the wind were constant reminders of the intended impermanence of the camp. A thin, older detainee whispered to us, "Don't be fooled by appearances. This camp is a lot worse than it looks." Journalist Michael Bociurkiw tells us why. In "Terrorized in the Camp of Shame," a graphic article on abuses in the camp, he reports that Indonesian guards allegedly beat detainees and sexually assaulted the women, while officials took bribes to recommend detainees for resettlement. At that time, 1993, the camp housed 14,330 detainees. In the article, a British aid worker familiar with the camp said, "These things don't surprise me," while a United Nations High Commissioner for Refugees country representative stationed in Indonesia dismissed the charges. "We're not saying it might not have happened at all," he said, "but I really believe it is very limited." He added, "Seventy percent of the time we have someone there."[12]

An American social worker, who had worked for one year in Galang counseling unaccompanied minors, spoke to us with her voice shaking. "I am appalled at the lack of protection for these kids and the way rules are changed on them. Girls are vulnerable to Vietnamese in the camp and to Indonesians. I don't understand how they can do this to the children. There is much sexual abuse in the camp, but because of the fear of retribution, people will not speak out." She also disapproved of forcing the children to make the decision to repatriate or remain in the camps. "We don't do this to children in the U.S.," she said. "These are children. They are put in an intolerable situation. We need to make the decisions for the children."

Hue: "An Indescribable Horror"

UNTIL THEY were finally closed in 1993, Thai camps along the border with Cambodia were among the most brutal in Southeast Asia.[13] As mentioned in Chapter 1, most of these camps held Cambodians along with a handful of Vietnamese. The Vietnamese asylum seekers had escaped from their homeland in the early and middle 1980s, traveling overland through Cambodia to

Thailand. Along the way, they had weathered attacks by Vietnamese soldiers, Khmer Rouge soldiers, and bandits, while also avoiding the many mines along the Cambodian border. Only 10 percent survived the journey. They were placed in and moved among various camps in an area known as Site 2. Because of an international bureaucratic foul-up, many of the Vietnamese languished in these camps for more than a decade.[14] Some of the children we interviewed had been in Site 2 camps for five years.

In the 1980s, Vietnamese occupation troops in Cambodia frequently shelled the camp, a collection of rickety rattan and thatch huts. Hue, an elderly woman and survivor of the camp, released in 1988 and now living in northern California, recalled those days for us. Unlike most of the people in the camp, she was considered a refugee and was allowed to leave in 1988. "In some months, shelling went on continuously, day after day. It was an indescribable horror. We would hear the screams and cries of the wounded, bodies were everywhere, and blood was all over the roads. We were terrified; our family simply huddled together, embraced one another, and cried."

For Hue, the nights were more terrifying. That's when the Cambodian bandits would come down from the hills and enter the camp. "They shot people, they raped women, and they took whatever they wanted—clothes and rations, especially rice. We were completely unprotected. We would hide in a corner and hope they did not find us."

But the greatest danger, says Hue, came from the Thai Task Force 80 camp guards. "They killed, raped, and beat people whenever they wanted. Almost every youngster was hit on the head with rifles two or three times. Once, the guards stopped three young Vietnamese men who were talking with a Laotian girl. They cut lines up and down the arms of the young men until blood flowed freely. Then they poured vinegar on the wounds to cause the young men great pain. After that, the guards buried the three of them alive. I saw that. I was there when they stopped a Cambodian woman from selling fried bananas in the market. She was not permitted to do that, so the guards took the boiling oil from her pan and poured it on her head. Her two eyes blew up and she died."

Hue continued, "You cannot imagine what it was like to be there, the horror of it was beyond description. I wrote to my relatives back in Vietnam, 'Do not escape.' With the never-ending hunger, the continuous fear of death and torture at any moment, the dirt, the lack of privacy, the exhaustion, the disease, and the uncertainty of what was to happen to us, we were easily swayed by rumors that we would be sent back to Vietnam. We did not know who to believe or what to do. We were always in a panic. We were not in a clear mind to make decisions."

Hue's remarks are confirmed by other observers. The Lawyers Committee for Human Rights reported that "Vietnamese fleeing their homeland frequently have been raped, robbed and sometimes killed by bandits or Cambodian guerrillas shortly before reaching the Thai border." They state that competing Cambodian factions (Khmer Rouge and Khmer Peoples National Liberation Front, or KPNLF) captured these people and held them as "virtual slaves — sometimes as human mine detectors." They forced them into military service, held them until relatives abroad paid ransom money, and sexually abused women and girls. Thai guards, the Task Force 80 rangers, also abused the asylum seekers. "Through early 1987, conditions for Land Vietnamese at Site 2 [Vietnamese Land Refugees] were dominated by robbery, rape and abuse by Thai rangers, KPNLF soldiers and armed bandits. Thai security officials referred to the Platform, the Vietnamese Section of Site 2 South, as a 'jail,' and considered the residents to be prisoners without legal protection or human rights."[15]

In 1988 Nguyen Dinh Huu visited Ban Thad, a Site 2 camp for Vietnamese, and our organization subsequently built a school for the camp's children. When the Vietnamese moved to Section 19, Site 2, we provided school assistance there. At the invitation of the people of Section 19 and with the permission of Thai authorities, we visited them in 1992. At that time, Site 2 was home to more than 200,000 Cambodians and less than 1,000 Vietnamese.

The shelling had long ceased. The Task Force 80 rangers, a poorly trained, all-male paramilitary force, had been replaced in August 1988 by the Displaced Persons Protection Unit (DPPU), a better-trained security force, and serious incidents involving Thai guards had ceased. Nevertheless, Site 2 remained a dangerous place. The camp was so vulnerable to attack by bands of Cambodian bandits seventy to eighty strong that by four in the afternoon, outside of a handful of Thai guards, all other government officials and international relief workers fled in car caravans to their homes in or near Aranyaprathet, some fifty miles southwest of Site 2, abandoning the camp inhabitants to the terrors that night brought. The bandits also attacked Thai villages near the camp, kidnapping the inhabitants, holding them for ransom, and sometimes killing them. North and west of the camp, the roads and villages were controlled by bandits day and night. Travel along these roads was highly dangerous. To reach the camp safely from that direction, as we did in January 1992, required a caravan, an armed escort, and a bit of luck. From time to time, the Thai High Command would launch campaigns against the bandits, but with little success. Even after the border camps were closed in 1993, the area remained dangerous. It was no place for children.

Chi Lan: Sent Away by Stepfather

SIKHIU IS a cheerless, forbidding camp in central Thailand notorious for its abuse of detainees. The camp, hidden from the main road along a narrow, dusty path, was surrounded by thick, gray stone walls, patrolled by armed guards, and divided into sections separated by high steel fences. Inside, the inmates lived many to a room in crowded beehives of rough stone, without privacy, dignity, or hope, while camp officials, guards, and UNHCR officers ran the camp, seemingly indifferent to the worlds of pain and loneliness that they oversaw. While the detainees of Sikhiu were surviving on meager meals sufficient to stave off starvation but not hunger, the United Nations was remodeling its building in Bangkok at a cost of twenty million dollars.

In the early years of its operation, the Task Force 80 guards of Sikhiu frequently killed, tortured, raped, and extorted money from their helpless prisoners. One former detainee now residing in the United States recalled severe punishments for minor infractions of rules, "The guards would hang us by our thumbs for hours until we passed out. They checked to see if we were really unconscious by burning us with lighted cigarettes." Another inmate described the beatings. "They would tie a man's hands behind his back tight on a pole and then beat him on the back with a rattan pole." This same man described killings, corruption, the stealing of food, medicines, and clothes intended for the inmates, gambling, drinking, and prostitution involving both the inmates and the Thai guards. The camp was closed to outsiders so that the horrors within would remain hidden. But former detainees of Sikhiu and other camps reported the abuses, and Western nations complained to Thailand. Sikhiu was closed in 1986. It was reopened in 1991 to house screened out post-CPA arrivals and those awaiting screening. The guards were new and the treatment of detainees had improved, but outsiders only rarely were allowed access to the camp. In 1992, we were the first nongovernmental organization allowed to observe the camp since it had reopened.[16]

We first interviewed Chi Lan, sixteen years old, in Sikhiu on January 2, 1992. Chi Lan had not been mistreated, but she was witness to all of the terrors of camp life. During our visit, the detainees frequently mentioned a recent shooting of two inmates by the assistant camp commandant. Chi Lan spoke to us, not of that incident, but of her hunger and loneliness.

"I don't have enough food to eat, but I try to make ends meet. I have less food than I did in Vietnam. I am hungry, but I try to survive with what I have. Because I am an unaccompanied minor, Enfants du Mekong [a French charitable organization] gives me three hundred baht [US $12] a month to supplement my food, but next month, the Ministry of the Interior will stop us from receiving that money. I have three pairs of clothes—one for church and two for at home. When they wear out, nothing can be done. Here in camp, I just go to school. I don't know anything else. This is better than in Vietnam, where my mother had to pay for my tuition. But I miss my mother. Soon after I arrived here, I received a letter from her. She was pleased to learn of my arrival. The last letter I got from her was in December 1990. She told me to take good care of myself. She said that my stepfather had a visa and that they would leave for America soon. I haven't heard from them since."

Chi Lan's story, while not as traumatic as many, speaks nevertheless of the formative events since 1975 that prompted people to flee Vietnam. In 1976, nine months after South Vietnam fell to the victorious North Vietnamese Communists, Nguyen Thi Chi Lan was born in a small hamlet of Xuan Dinh Village, Dong Nai Province, 25 miles northeast of Ho Chi Minh City. Although the war was over, its effects dominated Chi Lan's life from the day she was born. She never knew her father; he had been missing since 1975. Several years later, her paternal grandmother told her that he had been in the South Vietnamese army.

As Chi Lan was growing up, the new government imposed socialism on South Vietnam, as described in Chapter 1.[17] During these years of economic turmoil, Chi Lan attended school, completing the seventh grade. In contrast, most of her classmates quit after the second to supplement the meager incomes of their desperately poor families. Their parents would say, "If you don't work, you don't eat and you die. If you don't go to school, you can still work and eat." Chi Lan's adoptive mother, an agricultural laborer, was as poor as the other parents, but she went without food and clothes for herself to send her daughter to school. She had to pay for books, the maintenance of buildings, and extra tutoring from teachers whose salaries were otherwise not sufficient to live on. After school, Chi Lan helped with home chores and played with friends, but she always felt sad. "My friends had a father, and I didn't." Chi Lan cried as she recalled her loss.

In 1982, Chi Lan's adopted mother remarried, and in 1984 she bore a son. After that, Chi Lan's life became harsher, duplicating a situation experienced by many Vietnamese stepchildren. "Mother was very close to me, but my stepfather was not good to me. He didn't like me. He yelled at me and would stare at me."

Because Chi Lan's stepfather, a former major in the South Vietnamese army, had been incarcerated for seven years in a reeducation camp, he was eligible to be resettled in the United States under the Humanitarian Operation (HO) program. "I heard my mother and stepfather discuss going to America, but they never mentioned me. I became sad. I asked my mother to let me go with them. I heard about friends who went to the U.S.A. Mother said, 'I'll help you go to America, but in another way. I plan to send you out through Cambodia.'" Chi Lan became one of the thousands of children fleeing Vietnam without parents, an unaccompanied minor with nowhere to go, a casualty of war and oppression, international politics, failed domestic policies, and family disruption.

For Chi Lan, family rejection was utterly devastating. Like other Vietnamese children, her identity and character had been forged in her relationships with her family. Chi Lan's mother and grandmother had given her unconditional love and nurturance and had made great sacrifices for her. She was deeply dependent on them. To them she showed respect, unquestioned obedience, and a deep sense of moral obligation, which extended not only to living family members, but to those who had preceded her and would follow her.

But Chi Lan also felt a great sense of loss. She saw her life and family as incomplete because she had grown up without a father, a guiding, disciplined authority. Because of the war, tens of thousands of Vietnamese children lost their fathers. Like Chi Lan's adoptive mother, many war widows remarried; so did some women whose husbands languished in reeducation camps. Chi Lan found herself not only rejected by a stepparent, but also sent away from the family.[18]

Many of the children we interviewed in detention centers recounted similar experiences. We are especially aware of how deeply harmed they were by their loss because of our own experiences with Vietnamese families. Nguyen was reared in the Vietnamese family system, and Freeman lived for some time in the postwar period with a poor family in Ho Chi Minh City. Despite disruptions brought about by war and forced change, core Vietnamese values have persisted for many families: nurturance, dependence, obligation, and submission to and respect for elders. Feelings of separation, loneliness, rejection, and despair dominate the lives of unaccompanied minors in detention centers and repatriated minors in Vietnam. Their life stories are testimony both to their hopes and their disillusion.

In July 1990, at the age of 14, Chi Lan, along with several neighbors, took a bus into Cambodia. The bus driver paid off Vietnamese officials to let the bus proceed. In all, 47 people escaped. Chi Lan recalled the journey. "Along the way, Cambodian soldiers stopped us, and the owner of the bus gave them money. We did not know what faction these soldiers came from. I was not afraid of them because at that time I did not know what these soldiers sometimes did. The rest of our trip was safe. We arrived at the town of Kompong Som on the seashore, and from there we boarded a boat. We landed on an island, where we remained for one day. Then a Thai fishing boat arrived. A man from our group swam to the boat and told the fishermen that we were refugees. They gave us some food but not enough for all of us. Some of the adults went deep into the jungle. They brought back wild bananas, coconut, and manioc, cooked it, and gave it to the children. Later, another boat arrived. The fishermen gave us fresh water and some more food, but they refused to take us on their boat. After two days, a third boat found us. The men in this boat brought us on board, searched us, and removed our gold. No one dared to complain, and luckily there was no rape or abduction. They took us to the police. From there, we were taken to Lan Ngop Camp, where we remained for over twenty days. Then we were sent to Phanat Nikhom Camp. We arrived there in the month of August."

Chi Lan had expected to be resettled. Instead, she was told about the Comprehensive Plan of Action. Since she had arrived after the cutoff date, she would be interviewed by the Special Committee to determine whether or not it was in her "best interests" to be resettled or repatriated; most likely she would be told to return to Vietnam. "I had never heard of the CPA until that time. Even when I heard, I had no idea about that; I did not know what they were talking about."

When we first met Chi Lan in Sikhiu, she had been in Thai detention camps for nearly one-and-a-half years. Many unaccompanied minors in the camp had been advised to return to Vietnam. At that time, they were not sent back unless they volunteered to go. Since most refused to repatriate, the authorities tried to coerce them by curtailing their schooling and reducing their food. Others, like Chi Lan, were still awaiting the decision of the Special Committee, which might take one or two years.

Chi Lan herself had not even been interviewed until well over one year after she had arrived in Thailand. She had been completely unprepared for it. "I was told that I would be interviewed one day in advance. I had no idea what they wanted, but I was ready to answer anything they asked. They treated me nicely during the interview, but I could not understand all of the meanings, so I could not answer properly. I did not understand what they asked."

When we left Sikhiu, we did not know what would become of Chi Lan. We had told her to keep us informed of her situation. In early 1993, we received a letter from her. Officials had informed her that it was in her "best interests" to be sent back to Vietnam. She wrote, "I have decided to return to Vietnam. You know what this camp is like, so you know why. I hope you can visit me in my home village." We wrote to Chi Lan that we would meet her on our forthcoming trip to Vietnam, and we did in June 1993. Her story continues in our chapter on repatriation.

CHAPTER THREE

VICISSITUDES OF FATE

PHILIPPINE FIRST ASYLUM CAMP on the island of Palawan was the least harsh of the large Southeast Asian detention centers. Unlike the steel cages surrounding the Hong Kong camps, the perimeter fence in Palawan consisted of a few strands of wire that presented no barrier for detainees who wished to climb over them. But they didn't need to, since with only a cursory check they could freely enter and leave the camp at its two gates. Within the camp, they could move without restriction. Detainees were allowed to operate small businesses, and these dotted the camp: noodle shops, restaurants with full Vietnamese meals and regional dishes, jewelry stores, tailor shops, barber stalls and beauty salons, two bakeries, and sundries shops. The camp contained Catholic and Protestant churches, as well as Buddhist and Cao Dai temples. Schooling and vocational training was extensive, and health care was the best of all the Southeast Asian camps. An elected council represented the interests of the camp residents. A wide variety of social services, sports, coffee shops, fruit and vegetable gardens, social clubs, and leisure activities relieved the boredom of camp life. The standard of living exceeded that of local residents.

The Philippine government insisted on the humane treatment of the Vietnamese asylum seekers. As a rule, the guards of the Western Command dealt humanely with the detainees, though relations deteriorated markedly in the final months of the CPA, heralding the closing of the camps and the threat of forced repatriation. The major aid agency in Palawan, the Catholic-run Center for Assistance to Displaced Persons (CADP), was a staunch advocate of comprehensive services and the protection and humane treatment of detainees. Unlike other CPA countries, Philippine national interests were consistent with UNHCR's principles for the protection of asylum seekers.

Yet stresses were high in the Palawan camp, especially for those awaiting the decision on their application to be resettled as refugees. In her pre-CPA comparative study of camps, Linda Hitchcox suggests that for short periods of time, harsh physical conditions were less important as a stress-producer than other causes. Although camps in the Philippines, Hong Kong, and Thailand were organized somewhat differently, Hitchcox claims that internees at all these camps experienced similar frustrations. Those who stayed less than two years were affected less by barbed wire and guards than by how they evaluated their chances of being repatriated. This is why the levels of anxiety and depression in Palawan were comparable to the high levels of anxiety in the more harshly regulated Thai camp of Phanat Nikhom.[1] But the physical environments of the harsher camps took their toll on detainees who remained for more than two years, which was the situation for most post-CPA unaccompanied minors.

In our interviews in 1991, we also found that unaccompanied minors in Palawan camp were highly stressed. Friends, foster parents, and counselors tried to give them support, but they were no substitute for parents and blood relatives. Therapists whom we interviewed called attention to several issues, including fear of interviews and rejection, the boredom of daily life, uncertainty about

Minimal fence surrounding Palawan First Asylum Camp, the Philippines. Such fences contrast with the high barbed-wire fences of the Hong Kong camps. *Photo: James M. Freeman.*

the future, and mixed messages. Some people in the camp told them to hang on and they could get resettled. Others told them that if they had no parents in a third country, they would have to go back. Some children received letters from their parents telling them not to come home. An American therapist who worked with unaccompanied minors commented to us that a frequent source of stress was "unwanted pregnancies. While abortions are legal in Vietnam, they are illegal in the Philippines." There were complications from botched abortions. If she gave birth to a child, the young mother, although a minor, was not allowed to give up the baby for adoption; she feared rejection by her family in Vietnam and abandonment by her boyfriend. The children feared that they would be pushed into the violent political demonstrations that erupted in the camp. Separation from relatives was a major source of stress. Younger children, 9–11 years old, wanted to be in foster families and then were devastated when the foster family was resettled and they were left behind. Together, these factors left the children in a constant state of anxiety. When they were told they would have to repatriate, they became reserved and quiet. They did not eat, and they dropped out of school. Counselors tried to comfort them, but as one child said, "You will never understand. You are not a refugee. You will never know what the feeling of hopeless is."

Tuyet: Storms in My Life

IN 1991, our volunteer organization, Aid to Refugee Children Without Parents (ARCWP) sponsored a literary contest for unaccompanied minors in the Philippine (Palawan) First Asylum Camp. Tuyet, then 16 years old, wrote the prizewinning essay, an account of her personal anguish as she was rejected for resettlement and told to return to Vietnam. She called her story "Storms in My Life." Her title stands as a central metaphor for the stories of all of the children who sought asylum. She tells of her childhood in central Vietnam, her close ties to her family, her escape across the ocean, and why her family selected her to make this perilous voyage: they expected her to resettle and then help out her family in Vietnam, a heavy obligation to lay on a youngster. We have included an excerpt from her story that tells of her rejection.

Our group of 31 persons was sent to Palawan First Asylum Camp, where most Vietnamese refugees resided while waiting for resettlement. We were split up and sent to different barracks, depending on our individual situation.

When I arrived at the new living place for the first time, I felt the house was cold. The people living in the house were entirely strangers to me. It was a bit frightening. That was my first impression. As time passed, I lived a miserable life. I lived with my inside sadness. I went to school and got a job at the Social Services Section. Time gradually gnawed at my sadness.

I had no relatives in the camp, and none in other countries. Therefore I didn't receive any assistance from anywhere. Although I was deprived of material needs, I never complained or felt bad about this situation. Time was passing by, passing by, and I myself had to struggle to survive with the time, expecting a better future.

It was more than one year since I had arrived in the camp! More than one year of waiting, away from my homeland, separated from my loving mother, from everything.

On August 20, 1990, at noon, while following a narrow path home from the morning school, a strange feeling suddenly invaded me. I felt fatigued and irritated. I thought this was due to the hot weather, but it was not. I was falling into a dark hell. At that moment a girl of my group informed me that she had been "rejected." I knew that my refugee situation was similar to that girl. I could not think of anything else. I rushed to see our Vietnamese-American volunteer worker, who told me to go to the UNHCR office. I was completely desperate. Tears flowed from my eyes. The first drops were for myself. I was totally defeated. I had lost all my hope that I had been nurturing and believing in.

At 3:30 in the afternoon, I went [to] the UNHCR Field Officer at her office to inquire about her final decision about my future, I had already started crying profusely, knowing in advance that I had been preparing for an unavoidable fall down an abyss.

It was like a bolt from the blue. My application for resettlement had been rejected for reasons so simple I could never have imagined. I was a minor without relatives in another country. All of my parents were living in Vietnam. It was better for me to return to live with my parents in order to receive adequate care and protection!

I said a few words, but I already felt dizzy. All I knew was crying, only crying. I could not believe that my fate had ended in such a terrible way. No, no, no, I could not take it. I repeated this firmly to myself several times. I repeated that I could never return at this time. I showed the officer a letter from my father, who wrote that at any cost and under any hardship and adverse circumstances, I should stay and endure them while waiting for a brighter future. But the letter had no effect. With deep sadness and desperation, I bowed towards the UNHCR officer and left the room. I walked out but it was like nothing was in front of me. My feet automatically moved forward, but my head was in a whirl. It felt like I was walking in a dark area, a world that I thought I would never set my feet in. A somber space embraced me. I was like a wandering soul, moving, not knowing where I was going. Right then, two of my friends came to meet me. They guided me by the

A counselor from Community and Family Services International comforts a girl who was rejected for resettlement, Hong Kong. *Photographer unknown.*

hand; they anxiously asked me several questions, but I was speechless, shaking my head with two lines of bitter tears running down. They took me to their barrack. Several people there pressed me with innumerable questions. My sufferings had been contained at the bottom of my heart. Now I burst into sobbing, uncontrollably. I cannot describe the crisis I went through at that time. One of my classmates, who had suffered the same fate as me, started crying louder. The two of us were like crazy persons. It was a pitiful scene. We knew nothing but crying, and because of the same fate, condemned to a hell without any exit. I was hopeless and unable to find an escape because I was totally defeated. The only thing I knew was crying and blaming myself.

I hated myself for making my family, my loved ones, completely lose the hope they had placed in me. I kept asking myself why I had been defeated. Why, oh why was I forced into such a miserable situation? Why was I doomed to be such an unfortunate person? Oh, Almighty God! Why didn't you open your heart when seeing me writhing in deep agony? I fervently pray that you give me a favor, even a tiny one, to save this unfortunate human being.

My life, I have experienced enough so far. Like at this moment, I have tried unsuccessfully to open my eyes as wide as possible to see the world. My classmates felt pity for me, surrounded me, and consoled me, but my sobbing was louder than their words. I totally ignored everything happening around me. Everything was meaningless for me, and I continued to cry. My friends sat next to me and continued to comfort me. They took care of me, but I was exhausted; my arms and legs were paralyzed, and I collapsed like a dead body. I lay on a plank immobilized. Up to now, I had never experienced a situation like this. And now I could see who

Youths playing basketball, Palawan First Asylum Camp, the Philippines. Although the physical conditions and confinement were far less harsh than in Hong Kong, the stress levels were about the same. *Photo: James M. Freeman.*

I was at this time. I was no longer the same person. If I was, I should know how to think. But at this time, I only knew how to complain and to comfort myself with drops of lamenting tears, my eyes wandering to an indefinite horizon. I was tormented with questions. Where will I be going? Is there any reason that my future will be stopped at this place? No, it's impossible. My dad, my mom, my younger siblings were waiting every hour for news from me. They were placing their faith and hope in me. I could not fall down. I had to stand up, stretch myself, rise up against the storm and high waves which were ready to drag me out. No, I had to trample all my inside desperation, stand up and catch all of the available opportunities in life. So many people have put their hope in me; why let myself succumb? I still have friends around me; people turn to me, help me, so why do I consider myself totally defeated? Even though there is only faint hope, I still have hope. But at some moment of desperation, I would like to let go of everything and put my life in fate's hands. I wanted to disappear on the face of Earth immediately, because we all will return to dust some day. Long days in school have deteriorated my faint health; long hours at work also consume a large part of my time; long sleepless nights destroy me with unsolvable problems, and tears keep running on my cheeks. No, I cannot ignore this life because it was not for myself, but it includes my parents, my younger siblings who are expecting my success. I cannot let myself succumb; I have to make more effort. As Stefan Zweig has said, "Life does not grant

us anything, but anything destiny brings to us always has marked a discreet price."
I have to regain and consolidate my faith that almost got lost. I should know and
accept the failure, the challenge, the enthusiasm, then stand up with a new spirit,
high morale, with a new plan for my future, and realize that they cannot become
a reality if they lack my efforts.

Diderot has said, "The happiest persons are those who bring happiness to the
greatest number of persons." I don't see why I cannot bring happiness to anybody
else at all. There are plenty of people out there who have suffered more and encountered more failures than I have, and they continue looking for happiness and they
succeed. There is a future waiting for me. Whether that future is bright or dark
depends on me.

I know that at the present time I should have a strong self-confidence and
energy in order to produce a well-thought assessment of problems. This will save
me from collapsing again and will save other people from desperation.

All problems have happened to me in the past 20 months of anguished waiting. But I always try to find some relaxing moments to soothe my sadness. Since
the day I set foot in this camp, I have joined the scout group, where they teach
children both how to play and how to study. I also study arduously in school, where
I have completed 11ᵗʰ grade. I have just started the senior year, my last grade in high
school. I also participate in school activities, which I consider my duty and responsibility. I also put in a lot of time to improve my foreign language, which will be
our second language later.

I always dream and believe that I will have a better day in the future. That day
will be a shining one. I believe so, and so does my family.

Tao: Outside Looking In

TAO WAS born in 1977 near Cam Ranh. Tao's mother died when he was four
years old, and his father remarried and sent Tao to a rural area to live with his
paternal grandmother. Tao says, "While with Grandmother, I had no schooling at all. I did nothing but house chores. Grandmother offered me nothing."
After two years, she sent him to live with a cousin. When Tao was eleven, his
father came to him and said, "I have a new family. I don't have the possibility
of helping you. I will send you out. You have a chance to progress and possibly to study and prepare for your future."

Tao escaped by boat and arrived in the Philippines on June 9, 1989, eleven
weeks after the CPA cutoff date of March 14. In his interview with us in 1991,
Tao said, "We had never heard of the cutoff date. I first heard of it at the transit center but I did not have any idea about it. I did not have any idea about

refugee. I was totally ignorant. At first, I was not concerned. Later, I started to think about it. The more I thought, the more concerned I was. If screened in, what then? If screened out, what is my life, my future?"

One day Tao was called in for an interview. He says, "At that time, I knew nothing. The loudspeaker called out my name and told me to report the following morning. I had a high number so I thought I would be interviewed later, but I was called earlier, only four months after my arrival in Palawan." Normally the interview takes three hours, but Tao's lasted four hours. A Filipina conducted the interview. He describes her as "very serious." He says he responded to everything she asked, but he recalls in particular two questions: "What did you think about when you left Vietnam?" "If UNHCR decides to send you back to Vietnam, what do you think about it?"

Tao says, "These were bothersome questions; they disturbed me." To the first, he replied, "Father sent me out so that I would get a better education. Father told me he saw some Vietnamese go to the United States. They left as simple farmers. Now they are engineers. So go out of the country and get an education." To the second, he said, "My father sent me out to have a better future. I will be the last person to return to Vietnam if this camp closes." She asked him why he refused to go back. He said, "I believe Vietnamese overseas will do something because as Vietnamese they must help them [any Vietnamese who escapes] out." Tao says he believed he could be resettled. He told her, "If I go to a third country [he used the official term for country of resettlement], I would study. I love study. I want an education. If I return to live with my paternal grandmother, the end—no education."

Thirteen months after the interview, on November 1990, Tao received the decision: "*Bi da* ["kicked," slang for rejected]. I got the same form letter as every other kid. My feeling was very sad. I had a lot of hope, of great consequences in my education. Some of my friends have new changes in the situation of their family, so they submit for reconsideration, but for me it is hopeless. I have nothing to offer, to submit to change my situation. I have been called back two or three times to check my statement. Meanwhile, there is only one thing to do and that is to continue my education."

Tao then says, "I remember how my body felt when I was rejected. I felt sick for two to three days. I could eat nothing; I drank only a little water. I had the impression I was not really myself. I was outside of myself looking in. This lasted for one month. Then an overseas volunteer talked to me, consoled and counseled me, and I felt better. I resumed my education. After being screened out, my brain worked more than before. I thought more than before, about the future. What will happen to me? I remember a dream I had. It happened two days after I was screened out. A person told me he would take me out of here. Then suddenly I found I had returned to Vietnam. I woke up scared!"

Tao describes how he copes with his awful loneliness and how he tries to keep up his spirits in the face of deep disappointment. "When I am sad at night, I take music books and sing. During the day, I read, go to the library. Daytime is happiest for me; nighttime is the saddest. But the saddest time of all for me is during Tet, the Vietnamese New Year. Everybody is happy, but I am very sad. I miss my country, my hometown, my father, my siblings. I still have hopes for the future. I hope to go to a third country to study agriculture and then return to Vietnam, to help people in the countryside. Because there men have to pull plows instead of oxen. But realistically, I am scared because I am not prepared to return to Vietnam at this time. When I left, I expected something better. Now I return to what I had done before, with time lost."

Tao concludes sadly. "On display in this camp is a small boat used by 120 Vietnamese boat people. All of them died trying to reach freedom, yet one more lived: a dying woman gave birth to a child who survived. They died trying to reach this place, seeking freedom, but what is the freedom in this camp? I could not salute my flag nor hear my national anthem."

Cuc: One Who Was Fortunate

CHILDREN WHO arrived in camps with a parent had a very different experience than unaccompanied minors. The contrast was even greater among those, such as Cuc, who were screened in and subsequently resettled to third countries. From 1989 to 1994, Cuc was a detainee in Palawan. She suffered no traumatic experiences; on the contrary, she enjoyed living in the camp. But she recognized that not all children were as fortunate as she, and she describes the differences. In 1997, we interviewed Cuc, then fifteen, three years after her arrival in the United States.

I came to America in 1994, after five years in Palawan. Here in America I have many relatives: my mother and father, my maternal grandmother, my uncle on my mother's side, two older sisters, and a female cousin, and I have a lot of faraway cousins in the United States. I am the youngest sister. Eight people live in my house, six female, only two male. But we did not all come to America at the same time. My grandmother came two years ago and my middle sister and mother came a year ago. I pretty much get along with my middle sister because we're sort of like the same age, only one year apart.

I remember a little bit about Vietnam. I lived there until I was eight years old. Every morning I would get ready and go to school. After school I would come home for lunch and then take a nap. I had a lot of friends. My father and mother worked at home as tailors. Earlier, my father had been in the South Vietnamese army. We had enough food; we were average, not rich and not poor.

My father tried to escape from Vietnam fifteen times before he finally succeeded. One time, people found out, so the escape was called off. Another time he was discovered and sent to jail for eight years, his punishment for trying to escape. Finally, in 1989, he succeeded, and I went with him on that try. He tricked me; he said we would visit my uncle in Hue. Kids are blabbermouths, so he did not tell me what he was really doing.

My dad wanted all of us to escape. But my mom wanted to stay in Vietnam to take care of my grandma because she has kidney failure. I escaped with my father, my oldest sister, and two uncles on my mother's side. Dad wanted my oldest sister to go with him and he wanted me because I'm the smartest one in the family. Middle sister stayed behind in Saigon with my mother because she was more like a crybaby.

At two, Dad woke me up. There was this bus waiting for us. And then I remember my mom, she was on her motorcycle, and like, she's driving along with the bus, and then, for like fifteen minutes she went back. And like, we were going to this place. We transferred to another bus and drove for two to three hours until we reached the beach. There was a ship out at sea, and my dad had to carry me out. I can't swim; he swam out with me.

I was eight years old; I didn't know anything, and I was tired, too. The boat had two hundred forty-seven people. When my dad got on the boat, his leg was shattered by all the rocks in the ocean. We were pretty wet. And it was noisy. That's all I remember because I was like really sleepy. It was so crowded that you couldn't lie down, only sit. We were on the sea for seven days. We had enough water but not enough food, but pretty much it kept us going. We were not stopped at any time; we went straight.

On the trip, I remember Dad said to me, "Be happy; we're going to have enough food and to be free." At first, I missed my mother not being with us. I felt this for a couple of months, but then, later, I got friends. When we landed, it was on a small island called El Nido. We stayed there two days. Then we were transferred to Palawan.

I pretty much liked Palawan because there were a lot of Vietnamese people there, and like, really friendly to newcomers. The first week, we had to go to a separate camp. Later, they put the group in different houses. Our family stayed together. We lived in Zone Eight for two to three years. And then we moved again to Zone Eleven on the other side of the airfield runway. We stayed there for a year. And then we moved to Zone One. We stayed there until we got transferred to Bataan transit camp.

In the camp, my dad was sort of, like, famous or popular because he was one of the veterans. And he would strike for, like, our rights. So a lot of people liked him. And he was, like, a teacher too. He taught English. Lots of people know me because of him. And I make friends too. All the people at camp were my friends. I had a lot of good friends. We get along; we have fun. I like school because when we go we see each other. It is really fun. We have some good teachers, but I don't pay attention that much because I'm having fun. And I don't care about studying, stuff like that.

We played with little crystal balls. We had a game that we played using cans of condensed milk. After we finished off the milk, we washed the can and then we put it down to play a game. Whoever is losing has to take care of the can. And then we take this slipper and tried to hit the can. And when the can is hit, then we all run and then that guy have to chase one of us. And if he catch one of us, that person have to take care of the can.

And then there's another game. We had, like, rubber bands. Put them together. And then scissors, rock or hammer, plastic, and a well. Rock beats scissors, and then scissors beats plastic, well beats rock, and plastic beats well. We'd use three of the four. We had rubber bands. We'd sit on two sides of the rubber bands. And if you lose, we have this special dance. And then, like, we have to perform it. Or sometimes have to high jump, sort of like an exercising, using the legs.

In another game, we have to use our hands very quickly. We have, like, a tennis ball. Then we get some chopsticks, ten of them. We have this special pattern. We have to bounce the ball and put the chopsticks down; then we have to bounce the ball and pick up the chopsticks.

Usually we'd wake up around eight A.M. We went to school around three P.M. to seven P.M. in Palawan, and in Bataan, from nine to eleven or twelve. And so, except for when we're eating lunch and dinner, the rest were outside. We played all over. We went swimming, too, every week or something, because the sea was right there. We'd climb up the poles on the basketball court. I didn't play basketball, though. Near that there was, like, a coffee shop with lights. And next to that there was, like, a park where kids can play, with swings and slides and stuff like that. So if we stay on top of the poles, we can look out on the ocean; it was really pretty. We'd see the ocean and the moon, and the people, too. Around nine in the evening people would come out because it was hot inside. And on weekends, we'd have a special day for movies, with those big stands. It was really easy to put them together and carry them to the open space. Sometimes we'd be watching TV and it would crack apart and fall down, and, whew, everybody would fall down on top of one another. People got hurt sort of, but not really bad. The first two years, it was every day that we had movies, but later they reduced it to the weekends. It was a lot of fun being there because all my friends were there. These were my childhood friends.

Every Saturday, I belong to meetings of the Catholic youth. Actually, we have to go to church every day. But we have special mass for Catholic youth. I was like a leader of one of the small groups. Every month or two we have, like, this really special picnic, and as a leader we have to learn a lot of stuff, like Morse Code and special signs. Sometimes we camp overnight over the airport; we went to this place near the hospital. There were a lot of coconut trees. We'd pass that and go down a little bit. And there was this huge place near the beach. It had a lot of coconut trees there, and we'd camp there. It was pretty far, like a mile, two miles from the camp.

While I was in Palawan, there were a lot of strikes. I remember my dad said we're going on strike, so people like America would know about us and would, like, help us to come here. So we had really a big strike, like one week or so. They just came out there; they just sat there. They would sometimes yell out. My dad participated, but I don't because I have school. But I took food out for him. Some of them, they camp out there overnight. It was started by one of the Buddhist monks, who led the strike. It was sort of fun. People went out, were talking with each other, and later at night were camping out, and later were talking and stuff. I remember they make posters about human rights.

The camp authorities were not nice about this, actually. The strike went for seven days or so, and then the police, the Filipino [police] came with firefighters and they would, like, spray water on us and beat up some of the people and rocks were thrown. So it was getting violent. And later they broke down the strike and everybody have to go home. I heard about it. My sister and I didn't go. My dad didn't want us to go and we are Catholics. And on the strike, people don't eat. And we are Catholics. So the Father said we are Catholics so we don't believe in hunger strike; it is killing oneself, suicide, so we don't do that. There were two or three strikes that broke down after one to two days, pretty small.

We had gangs. There was a veteran who worked for the police, like security in the camp. And so he got messed up with gangs. And when he stayed in transit, in Bataan, he got beat up and later died on the plane. He was beaten up by the gang. I just heard about it.

I know some of the gang people in the camp, 'cause later they are kind of like normal gangs. So I know them 'cause my dad is popular in the camp. Actually I know everyone in the camp. They were not that bad, but don't mess with them both in Palawan and Bataan. They were, like, really nice too. They stayed in a group, about twenty-five to thirty years old, both males and females. They beat up one guy. He died and they threw him in the stream. Later, police found that guy, eaten by fish; his eyeballs got eaten, and his ears too, real disgusting. He messed with the gang. Two people were killed like that.

Usually, the gangs in each zone took care of the water. They have a water place. And so people have to use the water. If you want to use the water, you have to pay them money, and they let you use the water. If you don't pay them money, then

Protest against the policy of repatriation at Palawan First Asylum Camp, the Philippines. *Photographer unknown.*

Protest against UNHCR, Palawan First Asylum Camp, the Philippines. *Photographer unknown.*

you have to use it, like, really late, six or seven [P.M.]. And they controlled the food too. They worked at the food distribution place. And then, if there's good stuff, they take the good stuff for themselves. They took a lot more out than they could use, way, way more. Each of us is supposed to get a certain amount, but they weigh it. So they take more and we get less. These were not "gang" gang, but strong people; they beat you up if you mess with them. So we got a small amount of food and not good food unless we paid them. They would take the meat and we have half meat and half slimy fat. We had enough food to eat, but that's because my dad, he was a teacher and he got an allowance. So he could buy more food.

Generally we had meat once every three or four days, fish, canned fish, vegetables, a weekly ration of uncooked rice, potatoes and sweet potatoes, and bananas, which were usually bad, overripe. Clothes we brought with us from Vietnam. Sister Pascale gave used clothes to poor people. From an organization called International Organization for Migration we got washcloths, toothpaste, toothbrush, things like that. If we were sick, we went to the camp clinic. If we were very ill, we went to the hospital outside the camp.

Two to three years later, the gangs joined the security [Vietnamese security in the camp]. They became like good person. But if someone mess with them, they beat them up. They also joined the sports, a soccer team for one year.

We had a fair for Tet, the Vietnamese New Year. We had a lot of stuff and fun. The older people would give us money, and we would go to this place and they have lotto, and "gourd, crab, shrimp, fish" [bau, cua, tom, ca]. This is a gambling game for profit played at Tet. You have different items in the gambling game. It is fun. It was really fun when there were lots of people there, about five or six years ago.

The Vietnamese officials in the camp were my dad's friends. Usually they volunteer for some of the organizations. They went out and then we vote, and whoever got the highest vote got to be the official. They would run for security and to be elected representatives.

My dad had contact with the Filipino leaders. One of them was a general. He was really nice. He was friendly, and he would talk to us. We got more food when he was general and the food was fresher, like the fish. He was too nice, so they transferred him. The new person who replaced him was meaner. I stayed in Palawan for five years and a half. For the last year, they have a person who was mean, who try to convince us to go back to Vietnam. So he was not that friendly. And the food was not good; the fish was spoiled. The Filipino guards stayed outside the gate at the market and at the gate entrance house, and at the monkey house [jail]. I didn't have any contact with them.

In the camp were a couple of Filipino medical doctors. They were nice and they gave us medicines and helped us. One of them died from diabetes. They gave us medicines and stuff we needed.

We didn't go into the town [Puerto Princesa] that often because we have to pay the three-wheeler to go there [a mile or two down the road]. We didn't have lots of money, so we didn't go often, maybe once a year to buy clothes. Sometimes Filipino kids would come into the camp and sell us fruit, which they picked. In Bataan, they'd sell duck eggs with embryo [a Vietnamese delicacy]. They also came to us and asked us for food. There they were really hungry.

I knew all of the overseas volunteers and Sister Pascale, who was the head of the Center for Assistance to Displaced Persons. The volunteers, who were mostly Asian, were helpful; they taught us English and gave us good pronunciation. They were really nice. And there was an American priest who was really nice. He gave us food from his refrigerator. He loved us. And a Vietnamese priest who was there built a house at the sea, and we'd visit him. He gave us clothes from America.

Dad had an aunt. She and an aunt on my mom's side were in America. They sent us some money, which we changed to pesos. So we had some money to help us. Some people here had no breakfast. Life was really hard for them. The food was not enough. They have to work, but they don't pay that much. They don't pay for work, they pay sort of an allowance which was real low. So those without money had a hard time.

I never went to the UNHCR office. I never went in there. There was one officer. She was Japanese. She was really pretty, but I think she is sort of like mean. People said that she wants to send us back to Vietnam. And there was this one lady, I don't remember her name. She was Filipino. She was the one that called us for screening us. We called her something like "murderer," because we have to, like, bribe her to get in, and if we won't, she didn't care if you were, like, a veteran or anything, if she know you have a relative in America. And some of them, some of the guys, you'd have to, like, sleep with them to get accepted, or you have to give them money. I knew about this because there was this lady. She slept with them for, like, ten times or something like that. And she got pregnant. But he didn't do anything; he didn't even accept her to, like, go to America. And so she took him to court or something. But it was a Filipino court, so actually they didn't do anything. I know that lady, too, 'cause she's a Catholic too.

I knew about the bribing of people 'cause my dad, he is a veteran. He told me Immigration asked if he had relatives in America, and he said yes. And then she, like, failed him. He appealed and got an amendment or something and so got accepted. There were a lot of cases about her. If she knows you have relatives in America but if you don't give her money and stuff like that, she'll, like, fail you. Some people gave her money and passed easily. They were not even veterans and had no trouble in Vietnam, but they passed.

If a person bribed them they went to Bataan. They had a good chance to go to countries like Switzerland or New Zealand, even though you didn't have any trouble in Vietnam. Only tough states like Canada and the United States and

Australia would not accept these people. You have to, like, be able to show discrimination. So most of the people that bribe cannot go there. I had friends who did not pay and failed. Some paid, and they were gone.

I never went through the screening; only my dad did that; my sister and I were part of his family. You had to be eighteen or older to be screened. Unaccompanied minors were interviewed differently. My dad saw the UNHCR Japanese lady and talked to her because he was a representative of a committee. He was the secretary of the Veterans Association and could speak English very well, so he could talk to others.

I remember that in school, the guys were immature, nerds, like. All the guys would kick all the girls out of their classrooms. This was done at break time. All of us were each other's best friends. We could talk like anything about guys, stuff that happens in camp, things like that.

For me, camp was a happy place. But for the unaccompanied minors, they had to stay in different house[s] and different sections. Unaccompanied minors had a very hard time. They didn't know what was going to happen to them because most of the minors got, like, failed, turned down. Only about one-fourth or one-third of the minors passed the [screening] test. Most of them were, like, paying the bribes. They got it from the people who sent them the money. They would pay bribes up to a thousand dollars. Some of them told me this. They didn't pay right away. They would give the money to the officials in their house or outside of the office area. Cash only.

In America, I have not seen any of the people I knew in Palawan, but my sister has friends from the camp who are in Texas, Los Angeles, and Canada. They call each other and send postcards. Most of my friends were minors, and they got sent back to Vietnam. Some didn't pay for screening or the appeal, so they were sent back.

When we were in Palawan, no one volunteered to go back to Vietnam. They were sort of positive [i.e., determined] about things. Then later, when I had been in America for about a year or so, some people volunteered to return. I lost contact with them. But I still keep contact with my uncle. We call him every month or so. He's in Manila. He and some others went by boat, passed the guards, and went to Manila. They left the camp because they did not get any more food. He works in Manila. He has friends in Manila who went there a year before he did. He shares a house with a Vietnamese lady. Others in the camp are not as successful. Some have families with small child, so they are, like, stuck in camp and cannot go out.

When I think of my life, in Vietnam, the Philippines, and America, I liked my life best when I was in the Philippines. In Vietnam I was too small. But Palawan and Bataan, that was my childhood, and it was, like, a lot of fun, too, even though the life was really hard. Five people had to share one can of fish in a day, and so it was really bad. Bataan was better. We had more food, and fresher. We actually could eat the food. In Palawan, the fish was really spoiled, and some people got, like, allergies, got itchy from it. I was in Bataan for one-and-a-half to two years. It was better than Palawan, but I was not that happy. In Palawan I had friends, but then some of them don't pass the screening test, so they were left behind. It was sort of hard, but I got over it. I make new friends. Life was better in Bataan. We had more space and more food. In Palawan, we lived in a house. On the first floor, ten to twelve people lived, and another ten people on the second floor, with one bathroom. So there was a total of twenty people in that small house. In Bataan, we had more space and a bigger special bathroom. It was not as smelly. Only one family lived in a house in Bataan.

In Palawan, sometimes, when we have to throw the tissue, we have to burn it, and sometimes, one or two times, the latrine house caught on fire and burned, and so we had nowhere to go when we really needed to for our business. So we had to go to a friend's house. It was really fun. Sometimes, when the latrine caught on fire, it spread to nearby houses, which caught on fire. Because the wood was old and dry and the roofs were made of thatch. It was funny. People would run out, see the fire coming, pack their stuff, and run next door. Then, later, they would have to unpack. But the fire would go fast and might change direction. Then they'd have to pack up and run in the other direction. One time in mid-autumn festival, a house caught on fire, and the whole building of connected houses burned all the way to the ground. Sometimes in the rainy season, houses would get water inside, so we have to bring all the stuff, like pans, to catch the water.

That's how life was in Palawan. It was fun. Now that I'm in America, I have to work a lot harder. I have to try really hard in school, or Dad will ground me and I cannot watch movies or go to places. But if I do well in school, Dad gives me money. He's really strict and traditional. We cannot date 'til we are sixteen to eighteen. He calls home from his work to find out if I'm doing my homework. And I have to ask him permission if I want to go somewhere. He says, "If you do well in school, your life will be better later." He wants me to do any job that I like. Since I'm quite good in math, I want to go into engineering or accounting.

Metaphors and Life-Narratives

VIETNAMESE CHILDREN of the camps used a variety of metaphors to try to understand and cope with the disruption they experienced. They sought ways to create order out of chaos, but often found themselves stuck, terrified of making a decision that might lead to unforeseen consequences. Time and again, with fear in their eyes, children told us that they had no hope and did not know what to do. They felt pressure because of the uncertainty of their situation and the conflicting messages they received from authorities, relatives, and fellow detainees. Younger children felt abandoned. Older children felt betrayed and terrified of being repatriated. Many children spoke of their disillusion when their friends told them that they had bribed officials in order to be screened in. Some children gave up and sank into a lethargic depression; others exploded in anger and violence. Equally self-destructive were those who made futile attempts to escape, provoking harsh punishments.

Despite their fears and disillusion, many children clung to hopes, however unreasonable, that they would not be returned to Vietnam. Their stories show that their metaphors of success were ones of resettlement, education, freedom, saving the family, and a happy future. Resettlement was seen as the solution to ensure a favorable future. Refugee status or a best-interest recommendation for resettlement stood for acceptance of the children as persons. Rejection of refugee status signified rejection of the person—but even more, rejection of the hopes for the future held by that child's family.

Through resettlement, children would be free to pursue the education that would be denied them in Vietnam. Education became a metaphor for acceptance. With education, the children could improve their economic situation and assist their family back in Vietnam. In the aftermath of being rejected for resettlement, many children held on to the ideal of getting an education—or, failing that, becoming a productive person—as the means to achieve a miracle. Perhaps if they told officials that they hoped to be productive, or showed that they were good students, officials would overturn a negative status determination and recommend resettlement.

Assistance to the family was tied to the notion of obligation to the family. Only with the greatest reluctance did children give up these notions. The stories show that many children refused to face up to the reality that they would be repatriated. Instead, they became politicized, depressed, unable to decide to return when told that they had no choice.

In Vietnam, people believe that the vicissitudes of life are connected with fate. When misfortune falls to a person, a family, or a nation, the Vietnamese interpret this as fate. It is no accident that Vietnam's most famous literary work, *The Tale of Kieu (Truyen Kieu)* by Nguyen Du, highlights the role of fate in the life of its heroine, Thuy-Kieu. Older Vietnamese frequently liken their own experiences to the heartbreak and suffering of Thuy-Kieu.[2]

Vietnamese people use the family as a buffer against the turnings of fate, and the family was a frequent topic of discussion for the Vietnamese children of the camps. Both those who were separated from their parents and those who were true orphans tried to retain family values. For them, as for other Vietnamese, the family was a major source of their identity, the center of Vietnamese culture, and the model for the organization of Vietnamese society.[3]

Many Vietnamese describe themselves and their culture as both orderly and emotional, and they see the family as representing this combination. The father stands for discipline and authority that must be obeyed, the mother for nurturing and affection, the emotional and sentimental aspect of Vietnamese culture. Children have expected roles, varying by gender and birth order. A child expects to receive direction and guidance from the father, emotional support from the mother, and support or respect from siblings, depending on birth order. When these ideal family ties are disturbed, Vietnamese people are in turn disturbed to their core. Separation from the family removes a portion of a person's identity.

The story of unaccompanied minors, then, is one in which the foundation of normal life has been shattered. The causes of this are both economic and political. For a decade after the end of the Vietnam War, Vietnam was plunged into a downward spiral of economic and social chaos, poverty, hunger, and repression, including the imprisonment of people in reeducation camps. The disintegrative effects on Vietnamese families were immediate and far-reaching, including the flight of asylum seekers, of whom nearly half were children. The stories of the children of the camps reveal a deep distrust of adults in authority and a notion that life is unpredictable. "I have no hope for the future" and "I have no idea what to do or where to go" are frequent expressions. Younger children often conveyed a sense of emotional abandonment, either from being sent away or from the untimely death of one or more parents.

There is an important distinction in the Vietnamese family between consanguineal or blood relatives *(ruot)* and those related by marriage *(ho)*. The bond between full parents and full siblings is considered strong; that between a child and other relatives or stepparents is weak. Under conditions of extreme economic hardship and hunger, children tend to be pushed out of the family by adult caregivers other than biological parents. A number of those children left Vietnam and became unaccompanied minors in detention camps, often shattered by the experience.

A particularly heavy burden for those who had parents in Vietnam was the fear that they were not living up to the expectations of the parents who had sent them out of the country. Although they were placed in a situation over which they had no control and which prevented them from being resettled, they felt responsible. They saw their parents as sacrificing to pay for their escape;

at the same time, the younger ones felt abandoned by being sent out. The children were highly stressed by these contradictory views, which they were unable to resolve.

For many children in the camps, the model Vietnamese family did not exist in Vietnam. One or more parents may have died, parents may have separated, and many families were made up of stepparents and stepchildren. Economic hardships had further disrupted family ties. But the children clung to the values of an intact family as a way of creating a sense of order in the chaotic environment of the camps. Some children whose parents had died when the children were very young expressed regrets that they did not know their parents. They missed the guidance and emotional support they would have hoped to receive. They also missed the sense of identity from being part of a family. Perhaps most painful, they did not even have memories of their parents to sustain them during their years in the camps. That is why so many children remarked that they had nothing to look forward to, no hopes for the future—for without family, they were incomplete persons.

CHAPTER FOUR

THE UNBEARABLE LIFE

THE CHILDREN OF THE camps clearly were victimized in numerous ways, but they were anything but passive. Though intimidated by officials, terrorized by gangs, manipulated by adult leaders, and ripped off by food contractors, the children found ways to resist and to fight back, sometimes openly, often in hidden ways. The resisters at High Island, Hong Kong engaged in public protest, as did many children in other camps. But even more widespread was the refusal of children to repatriate when they were asked to do so. "They'll have to carry me out of this camp," was a phrase we heard over and over. A sixteen-year-old youth in Palawan described how his friends encouraged each other to resist. "Not one of my friends has been willing to go back. Not one has chosen voluntary repatriation. My friends tell me, 'Think of the future, not the past. Even if you are rejected, don't be discouraged. Don't worry. Devote your time to study. Maybe some day something will change.'"

Hung: "I Dream of Doing Good for the Human Race"

WE MET Hung in 1993 in Whitehead Detention Center, Hong Kong, where he was working in the office of International Social Service (ISS), an organization that provided educational and recreational services for children in the camp. Hung was eighteen years old, tough, articulate, and politically savvy. He was the kind of youth who UNHCR and Hong Kong officials considered especially troublesome—screened out, aged out (over sixteen), refusing to repatriate, and claiming that he had lost contact with his parents and did not know where they lived. Officials told us they did not believe him. Although he presented himself as a human rights activist and a person who wanted to help others, officials dismissed this as puffery, and they said his story sounded too well rehearsed to be true. They said that he had falsified the location of his parents so that they could not be located. By contrast, lawyer and human rights activist Pam Baker of Refugee Concern Hong Kong considered Hung to be truly concerned about human rights, a genuine victim of persecution, and an example of a youth who should not have spent four years in a detention camp.

Many children tried to maintain a sense of hope in the future, even when they had no reason to believe they would succeed. Hung held onto the notion of education as a way to escape the camp. Like many youngsters, he persisted in the belief that if he did well as a student and could show that he would be a productive citizen, he might be selected for resettlement. Hung had been told that educational success had no bearing on his refugee status, but he refused to relinquish this last shred of hope. Education, along with persecution, is prominent in his story.

I was born in Quang Ninh Province, in north Vietnam, in 1975. My father, an electrical engineer, struggled to aid workers. He was a leader of a demonstration at a coal mine at Halong in 1989. My mother was a bookseller assistant. So I read books and I knew about the outside world, ideas, and the ways of capitalism. I knew that it differed from Vietnam's communist system. I read about that when I was twelve or thirteen years old.

In 1989, my father was arrested. About a month later, my mother was also arrested because her husband had gone against the government. My father saw that workers suffered a lot and were treated unfairly. Some people took things for themselves. When they were ill, they had no medicine or not enough. They were forced to work overtime, ten to twelve hours instead of the usual eight. A car collapsed and turned over, and lots of workers were killed. Their families were given no compensation for that. So my father led a demonstration.

I didn't see the demonstration because I was in school but my uncle told me about it. He also worked for the coal mine company. The workers gathered with banners and slogans. "Buy Uniforms." "Compensation for Workers." "No More Overtime." My uncle also demonstrated against unfair practices and was arrested. After that, I lost contact with my parents.

I had dreamed of doing something worthwhile, of becoming a medical doctor, but because of the activities of my parents, I lost all my friends. None stayed with me because they considered me antigovernment. Other students also accused me of going against the government and said bad things to me. They wanted me to be kicked out of school. I knew I could not be in the school. I could not study, thinking about all of this and what happened to my father and mother. Then I was dismissed from school. The letter of dismissal stated that I must leave because my parents are antigovernment. I felt bad, abandoned by the school. It hurt to be made alone.

My uncle escaped and hid from the authorities. One day he came to get me, and on May 14 we fled Vietnam by boat. We arrived in Hong Kong on June 6, 1989. I had to leave. I wanted to be a good student, to go into higher education for myself and for the human race. That was my dream. I dream of doing good for the human race.

I was the oldest of four children, so my uncle took me. The others, who are very young, are staying with their grandmother. When we left, it was very painful for me; I was leaving my country. I felt bad because my mother and father were left there. I felt sad, sorry for my parents. They did the right thing. They spoke out against injustice. People elsewhere can speak out, but not in Vietnam. Now I am eighteen years old. I want to live in the land where I was born. I have never received a letter from my mother, father, siblings, or grandmother, and I am very concerned. My grandmother is very old now.

My uncle is in Section 3 in Whitehead, but he has his wife and son with him. I have grown up alone. I play tennis, and I study by myself. I'm old enough to take care of myself, but Whitehead scares me.

In May 1991, after almost two years in Whitehead, I was interviewed by Hong Kong Immigration. The Special Committee interviewed me, since I was under sixteen. The interpreter told me to speak in Chinese. But I speak Vietnamese. So a Chinese interpreter was used. The Hong Kong official spoke English. So the interview was in Vietnamese to Chinese to English, and back again. It was complicated. The interpreter threatened me if I say anything. He said, "Your father is still alive, but you said he was dead." This is not what I said, but it made me scared, and I could not respond naturally.

Four weeks later I received word that I had been screened out. I met a lawyer from the Agency for Volunteer Services, a tall Dutch woman with long hair. I wrote an appeal letter, which was sent to the Review Board; eight weeks later, I received their refusal. The board noted that my father and mother had been arrested because my father had been demonstrating; they also observed that I had been dropped from school. They said this is "not discrimination" because I had completed the third grade. Therefore I was not denied an education.

My uncle also has been screened out. Vietnam has sentenced him without being in the country to twelve years in jail for protesting and escaping. He dare not return. But Hong Kong Immigration screened him out and denied his appeal. Now he is in the mandate appeal. UNHCR has said he has enough evidence for a mandate appeal and they have recommended him. But the mandate is not finished; he is waiting for a decision. My uncle is very worried about this, but also that he has a five-year-old son, who has spent four years in the camp. Even if my uncle gets the mandate, I will not be considered part of his family. So I have to go back.

Being screened out has affected my whole life. I worry about it; they will send me back. I have nowhere to go. I have no home and no parents. I don't know what happened to them. I am scared because if parents do something wrong, in Vietnam the son suffers for the parents. I cannot achieve what I dream of, doing good work and being praised by people.

I try to keep busy in the camp. At six-thirty A.M. I wake up and do some exercises. Around eight-thirty I bathe. From nine to noon I work at the ISS office, where I manage recreation. They pay me a salary of one hundred eighty Hong Kong dollars. I give one hundred dollars to my uncle and keep eighty dollars for myself. Some of the families here are so poor they have no money for food. Their children are hungry. I give my money to them. I eat lunch in my section of the camp, then return to work from one-thirty to five P.M. Around five-thirty, I play some sports, either tennis or volleyball. At six P.M., I bathe. From seven to nine P.M. I study. My subjects are Chinese, English, Italian, and academic subjects such as chemistry, physics, and mathematics. I do this all on my own, though some teachers help me. I study English, but also teach it to others and translate for others. I eat dinner around nine or ten P.M. at my aunt's place. But I sleep in my own place. On Saturdays and Sundays I play tennis, and I study the guitar and the saxophone, which I do not play well. In the evening, I study. My books are my good friends. All of my friends in camp are unaccompanied minors.

I have been in the camp for four years. I want to return to Vietnam, but not until human rights are restored. Now I am ashamed of Vietnam. It has a very poor standard of living and no human rights. How can Hong Kong force a person back who went against the government?

Resistance at High Island

UNHCR ADVOCATED the repatriation of asylum seekers who had been screened out, vigorously tried to persuade them to return, and actively participated in their reintegration to Vietnam. Because of this, many asylum seekers felt that UNHCR did not protect them. Detainees in camps organized protests against UNHCR and the countries of first asylum that would send them back. On occasion, this resulted in violent confrontations with guards and officials.

We experienced a hostile confrontation first-hand when we were mistakenly identified as UNHCR officials during our visit to Hong Kong's High Island Detention Center in the summer of 1994. We went there because we were establishing a children's shelter in central Vietnam, and most of the detainees had come from that region.

High Island, which held close to 7,000 detainees, was located at the edge of a bay, surrounded by steep green hills in an isolated section of the Sai Kung country park. This breathtaking view was spoiled by a tangle of metal walls topped by barbed wire that encircled 22 large Quonset huts. Each hut housed the equivalent of 120 family units, placed in two rows of three-tiered bunks measuring six by five by three feet per family. The heat inside was stifling. High Island was divided into two main sections, plus a third, small one for troublemakers. One large section contained north Vietnamese; the other mixed people from the north and south.

We went to the section of the mixed population. The detainees looked at us sullenly. We entered a room, several children followed us, and we asked them their names. A thin youth, about eighteen years of age, wearing a faded blue shirt, spoke harshly and brandished his fist. "I'm not telling you my name! I want you UNHCR to be as disturbed and embarrassed as possible for returning me!" He then turned to a seventeen-year-old female and commanded, "Don't answer them!" Another youth outside the room looked in the window and shouted, "Don't talk to them. They're UNHCR! Why are you in that room? Stay away from them!"

We told the children, "We are not UNHCR and we are not here to tell you what to do, whether to remain or to repatriate. That is your choice, and

Unaccompanied minors protest at High Island Detention Center, Hong Kong. *Photographer unknown.*

only you know in your hearts what is best for you. We do not take political sides; if we did, we would not be allowed in the camp. If you do go back to central Vietnam and need some assistance, we'll be there to help you. But we work without noise."

A fifteen-year-old youth replied softly, "Yes, like a quiet stream." Only when they realized that we were in no way associated with UNHCR and would not coerce or cajole them to repatriate did they calm down and speak to us about their living conditions, needs and hopes.

Trung: "Thanks for the Advice, but No Thanks"

TRUNG'S STORY reveals the extent of distrust the children had for officials. We interviewed this seventeen-year-old youth in the crowded, dusty, Thai camp of Phanat Nikhom in 1992. His parents in Vietnam had received immigrant status and were preparing to leave for Canada. To accompany them, Trung had to return to Vietnam. He refused, disregarding the pleas of officials and volunteer workers, thereby forfeiting his opportunity for resettlement. He explains the reasons below.

I was born in Saigon in 1975. My father is a farmer, but formerly he was a policeman, while my mother is a housewife. I have two older brothers. One is a farmer. The other escaped from Vietnam in 1979 and resettled in Canada. Because of him, my family has been accepted for the Orderly Departure Program for emigration to Canada. They tell me that I'd be eligible to go with them if I return to Vietnam before they leave. But I don't believe any of this, and I won't return.

I was in the ninth grade when I left Vietnam on April 29, 1989. I left from Kien Giang Province [southwestern Mekong Delta]. I started off with my father. We took separate routes to get to the boat. I made it, but on the way, he got lost and didn't get on the boat in time. He was stuck in Vietnam. I had no relatives or acquaintances on the boat. The adults on the boat protected and helped me. We arrived on June 22.

The first camp I was put in was Long Muon. Then I was moved to Ban Thad on the Thailand-Cambodia border. About three months later, I was moved to Phanat Nikhom. That's where they put post-cutoff people for screening. During that time, I received letters from my family, but not so regularly. My family was all right in Vietnam. My brother was still farming.

I don't remember the date I was called for an interview, but it took place around February or March 1990. I don't remember when I received the result, only that I was rejected for resettlement.

I felt sad. I figured I'll just stay here and try to study, and hope someday I'll be resettled, sooner or later. In the camp, the only thing I could study was English. I thought, now that I had to leave my home country for this place, a free country will accept me for resettlement. They would help me to realize my dream. ["They" were the free countries and UNHCR in particular.]

I don't like camp life very much, but since I came here, I want to wait for resettlement. Life in the camps is not as comfortable as in Vietnam. I miss my family and I have to stay in a restricted area. During the past three years, I've had no education. I have to deal with many difficulties. It's crowded, there's no education. Still, I want to stay for resettlement. I get money from my brother in Canada, about fifty dollars a month for food, clothing, books. I read English. My other activities are soccer and attending the Catholic Church. My parents want me to stay in camp and study.

UNHCR recommends that I return to Vietnam and reunite with my parents. I feel sad, but I hope sooner or later I will be able to depart from here for resettlement. I think a free country will have pity on us who had to leave their country and will resettle us instead. I know that nobody who has been denied has been resettled. But not only I, but also many others think we will be able to go to a third country. UNHCR says if I want to go to Canada, I have to return to Vietnam first and go with my parents. But my parents did not ask me to return to join them to go to Canada on the Orderly Departure Program. So to UNHCR, I say, thanks for the advice, but no thanks.

I'll agree to return to Vietnam only on two conditions. First, I want a written guarantee from the Vietnamese government that I will not be subjected to further persecution. Second, I want a document from the Canadian government that my family will be resettled in Canada and that I am included on that list. When they do that, I will return.

Chuong: "The Police Shaved My Head for Punishment"

SUNGEI BESI, a camp of two- and three-story cinderblock structures, located near Kuala Lumpur, Malaysia, was not as forbidding in appearance as the Hong Kong camps, but it had its problems. Because Pulau Bidong, Malaysia's other camp, had closed a few months earlier, Sungei Besi now held the people from that camp, too, creating conditions of severe overcrowding, and, with them, heightened tensions. We were in the security office when a thin boy entered the room. His head was shaved, and we asked him why. The security officer laughed and said, "Tell them, Chuong."

Chuong gave an embarrassed smile. We said we would like to know what had happened, where he came from in Vietnam, and how he arrived in Sungei Besi. Chuong described how he was drawn into the furtive life of black-market trading in Sungei Besi Camp. The year was 1992.

I was born in Saigon ten years ago, and I completed the first grade in Vietnam. Now, in the camp, I'm in the third grade. My parents took me to a boat to escape from Vietnam. But the boat was too small, so my parents got out. My mother said to me, "Go. If life is good, tell me and I'll try to come. If it's bad, tell me and I won't go."

I got to Malaysia, and I was put in Pulau Bidong Camp. Although I was very small, I had to cook my own food. That meant I had to carry water long distances. If I was unable to cook, I had to eat the food raw. Then I was moved to Sungei Besi [from Pulau Bidong Camp]. I like it better here, even though it is a lot more crowded, because I don't have to cook or carry water, and the food is enough.

At first, I lived with my aunt. But she did not treat me nicely, so I was separated from her. I go to school from two to four in the afternoon. Other than that, I eat and watch TV. I like Chinese kung fu films. My favorite is *I Kick You to Death*. It's in Cantonese. I've seen it many times. After seeing it, I also do some fighting.

In Sungei Besi, I got myself in trouble with the police. They arrested me. Some people in the camp asked me to buy pork for them. What I did was throw money over the fence. Some Chinese-Malay people would then throw pork over the wall to us. I'm Chinese-Vietnamese, so I could do business with them. Each time I did this, I got two ringgit. So the police arrested me and shaved my head as punishment, and for one month, I have to present myself to the police station every day. I won't do it again. It wasn't too heavy a punishment, but I have grandparents in Australia. I was screened in. I don't know the reason. I don't want to be prevented from going to my grandparents.

Lan: "I've Got a Five-Month-Old Son, So I Can't Go Back"

IN SUNGEI Besi, we also met Lan, whose situation was one that was seen all too often in the camps. Young girls alone in the camps were especially vulnerable. For protection, many of them took up with older men and a number of the girls bore children. In countries such as Malaysia, abortion was prohibited. Often the men abandoned the girls and their babies or were separated from them during the process of resettlement or repatriation. Many of these girls did not want to return to Vietnam, first because of the shame they had brought their families, but also because, burdened with a new child, they would have difficulty finding work.

I'm listed as fifteen years old, but actually I'm seventeen. I was born in Can Tho in the far south of Vietnam. My parents decided I should go abroad for a better future, so I escaped and arrived in Malaysia on April 13, 1989. I missed the cut-off date by less than a month.

My parents wanted me to leave Vietnam because of the way they were being treated. Public Security searched our home many times. In 1980 and 1981 they confiscated merchandise and gold and they accused my parents of smuggling. So my parents sent me out of the country.

I was in Pulau Bidong, and I liked it better than Sungei Besi. I could get fresh chicken and eat anything I wanted. Here I get tofu, chicken, and fish, but there's not enough food and food distribution is not regular. Here in the camp there is no school, only some English language training. [Her statement is inaccurate; schooling was available in the camp at that time.] I completed the fifth grade in Vietnam.

I have cousins who live in Texas. In June 1991, one of them came to see me and gave me some money. Since then I haven't heard anything from them. I have been screened out, so I don't have a long-range plan, but I don't want to go back. I will stay here until they close the camp. I've got a five-month-old son, so I can't go back. My boyfriend has not been screened yet. He's twenty-eight years old. In Vietnam, he was a businessman. Now we live together. But with my son it would be very difficult for me to return home. If they authorize my stay in Malaysia, I will do it.

Hao, Van, and Dien: Hunger

IN EVERY camp we visited, children complained that they were hungry. Yet official records showed that adults and children received rations that were supposed to be sufficient in calories and nutrition. Both children and adults complained that rations were reduced when the CPA was started and when people refused to repatriate. Hao, Van, and Dien, three friends in Palawan, were screened-out, aged-out teenagers who reinforced each other in their decision not to repatriate. They wished to be interviewed together, and a major issue for them was their hunger. Hao, seventeen years old, recalled seeing how the contractors who brought in food shortchanged people. "I saw a family that got their ration of food weighed on a scale at the distribution center. The scale said twenty-seven kilograms, but when they reweighed it at home, they found it weighed only twenty-five kilos. The center scale had underweighed the food. After that, I returned and used the other scale. It showed less than twenty-seven kilos. I brought back the rice and told them to reweigh it again. It showed a difference of two to three kilos. I reported this to security. They told the distribution center to give us more rice."

Unaccompanied minors at mealtime, Palawan First Asylum Camp, the Philippines. *Photographer unknown.*

Hao continued. "In the morning, I am hungry, but what can I do? I wait until lunch. If I go to class, it's hard to concentrate. I have to accept it. Dealing with my hunger is too difficult, but I have no other solution. The food distributed at the center is enough only for one meal, but we must divide it in two. If someone throws away a rotten banana and I see it lying on the ground, I pick it up and eat it. If someone throws away a carrot because it is too green, I eat it."

Dien, sixteen years old, said, "We often eat rotten food. The fish we get is almost always rotten." She added, "The fish is rotten, and we got a rash from eating it. We are allergic to it. All three of us got it, and so did a lot of other people. We had a rash all over our bodies. I couldn't sleep. I get it from time to time. I use an ointment and it goes away."

Van, seventeen, added, "When I get the rash, my mouth swells up and red spots appear on my arm. We have to eat."

Hao exclaimed, "Today's fish is half-rotten. I'm a fisherman. I know. A rotten fish is not hard but smooth, and it has a bad smell. What can we do with rotten fish? There's nothing to do but eat it."

Van said when he first came to Palawan, he was lonely, and he was upset by the behavior of people. "What I saw here at first was very discouraging. People fought over water. They killed over water. They didn't stay in line. Some people would monopolize, fight, and kill. One man died. I saw that. He was stabbed to death. People also fought over food because there was not enough. This discouraged me. I wrote a letter to my parents asking them to allow me to return. They wrote, 'Have patience. Stay where you are. Think about your future.'"

Hao, Van, and Dien had been screened out. They referred to this as *bi da* ["kicked," rejected]. Dien says she had never heard of screening in Vietnam. In the camp she was told she would have to go through screening. She said,

An unaccompanied minor with his rations of day-old fish and overripe bananas, Palawan First Asylum Camp, the Philippines. The children frequently complained that the food they received was rotten and insufficient. *Photographer unknown.*

"The afternoon before my interview, a loudspeaker announced my name. 'Tomorrow, Dien must go for an interview.' I had no preparation for this. No one gave me any information about what the interview was or what it meant. Nobody told us about a cutoff date. I only heard about this from other refugees. The next morning I got the announcement from UNHCR about the cutoff date. I got this from the loudspeaker, not from any official."

Dien said she felt nothing at the time, because "I didn't have any idea what screening was, what an interview was. I had never had an interview of any kind in my life, and neither had my two friends here."

Van said he was not worried, "until the day they called my name for interview. Then I worried. I was scared when I went into the interview."

Hao added, "I could not sleep. I did not know what they would say." A Vietnamese woman who was an overseas volunteer interviewed him. He says she was very nice in demeanor and made him feel at ease. He had been in the camp for nine months before he was interviewed in January 1990. He received his denial thirteen months later, in February 1991. He concludes, "I won't return to Vietnam. I'll only return when there's no Communism. I'll stay until they carry me out."

Van added, "Me too. I'll stay until the day they carry me to the airplane."

Tai: "My Family Escaped but They Haven't Been Heard From Since"

OUR INTERVIEW in 1991 with Tai, twelve years old, in Palawan, calls attention to the credibility issue of children claiming that their parents are deceased. In checking these claims, UNHCR found that many children had fabricated their stories, hoping to be resettled as orphans. Tai's ironic concluding statement is testimony to the extent to which children felt intimidated by the authorities who cross-examined them.

I was born in central Vietnam in October 1979. I escaped with my brother-in-law from Qui Nhon, near Nha Trang, and we arrived in Palawan on June 16, 1989. In June 1991, my family escaped, but they haven't been heard from since. I contacted the Red Cross and UNHCR, but they cannot locate them. I was interviewed on March 15, 1991, by a Philippine lady. She treated me okay. The interpreter was a refugee in the camp. I learned that I had been denied on December 19, 1991. The day before, thirty to forty of us were called to a meeting. A Filipino man told us that we would receive the decision the next day. Those who were accepted would be processed to go to Bataan to prepare for resettlement. Those who were denied should prepare to return to Vietnam. He said, if we are rejected, it would be better to return to Vietnam to continue our education. We would get fifty dollars for returning and thirty dollars a month for a year. When we return, we could qualify for a loan to set up a business, and the loan would be repaid to the bank.

I don't want to return. My parents have already escaped, but they have disappeared. If I went back, I don't know with whom I would be living. I listened to that man, and I felt normal, not happy or sad. I figured, no matter what that person said, I wanted to stay here.

I've been told that at UNHCR they have received reports that, of thirty unaccompanied minors, twenty-eight claim like me that their parents are lost or dead. These minors are asking for a review because their parents are dead. But UNHCR doesn't believe them. They are checking on the truth. Many minors are afraid to go and ask them. It's funny, they risk their lives to get freedom, but they're afraid to talk to those officials.

Thu: "I Don't Know How to Deal with My Fear"

A RECURRENT theme in the accounts of the unaccompanied minors is the disruption of their lives that results from their incarceration in the camps, their fears, and their despair. Many children spoke about their Special Committee interview, claiming that they did not understand the questions. Their claims contrast sharply with the presentation in UNHCR documents of guidelines for protecting, interviewing, and communicating effectively with unaccompanied minors.

According to those guidelines, the interviewers should collect the detailed social histories of children, look for nonverbal forms of communication, use nonverbal (drawings, games) as well as verbal measures for collecting information, and create an environment of trust. Questions should be phrased in ways that are appropriate to the age, culture, and circumstances of the child. Appropriate questions include inquiries about family relationships, persons who accompanied the child, the separation of the child from the family, events that might have led to the previous breakdown of normal life, reasons for leaving the country, whether or not parents sent the child out, and if so, why. The interviewer should ask if the child has special problems or needs. Sample social-history forms are included for the interviewer. These are based on a 1988 publication of International Social Service.[1]

While a few children said that the interviewer put them at ease, others said they were terrified. They indicated little or nothing to suggest that they were treated according to UNHCR guidelines.

Thu was fourteen years old when we interviewed her in Chi Ma Wan Camp, Hong Kong, in 1991. Her narrative illustrates themes of betrayal and abandonment and the ways in which bureaucratic rules are used to devastate a child's life.

I arrived with my elder brother in Hong Kong in July 1988, one month after the cutoff. I was eleven years old and he was twenty-one. My family comes from Hue, where they were farmers. My parents also escaped, but in a different boat, and they have disappeared. We have not heard from them since. My brother got married to a screened-in wife, so he moved with her to Pillar Point, and I was left alone here. I have been interviewed and denied twice. Now I will stay here until UNHCR reviews my case.

When I left Vietnam I had completed the fourth grade. Now I'm fourteen years old and I am in the seventh grade in camp. I study for about two-and-a-half hours a day, but for the rest of the time, I have nothing to do. The boys have some opportunity for exercise, but we girls do not. I just sit.

In this camp, the food is not nice. We have soup, which is some boiled water and some vegetables, but it is not enough, and I have lost a lot of weight. We eat rice and once in a while a piece or two of meat. But our food is like that of the communist soldiers in Vietnam. We lived next to the security people and I saw them and what they ate. I don't have enough clothes. The only thing I have is what I am wearing. Only if you have relatives who send you money can you have clothes.

What worries me is when I will be forced to repatriate. This is on my mind all the time. I am afraid of that always. I don't know how to deal with my fear. There are other children like me in this camp without parents. They were accepted for resettlement and I was not. I was surprised at this because the other cases were identical to mine. We are unhappy here, but most of us have not volunteered to repatriate. The only one who has is Liem. [See Chapter 2].

Xuan: "I'm Screened In but My Parents Are Screened Out"

PILLAR POINT, Hong Kong, was an open camp, built of cement and stone, which housed screened-in asylum seekers until they were resettled to a third country. Because they were classified as refugees, the adults of the camp were allowed to leave during the day and hold jobs outside the camp. Eventually, most of the refugees were resettled, but a few, because of their criminal records or medical disabilities, could not find countries that would take them. The most difficult cases were of people who were classified as "stateless" persons, since they could not document their country of origin. The Hong Kong government eventually allowed them to remain in Hong Kong and closed the camp in June 2000.

We interviewed Xuan, who was twelve years old, at Pillar Point in 1991. Like Thu, Xuan was caught in a bureaucratic nightmare, but his situation was the reverse of hers. He was classified as a refugee because he arrived before the cutoff date, but was not resettled because his parents arrived after the cutoff date and were screened out. When we interviewed him, he had been stuck like this for four years.

I was born in Haiphong. I am twelve years old. I don't know the occupation of my parents, but I know my grandparents are fishermen and my grandmother buys and sells old newspapers and old things. In 1987, I arrived in Hong Kong with my uncle and aunt. We left to go for freedom, and once we resettle in another country, my family will find a job. Because we came early, we are refugees. But my mother and father arrived later, after the cutoff date, so they're not eligible. That's why I've been stuck here since 1987. I remain in a transit camp for refugees, but my parents are in a detention camp. The Hong Kong government doesn't know what to do about this. I see my parents only once every two months because I have no money to visit them. UNHCR provides a person to accompany me when I visit my parents. I need about one thousand Hong Kong dollars to buy food and clothes for my parents. They are living in a terrible detention center, and my parents look very bad. I save money to help them. The money is from a weekly allowance I get from Caritas. The money pays for the transportation, food, clothing, and money for my parents. I've been in this camp since I was eight years old. I miss my parents, but what can I do? I don't know how long I will be here.

Tam: "I Didn't Understand Any of the Questions"

TAM, a thirteen-year-old boy who we interviewed in Sikhiu, Thailand, in 1992, is one of many children who claimed they did not understand anything when they were interviewed by the Special Committee, but like many children, he did not discuss the particular questions that confused him.

I was born in Long Thanh, near Bien Hoa, in Dong Nai Province, southern Vietnam. My father died about when I was born. My mother disappeared soon after I was born, and my paternal grandmother took care of me. I had no brothers and sisters, only an aunt who lived with us. My grandmother never talked to me about who my mother was. My grandmother is now very old, about seventy-five. When I think of her, I am very sad. I cry because I miss her a lot.

In Vietnam, I completed the second grade. After that, I could not go, because I had to pay tuition, and we did not have enough money, so I quit. I did whatever my grandmother told me.

It was my grandmother who sent me out of Vietnam. I went with a group of neighbors. She told me that now she was too old to take care of me, but if I went, someday I could grow to support myself. So she was sending me out.

I left Vietnam on August 19, 1990. I was twelve years old. We went by foot through Cambodia. We had twenty people in our group. We were seen by Cambodian soldiers, who shot at us. This happened twice, but nobody was hurt. We ran away. I was very afraid then.

Finally, we reached the Thai border. We stayed someplace one night. When I awoke, all the others had disappeared. So I went to the police station and presented myself to the police. They sent me to Bangkok, where they locked me up in a prison called Suan Plu. I stayed there for four months. It is for detention for people who violated the immigration law. Both older people and children lived there. I was not afraid. Vietnamese people were there, so I had people to talk to. I didn't know what would happen to me, but I was not afraid.

They sent me to Phanat Nikhom, to the center for unaccompanied minors, but it was full and I was not accepted there. There was a demonstration, so the minor center wouldn't take any more people. I had to live outside the center. A man was supposed to take care of me, but he didn't. Then I was given to another lady to take care of me. She did this until she got married. Then I was alone again.

Then I was moved to Sikhiu Camp. I had to stay with a big person, who was eighteen years old. I stayed with him for four months. Then he went back to Vietnam. Meanwhile, in September 1991, I was interviewed, but now, four months later, I have not heard any result.

I go to school. I'm in the third grade. I like all subjects and I find them easy. After school, I collect stamps. A friend of the man who returned to Vietnam gives me the stamps. In the camp, I have a lot of friends. With my two closest friends, I play checkers, and we play jokes on one another.

The food here is different than in Vietnam, and not as good. It is less and the quality is poorer. It is enough, so I am not hungry. But I have no special desire for anything. I like to watch the video when I can, anything. I like it all. The video belongs to UNHCR. My clothing is not enough. I have one shirt and one pair of pants, which was given to me when I was in Bangkok. That was given to me by someone who returned to Vietnam. It was given to me because I had no brother or sister or anybody to help me.

My grandmother sent me out of Vietnam. I did not know why. I had never heard of anybody doing anything like that until I left. When in Vietnam, I had never heard of the Comprehensive Plan of Action. I heard of it only when I arrived in Thailand. Then people told me I had arrived after the cutoff date so I had to be screened. I did not know what they were talking about.

When I was interviewed, I didn't understand it. I was worried at the interview. I agreed to be interviewed, so I was on the list. I decided to come for the interview. If I came first, I'd get a quick interview. If I didn't, then I'd have a later interview. The interviewer was nice, and I felt comfortable. I did not understand any of the questions, but I felt comfortable. I don't worry about the result, and I don't have a preference because I don't know about these things.

Cooking rice in Sikhiu Camp, Thailand. *Photo: James M. Freeman.*

Minh and Nga: "I Miss My Parents Very Much, Especially at Nighttime"

ONE OF THE great tragedies of the Vietnamese exodus was that relatives often sent small children out of the country at great risk to the children. If they survived, they had to learn to cope without family or relatives to help them, as did this twelve-year-old brother, who took care of his six-year-old sister. We spoke with them in Phanat Nikhom Camp, Thailand, in 1992.

My name is Minh, and my sister is Nga. I was born in 1979 and my sister was born in 1985. I am the oldest and she is the youngest. Our father was a medical doctor and our mother ran a coffee shop. We come from An Giang Province [a southwestern province next to Cambodia]. Father left the family long ago. Our mother had no news from him, and after some time she died. So we are orphans.

We lived with our father's younger brother, and it is he who arranged for our escape. He asked us to follow him. Then he put us in a small boat. It was at night. Then we reached a bigger boat. Still, our uncle didn't tell us anything, and we did not know anyone else on the boat. We left on October 13, 1989.

At that time, we did not know what happened to us. There were thirteen people on the boat. The only thing we took with us was some clothes. We did not have any money or documents. We just knew our age. When I went to school in Vietnam, my mother told me I was nine years old. So I knew about this. And when we got to the camp, an adult told me to count our age, and I could do that.

I don't remember how long we were in the boat. I remember being seasick and that we did not have enough food and water.

NGA: I remember that I was scared. I didn't know anything about the trip, but I was afraid. But my uncle asked me to go.

MINH: Our uncle was married but had no children. When we moved to live with him, he was a farmer. We stayed with him for a year. During that time, life was very hard. We did not have enough food. I couldn't go to school because I had to help my uncle farm. I helped him grow corn.

NGA: I didn't go to school because I am of small age. I would just eat and sleep. My brother is good; he never beat me.

MINH: I remember that Uncle told me, "Just go and study hard." At that time, I didn't know where he meant.

NGA: Uncle didn't tell me anything.

Minh's narrative continues:

When we reached Thailand, we were put in Long Muon Camp for a month. Then we were transferred to Phanat Nikhom. When we first arrived, we were put with a couple with children. They loved us and took care of us. Then we were sent to a transit camp, and I no longer have any contact with them. They moved to Sikhiu Camp, and we were sent to the minors center. But the minors center closed, so we were moved to the transit center under the care of a Catholic priest. We have no relatives; we are alone, so the only help we got was from Enfants du Mekong, which helps children. Every month, each of us receives three hundred baht. We give it to the priest, and he takes care of everything for us—clothes, and payment for someone to cook for us.

We get enough food, and life in the camp is a little bit better than Vietnam. We have enough food, we go to school, we have a caretaker, I'm in the third grade, and my sister is in the first grade. She is just starting to learn how to spell. But for me, some of the subjects are hard and others are easy. Our life is better since we moved in with the Father. Before that, we were helped by people in our section of the camp, but it was not as good.

I miss my parents very much, especially at nighttime. Sometimes we cry when someone asks us about our family. When we think of our parents, we are sad. After two years in the camp, I still feel this way about my family, but I don't want to return to Vietnam because of the hardship in our country.

Girls' quarters in Phanat Nikhom Camp, Thailand. *Photo: Nguyen Dinh Huu.*

We were recommended to be resettled to New Zealand, but so far the delegation has not yet come to camp. We were also told that their immigration service will see us, but I am still waiting. I prefer the United States because it has better education.

I remember Father and Mother, even though Mother died, and I have no image of my father since he left long ago. But I still feel about them and dream about what they would be like. I don't actually dream of them. I have no dreams, except once I dreamt that I was rejected by a delegation. We came to see the delegation without our shirts on, and we were there with others, Laotians. Later, I saw a list of the rejected, and I saw our names. My sister has no idea about things. She cannot talk; she simply follows me.

We were screened, but we knew nothing about it. We had never heard of screening, and we had never heard of the cutoff date of March 14, 1989. It was only after we arrived in the camp that we heard of screening. I didn't believe and I didn't worry about that. Now my only worry is how long we have to stay in the camp. When we were called for the screening, I was interviewed by a Thai official. She spoke Vietnamese and she asked me questions. I understood the interviewer well, though sometimes when speaking Vietnamese, I couldn't catch what she said, and I asked her to speak again. She did it. When I came to the interview, she asked me and I cried because it reminded me of my mother and father. We were interviewed three times, by different interviewers, but they spoke Vietnamese perfectly.

NGA: I didn't say anything. Brother said everything.

MINH: We wish we had somebody to help us finish our education. I don't know what I will be, but I want to be a medical doctor, be successful, and make good grades in school. I know I have a responsibility to help and love my sister.

Thuy: "I Miss My Mother and Father. I Want to Go Home," as Reported by Thuy's Uncle Vuong

IN VIETNAM, rumors circulated that adults escaping with children would automatically be resettled, and for this reason, some children were brought to the camps by relatives or by others who were not their biological parents. We have frequently criticized the separation of children from their long-term caretakers, but we believe there are times when separation is justified. Thuy's case is an example. One evening in 1991 in Palawan, we saw a little girl walking around the camp unattended. She was wandering around the temporary bleachers put up by the camp residents to watch evening videos. "Who are you?" we asked. "*Con bi da* [I've been kicked]," she responded, referring to her rejection for resettlement. We asked some spectators if they knew who took care of this little girl. One of them said, "She's an *unam* [unaccompanied minor]. She has an uncle around here somewhere." After searching for nearly an hour, we found her uncle sitting in a coffee shop, oblivious to the whereabouts of the child. His name was Vuong. He was thirty-six years old, and his niece was four. We asked if he would tell us how he and his niece came to be in Palawan. The following morning, he told us his story. We sat on the steps of the office of the Center for Assistance to Displaced Persons (CADP), an NGO funded by the Catholic Church. Thuy was playing nearby.

I am Thuy's paternal uncle, her father's elder brother. I was not allowed to leave my village near Nha Trang because I had been in the South Vietnamese air force. I didn't have a family registration book and I left my village for two weeks without permission. The local authorities accused me of going to the city to join an antigovernment organization. They arrested my wife and forced her to call me back. I refused to return because I knew I'd have trouble with the local authorities. They'd put me in jail. So I headed for Saigon, where Thuy's father lived. He was too young to have been in the South Vietnamese army, so he did not have any trouble. In 1984, we moved back to Nha Trang, and he married Thuy's mother. My brother and I worked as helpers in a bakery. I was working there illegally. I'd work there at night and then return home, where I'd hide during the day.

Thuy's mother became pregnant, and Thuy was born prematurely at seven months. For the next two years, I helped care for my small niece. But my life was too dangerous, hiding during the day and working at night. I had seen no chance to get out of this, so I decided to leave the country. I had been taking care of Thuy for a while, so I asked her parents if they would let me take her out of the country. They agreed. Her father was busy working in the bakery. Her mother was selling things every day to support the family. So the attachment was between Thuy and me. My brother trusted me so I was not worried.

Vuong's story did not ring true to us because he neglected his niece to the point of endangerment. We asked him about Thuy's reaction to being removed from her parents. His answer did not sound believable.

Thuy was close to me. Even in Vietnam, wherever I went, Thuy went with me. When I returned from work, I took care of her. And when we left Vietnam, Thuy did not show that she missed her parents.

I had left my wife long ago. She took our three children and moved out of the city of Nha Trang. I have not seen her since. For a long time I did not know what had happened to her. Then I heard that she had escaped and had gone to Norway.

Here in Palawan, I was screened in on the basis of humanitarian considerations, to be reunited with my wife. But then I learned that my wife had remarried in Norway and has had one child with her new husband. So I will go to a sister in the USA. She lives in Kentucky. She has sponsored me.

Meanwhile, Thuy has been denied. When I saw the list of the people screened in, I was surprised to see that Thuy was not on the list. The letter informing me that I had been screened in made no mention of Thuy. So I asked the UNHCR official why Thuy was not on the list. She said she did not know; it is the problem of the Special Committee working on minors. She advised me to write a letter requesting to stay in the camp until Thuy's situation is settled. One of the officials at UNHCR offered to go back to Vietnam to return Thuy to her parents. He also offered to try to get Thuy screened in so she could accompany me to America. This mess happened because they used two committees and did not consider us together. When I was interviewed, Thuy accompanied me. I told the committee that I had taken care of her all of her life. The CID [Immigration Service] said that Thuy was my niece and that they would consider her with me, but later on UNHCR informed me that they would examine Thuy's situation separately.

They took her to be interviewed. The interview lasted two days. The interviewer was a young Filipino woman, assisted by a Vietnamese woman in the camp who served as the interpreter. They asked her, "What reason made you leave your country?" Thuy didn't understand. "What does 'reason' mean?" she asked. They asked, "Do you want to return to Vietnam to be with your parents?" Thuy replied, "No, I want to go with my uncle." Then they asked her, "How about your life here? Is it happy or unhappy?" She replied, "I like to stay here and play with some toys." They screened her out. She is four years old.

As Thuy's uncle finished his story, Thuy came up to us holding a piece of paper. It was her rejection notice, written in English, addressed to this four-year-old child at the Philippine First Asylum Camp, Palawan. It was from the Republic of the Philippines, Department of Justice, Bureau of Immigration and Deportation, Manila. The letter read:

The Special Committee on Minors (attached and unaccompanied) and Individuals of Special Humanitarian Concern of the Philippines examined your case on 14, November 1991. The Committee has decided that it is in your best interests to be reunited with your family in Vietnam. I would like to suggest the following for your immediate action.

1. Notify your family in Viet Nam concerning the decision of your case by the Special Committee.
2. Inquire from the UNHCR, Palawan Field Office the assistance it offers concerning voluntary repatriation.

This notice was signed by Leonardo Aguilar, Jr., Chairman, Committee on Unaccompanied Minors and Individuals of Humanitarian Concern.

The interview with Thuy's uncle was over. He went to meet some friends at a coffee shop. Thuy remained playing on the steps of the CADP office, unattended. We asked Thuy, "Do you want to stay with your uncle or your parents?" Thuy replied sadly, "I miss my mother and father. I want to go home. I miss my home."

We alerted the UNHCR office that Thuy was neglected and wanted to return to her parents. Soon after, she was repatriated.

Psychological Scars

A DETAILED account of the psychological condition of the children of the Hong Kong camps appears in *Living in Detention: A Review of the Psychosocial Well-Being of Vietnamese Children in the Hong Kong Detention Centres*. This report, prepared by Margaret McCallin, was based on her questionnaire survey of 603 children. This was supplemented by fifty-six in-depth clinical interviews conducted by James Garbarino and Edgardo Menvielle, who have done extensive interviews worldwide with at-risk children. Children were selected according to two criteria. The first was the time of arrival, with those who arrived in 1988–89 distinguished from those who arrived in 1990–91. The second criterion was the type of caregiving the children experienced, with subjects divided among unaccompanied minors, "attached minors" accompanied by a family member who was not a parent and not previously a principal caregiver, and "accompanied minors," who were accompanied by one or both parents.

Many visitors to the camps have given impressionistic accounts of the sorry psychological state of the children. The voices of the children confirm this, as do the remarks of the therapists in the camps who worked with them. McCallin's report adds significantly to the evidence that the condition of the children was far worse than many critics had imagined. The majority of the children were depressed and anxious. Their response to the events they experienced was "sadness, lack of energy and a disinterest in what [was] going on around them." The two major sources of stress in their lives were their considerable fear for their personal safety and their great concern about their family back in Vietnam. Their anxieties surfaced in psychosomatic symptoms. The children were restless and unable to concentrate because they remembered distressing events. They felt that people had not helped or guided them, and they expressed "a need for affection."[2]

McCallin expands on several of these points. A sampling of her comments should be deeply troubling to those who found excuses for keeping the children in the camps. "Many children evidenced a deep sense of loss and abandonment, due, for example, to parental loss through death or remarriage. Their losses were recalled with painful intensity, and many children appeared as 'psychologically wounded'. . . . Many of the children are suffering from depression . . . characterized by a profound lack of initiative and sense of hopelessness. Two thirds (particularly girls) said that they spend whole days in their bunks because they are sad or depressed." Their accounts of their lives in the camps revealed a "strong sense of passivity and powerlessness." They felt deprived of the normal activities of adolescents and they avoided thinking about the future. They spoke at length about their fears for their personal safety and their ways of coping with this. "Girls fear sexual assault and harassment and boys are fearful of bullying by older, more powerful males and the system of threat and intimidation that operates, especially in certain camps. Many children reported a strategy of invisibility, withdrawing into reading or studying or neutralizing their appearance through dress, posture etc. to appear younger, as a way to avoid being noticed and therefore attacked by predatory elements within the camps."

In addition to the fear of violence and separation from their families, the children also mentioned other stresses. These included confinement in a prison environment, unappetizing food, and lack of clothing. Of greater concern for McCallin were the children "who reported no problems whatsoever, despite acknowledging their awareness of the existence of events such as fights, rioting, and violence against women in the camp." Traumatic events were frequent. A girl who was a witness to the gang rape of older females was told to look away, but she heard their cries. A boy described a stabbing he had seen. "Posttraumatic symptoms such as feelings of terror during the incidents, recurrent nightmares and flashbacks, and persistent fear were reported by children who had been traumatized." The children received little help in coping with these.[3]

The investigators used a stress assessment schedule to measure levels of stress (high, middle, low) of children who had directly experienced traumatic events, both en route and in detention. The greater the number of traumatic events a child experienced, the higher the score on the stress assessment schedule. Over 40 percent of the children scored in the high-stress areas from their experiences en route or in the camps. The seventeen stress indicators included having night-mares, waking feeling afraid, feeling like crying, trembling/fast heartbeat, feeling alone, loss of interest in life, and inability to stop thinking about distressing events. The 2,083 traumatic experiences en route that the children reported included lack of food/water, seasickness, robbery, boat breakdown, storms, sexual assault, physical assault, and traumatic separation from family.

The 1,958 traumatic experiences in detention camps that the children reported included sexual assault, physical assault, bullying, coercion, imprisonment, witness to suicide, hunger strike, demonstrations, weapons searches, teargassing, forced relocation, and forced separation from family and friends. Children perceived violence directed at the individual child as more threatening than danger from natural forces such as storms or mass events like being carried along in a riot. The high-stress children experienced 50 percent or more of the total events reported involving direct threats or violence both en route and in the camps. Of particular concern to the authors was that the children had no escape or relief from, and no way to come to terms with, ongoing events in the camps such as violent demonstrations and teargassing.[4]

Not surprisingly, attached and unaccompanied minors showed increased stress the longer they stayed in the camps. The status determination process was a significant source of stress. Rejection was not explained in a way that the children could understand. Earlier arrivals experienced more traumatic events en route and in the detention center, and had significantly higher total scores on the stress assessment schedule than later arrivals. Because of this, McCallin called "for immediate attention to the needs of the long-stay children." Another point of concern was that children who had experienced high levels of trauma developed feelings of isolation, detachment, and loss of confidence.[5]

Significantly, caregiving arrangements for attached and unaccompanied children made no difference in the emotional well-being of these children. The researchers found no evidence that attachment to a caregiver other than a parent provided adequate protection. Those who were accompanied by at least one parent were a little better protected from the detention center experience, but the well-being of all of the children deteriorated over time.[6]

McCallin's findings are based on children who had been in the Hong Kong camps for less than three years. Subsequently, children remained in the camps for three to five years or more, suffering and coping in an environment of increasing political tension, resistance to authority, violence, and ultimately despair, as thousands of reluctant asylum seekers were forcibly repatriated to Vietnam against their will.

Traumatized Children Elsewhere

GUUS VAN der Veer has summarized studies on the traumatization of children and adolescents elsewhere that might also apply to Vietnamese refugees. His observations are similar to the conclusions reached by McCallin. As a result of experiences with extreme violence, children may manifest symptoms of post-traumatic stress disorder, including nightmares, intrusive thoughts and concentration problems, becoming easily frightened, repressing their feelings, and trying to avoid situations which remind them of the traumatic events. Van der Veer refers to the studies of L. C. Terr, who distinguishes between two types of traumatic conditions: children who have suffered from unanticipated single traumatic events have symptoms that differ from those who suffer from more continuous, repeated, and anticipated ordeals. Single, shocking events trigger "detailed memories, misperceptions, hallucinations and mistiming," and a belief by children that they can predict accidents and disasters. This belief is also seen in adolescent refugees who have been severely tortured or were forced to witness executions. Terr's explanation of this, as summarized by van der Veer, is that "children who have been rendered totally helpless and placed in a frightening situation later try to make these experiences controllable. The child prefers to attach feelings of responsibility or guilt to the events than to accept helplessness and coincidence as reality."

By contrast, long exposure to traumatic events may result in emotional reactions that include "an absence of feeling, a sense of rage, or unremitting sadness, and of course, fear. The absence of emotional reactions is the result of denial (the child tries to look normal, whatever has happened and avoids talking about himself), psychic numbing, self-hypnosis and dissociation. Rage may be acted out in self-mutilations, physically damaging suicide attempts, or anti-social behavior. It may be covered by extreme passivity." The emotional reactions of children may be more intense than their parents or adults realize. The child's mental health and relationship with parents prior to traumatic experience also influence a child's post-traumatic reactions.[7]

Van der Veer divides the problems of adolescent refugees into three developmental themes. The first is finding a socially acceptable way to deal with aggressive and sexual impulses, a task made more difficult when an adolescent has been subjected directly or indirectly to traumatic experiences.

The second developmental theme involves separation from parents. Adolescent refugees need their parents' emotional support, but often have been separated from them for years. This occurs at a crucial time in their development, interrupting their process of individuation. "They are often very worried about their parents and feel they have failed in their responsibility towards them," yet it is often difficult even to maintain contact with their parents. "The feelings which young refugees have towards their parents are usually very complex. They miss their parents' emotional support but feel hindered by the expectations and norms which they assume their parents have. They feel guilty about not living up to these expectations or violating these norms."

The third developmental task is building an independent future. This becomes difficult for young refugees when the expectations of the future which they had before they fled have been "destroyed and their world view and self-image have been shaken by their traumatic experiences. As long as their request for asylum has not been granted they are not sure whether they will be able to build a new future in exile."

Adolescent refugees/asylum seekers who come with their parents have to carry out the normal developmental tasks of adolescence under circumstances which they find strange and hostile. They often have conflicting feelings—for instance, feelings of contempt and resentment versus ones of solidarity—about their parents, their fellow refugees, and their native country. Youngsters who were not consulted about their flight may feel helpless, while still feeling a bond with their parents because they share a similar culture, social status, and refugee experience.[8] Van der Veer is commenting on refugees who have been resettled, but his remarks apply with even greater force to adolescents stuck in the camps without a parent or relative.

CHAPTER FIVE

SCREENING AND ITS CRITICS

Unfriendly Welcome in Hong Kong

BECAUSE OF its far-reaching consequences, nothing in the CPA provoked as much controversy, criticism, and heated emotion as screening. Everybody involved had a vested interest. Asylum seekers sought to be resettled as refugees, often risking their lives and those of their families. Countries of first asylum tried to get rid of the asylum seekers quickly. Countries of resettlement took as few of these people as possible. UNHCR maneuvered to "wrap up" the Indochinese problem, as one official put it, so that they could turn to other, more pressing issues. Some voluntary agencies and news media capitalized on these controversies, highlighting alleged human rights violations and unfair practices in screening and in the treatment of the asylum seekers.

Hong Kong had a long tradition of allowing dissent to be aired. While some human rights activists, journalists, and prominent citizens expressed concerns about human rights abuses, others, including many officials, were vehemently opposed to the Vietnamese influx and expressed their views favoring harsh treatment in numerous newspaper articles and letters.[1]

Hong Kong's negative reaction to the Vietnamese boat people was fueled by the tens of thousands of asylum seekers who landed there. Hong Kong saw no reason to be more lenient with the Vietnamese than they were with illegal immigrants from the People's Republic of China, whom they routinely sent back. To discourage the Vietnamese, Hong Kong initiated screening in June 1988, a good nine months before the CPA came into force in other countries.

The Hong Kong government justified the start of screening in 1988 and the treatment of all Vietnamese immigrants as illegal immigrants by the "falling rate of resettlement and the changing nature of those arriving from Vietnam." By "changing nature," the Hong Kong government indicated that, as many critics had claimed, they had made a prior judgment regarding the status of the new arrivals. In fact, one government document noted that "the great majority [are] northerners who have left Vietnam for economic reasons. Most are therefore unlikely to qualify as genuine refugees." The government asserted that "screening is in accordance with internationally accepted practice for the determination of refugee status." All Vietnamese arrivals would be held in detention centers pending screening, "subject to security requirements." The principle of screening was to "identify genuine refugees." Through June 1994, those screened in through first-instance decisions constituted about 11 percent of arrivals. On appeal, another 4.5 percent were screened in, for a total of 15.5 percent, well below the percentages of other first-asylum countries.[2]

There were widespread complaints about flaws and bias in the screening process, especially in its first years. These included the denial of access to screening, the lengthy interview process, incompetent interpreters, insufficient interviewers, denial of access to independent lawyers to provide legal aid for applicants, lengthy appeals, variations in the implementation of refugee instruments, and "the most intractable problem . . . what to do with the screened out cases."[3]

Asylum seekers were not given adequate information to enable them to make informed decisions either at the first level or on appeal. Those who were screened early received no assistance from UNHCR or other organizations in advance of the screening. The interpreters did not know the dialects and idioms, especially the communist phrases and expressions used by the former north Vietnamese, and the information requested varied from one case to another.[4]

Attorney Janelle Diller, writing in 1988, expressed concern that the voices of asylum seekers speaking in their own defense were not heard. "Even after participating in screening interviews, some asylum seekers appeared confused about the process. In addition, asylum seekers receive no notice of the right to contact UNHCR, nor does UNHCR provide any contact or written materials pertaining to upcoming initial interviews. The asylum seeker is thus denied such simple advice as attempting to remember details of incidents pertinent to hardship in his or her life in Vietnam, including sources to document or corroborate those incidents. Such details are likely to escape memory during the frightening moments of the interview itself." Interpretation services were inadequate. This "denies the applicant a real opportunity to be heard. No record is kept of the original Vietnamese statements of the applicant. Since the file of each case contains only the examiner's notes reflecting the government interpreter's translation, the original meaning intended by the Vietnamese asylum seeker, if distinct from that interpreted, is lost forever."

Because the original Vietnamese text was not included, there was no safeguard on appeal to identify cases of erroneous interpretation. Equally serious, there were no special procedures that might address psychological and cultural difficulties faced by an asylum seeker during the interview. Diller accused the examiners of having "no special training in psychological, interpersonal, or cultural skills." She also observed that certain aspects of the interview might intimidate rather than encourage free speech. In addition, "the procedures also fail to contain mechanisms for dealing with cultural inhibitions which may prevent Vietnamese female applicants from producing full personal accounts of their lives to male examiners or interpreters."

Finally, Diller noted that "no separate and appropriate procedures exist to deal with unaccompanied minors, despite recommendations otherwise." She specifically criticized the role of UNHCR in the refugee determination procedures, because they only monitored 20 percent of all cases while 90 percent of all cases were being rejected, because the effectiveness of the monitoring was questionable, and finally because their assistance on appeal was deficient.[5]

Three years later, Anne Wagley Gow, a former UNHCR field officer in Hong Kong, reiterated Diller's concerns and added some of her own. Of particular concern to Gow was that the Hong Kong government had determined in advance the percentage of Vietnamese they expected to grant refugee status. Even before status determination procedures were started, the Hong Kong government announced that they expected about 10 percent of the people who sought asylum to be refugees—and that was the percentage actually screened in. Although acknowledging that changes and improvements in the status determination procedures had occurred since the earlier critiques of Diller and others, Gow cautioned that those who were screened out in 1988 and 1989 were "particularly vulnerable to having been wrongly denied refugee status." She quoted an Amnesty International report, which claimed that screening in Hong Kong still lacked safeguards. Furthermore, the screening did not identify all those who might be genuine refugees, and a weakness was revealed in the review process by the very fact that large numbers of refugees were initially screened out. The informational brochure belatedly issued by UNHCR to asylum seekers in 1990 was considered by some legal scholars "grossly misleading," omitting essential information and misstating the law.[6]

"I Know What Is in the Best Interests of Children"

EACH UNACCOMPANIED minor was interviewed by a social worker employed by International Social Service, a nongovernmental agency. The child's case was then presented to a panel of two UNHCR legal consultants and a senior social worker. They made a recommendation for the child's status and durable solution (resettlement or repatriation). This was then presented to Hong Kong's Department of Immigration.

Special Procedures did not begin until February 1990, over one and a half years after Hong Kong initiated its status determination procedures. By November 1990, only 100 cases out of the 2,500 unaccompanied minors in the camps had been decided. Similar delays also occurred in other countries of first asylum.

In 1993, UNHCR, under heavy criticism for these delays, assigned Christine Mougne to respond. This UNHCR Senior Regional Social Services Officer was the architect of the model for the Special Procedures for unaccompanied minors. She had also come up with the controversial theory that unaccompanied minors were "economic anchors," who had been sent out of the country to be resettled so that later they could bring over their parents. At a conference on the CPA, Mougne explained what went wrong with the Special Procedures. "Bureaucratic delays conspired with practical problems such as recruiting suitably qualified interpreters," with the consequence that the procedure got off to "a lamentably slow start." This caused a large backlog of cases. She found this "discomforting" because "children had already spent a wasted year alone . . . all too often unprotected in the camps waiting for the procedures to begin. For me, the tragedy [of the delays] is that the unreasonably long time spent in camps has inevitably taken its toll on these children and young adults. After two, three or more years separated from their families and exposed to the violent and lawless camp culture, the rate of delinquency and other disturbance is all too high. Reintegration in these circumstances is not going to be easy."

Mougne maintained that, overall, the Special Procedure was a major advance in setting up a system in which, on exceptionally compelling humanitarian grounds, a child who had been denied refugee status nevertheless might be resettled. But in fact children were screened out and separated from screened-in adults, often their relatives, who had been their de facto parents for years. Many children had fled, not with their parents, but with other relatives who were part of an extended family. The "Note on Unaccompanied Minors" stipulated that "minors not accompanied by their own parents may be linked with other relatives or other families in the camp and care should be taken in assessing the nature and implications of these relationships."

Over the protests of many critics, the decision was made that "minors *in camp* without their parents would only be linked for the purposes of refugee status determination with adults who qualify as principal caregivers in place of the parents" (italics theirs). Mougne stated that this was not due to disrespect for Vietnamese family traditions, but rather to protect each child's options. This gave the child his or her own claim on refugee status, not dependent on the relative, and also enabled the child to have a thorough examination into the durable solution that would be in that child's best interest.[7] The consequence of this decision, however, was that many children were separated from their relatives who were given refugee status and resettled; the children remained behind in the camps, awaiting their interview by the Special Committee.

In Hong Kong, UNHCR was accused of creating other difficulties. Social workers from International Social Service recommended against repatriation of unaccompanied minors. They were overruled by UNHCR and prohibited from submitting appeals for these children: "The UNHCR refuses to acknowledge the receipt of appeal submissions, stating an appeal process does not exist for durable solution decisions for unaccompanied minors." Subsequently, but also with considerable delay, an appeal process was set up through the Refugee Status Review Board.[8]

Christine Mougne also defended UNHCR's actions in *Refugees,* a UNHCR publication. She wrote that a major aim of UNHCR was to discourage the escape of children from Vietnam. Presenting her "economic anchor" theory, she stated that deterrence would "only happen when parents in Vietnam realize that sending their children out alone will no longer lead to their own resettlement."

Anne Gow, the former UNHCR field officer, responded with a blistering attack. "Attributing such motivations to Vietnamese parents is both culturally insensitive and erroneous. Multiple factors enter into a parent's decision to send a child to seek asylum, most obvious of which is a desire for the child to be free from a future of persecution due to the family's social or political history. The decision is an agonizing one, and simplifying and generalizing the intentions of the parents does not contribute to an understanding of the situation of individual unaccompanied minors."

To illustrate her contention that UNHCR was not a neutral party, Gow cited the highly publicized case of a fifteen-year-old unaccompanied minor, Nguyen Ngoc Toan. Toan was denied refugee status, while his seventeen-year-old brother, who had arrived before the cutoff date, was resettled in New York. The social worker from International Social Service had written a summary favoring refugee status for the youth. The UNHCR Special Committee omitted this, but its own recommendation to deny refugee status was forwarded to the Hong Kong Immigration Department. High Court Judge J. Bokhary overruled the Hong Kong Immigration and UNHCR recommendations. The judge found that the decision-making process did not allow Toan to have his case "fully and fairly presented."[9]

Of particular interest was the judge's summary of discrimination against Toan's family in Vietnam. The persecution directed against them was systematic and pervasive. Authorities confiscated the working tools of Toan's father because he had worked for the Americans, and they refused to let him earn a living legally. The security police spied on Toan's family and they destroyed the family's Buddhist temple. They would not let Toan's brother earn a living; this showed that Toan's generation also was being persecuted. Toan's father had to do forced labor two or three days every two months because he was a member of a disfavored group. For the same reason, Toan had to do extra labor at school. Other children at school taunted and abused him physically. The teachers both allowed this and treated him worse than other students. Despite this, the Special Committee recommended that Toan be denied refugee status. They reasoned that the discrimination and harassment directed at Toan and his family "do not amount to a well-founded fear of persecution." The Special Committee stated, "It is in Toan's best interest to return to his family in Vietnam, emphasizing the advantages of a person of his age living with his parents." The judge disagreed, and went with the recommendation that Toan be reunited with his brother in New York.[10]

UNHCR and Hong Kong officials admitted, publicly and privately, that the length of time taken to establish the Special Procedures for unaccompanied minors was excessive, but in other respects they justified their screening decisions as being appropriate. Typical of this group was the Chairman of Hong Kong's Refugee Status Review Board, a retired judge of European descent whom we interviewed in his spacious office in December 1991. Although many of his decisions were considered controversial, he defended his actions and those of his board by saying, "I was a senior judge in the family court, and I'm the father of three children. Therefore I know what is in the best interests of children." He denied that there was a bias in the evaluation process as held in Hong Kong. "I don't care if a person is screened in or screened out. I only care that a person who deserves refugee status not be missed. The Hong Kong government has never once given us a quota for in and out. It never tries to interfere with our duties." The board overturned under 7 percent of the screened-out cases. He justified this by saying, "The basis on which refugee recognition takes place is shifting. Vietnam is changing. What might lead you to have had a well-founded fear of persecution a couple of years ago has changed now. An example is religious persecution. I know because I go to churches in Vietnam and I look for trouble, but I don't see it." While acknowledging that the evaluation process for children took too long, he claimed that his interpreters for interviews, all of them Chinese, were the best, and said that there was no possibility that the Review Board was biased. The chairman concluded by saying, "I think I know the Vietnamese well. They are a gentle people. I don't blame them for trying to embroider their stories."

"The Procedures Performed, in General, Remarkably Well"

NOT ONLY the government of Hong Kong, but also UNHCR vigorously defended its actions. Under heavy criticism from many groups, UNHCR responded with its Bulletin of August 1995, "The Comprehensive Plan of Action," which justified its activities both in Hong Kong and other first-asylum countries and summarized the principles, procedures, and problems of the Comprehensive Plan of Action. UNHCR stated that its role was to safeguard asylum seekers in their application for refugee status. This was done by UNHCR-appointed legal consultants in some countries, or through UNHCR representatives on appeals boards in others. "If there was no consensus, UNHCR was able to exercise its mandate—in other words, could independently declare that an individual merited refugee status. Essentially, UNHCR provided a quality-control 'safety net' for screening." With regard to Hong Kong, UNHCR appointed legal counselors who examined the case of each asylum seeker. These counselors intervened in support of asylum seekers when they felt the case deserved such action. When their judgment differed from the Review Board, they would exercise UNHCR's mandate to recommend refugee status, and they did so in more than 1,500 cases in Hong Kong. UNHCR concluded, "Though there may be a few egregious cases—which UNHCR remains open to reviewing—the procedures performed, in general, remarkably well."[11]

UNHCR also responded to accusations that their participation in screening was inadequate. For example, people arbitrarily detained in Vietnam for several years had been denied refugee status because "no torture was involved," and UNHCR went along with such decisions.[12] In several countries, asylum seekers claimed that refugee status was bought for sexual favors or money. In bulletins and public letters, UNHCR responded emphatically and in detail that they had looked into these accusations and that the claims of corruption and sexual exploitation were unproved.[13]

In "The Comprehensive Plan of Action" and "UNHCR Report on Alleged Corruption in the Refugee Status Determination in the Philippines," UNHCR maintained that they trained government officials to establish the procedures used to screen refugees. They also gave regular workshops for government officials on the CPA, refugee status determination procedures, interviewing techniques, and the current situation in Vietnam. UNHCR monitored a "significant proportion" of the interviews held by Philippine officials. This was in addition to UNHCR's own interviews of all asylum seekers prior to pre-screening. Finally, they "carefully reviewed" all of the files of the people who had been denied in the first interview. UNHCR concludes, "Through such close involvement in the procedures, UNHCR was able to identify and intervene on all deserving cases."[14]

The most damaging criticisms were allegations of corruption among immigration officials and police in the Philippines, Indonesia, and Malaysia, and among consultants hired by UNHCR. These allegations seriously called into question the credibility of both the CPA and UNHCR as a protector of refugees. In the two publications mentioned above, UNHCR responded in carefully measured language, distancing itself from those who might taint the organization. "Corruption cannot be ruled out, particularly in situations where asylum-seekers and government screening teams frequently lived in the same camps, with large sums of money being remitted from family members overseas. . . . UNHCR would find it intolerable that a genuine refugee be denied protection because of corruption." Because of the extensive review and appeals process in which UNHCR was involved, they conclude that "very few refugees— if any—were unjustly screened-out because of corruption or malfeasance." Thus, they have fulfilled their mandate to protect refugees. They are less concerned that some people may have been given refugee status without deserving it. "In certain specific cases brought to UNHCR's attention, some people may well have paid bribes in order to be screened-in." A possible indicator of this was seen in Indonesia. "UNHCR's internal review indicates that an untypically large number of people were recognized for refugee status by the authorities, despite UNHCR's recommendation that they did not qualify for refugee status. UNHCR does not, as a rule, question governments when they adopt a more generous interpretation of refugee criteria than its own." They did, however, request that authorities initiate criminal investigations in Indonesia.[15]

Robinson reports that UNHCR reviewed the screening charges in Indonesia as a result of increasing pressure from refugee advocacy groups and the U.S. Congress. He observes that the review was done in-house. UNHCR did not re-interview any of the asylum seekers and it did not investigate specific corruption charges. "UNHCR seemed principally concerned with whether any deserving case might have been screened out unfairly. . . . Their conclusions were never released publicly, but according [to] a report by the US General Accounting Office, the UNHCR review upheld the screening decisions in 481 of 486 cases." The General Accounting Office report concluded that corruption did have an impact on screening. Strong cases were not denied; however, though rarely substantiated in the case files, corruption accounts for the high number of positive decisions in weak cases.[16]

In their more detailed public response to specific allegations of corruption in the Philippines, UNHCR investigated but could not find evidence of sexual and monetary demands made by screening officials.[17] "UNHCR staff made repeated efforts to obtain reliable information about rumored bribery. *UNHCR made it known that protection would be given to anyone who provided such information*, **No one ever came forward**" (italics and boldface theirs). Intermediaries such as interpreters might have been involved in bribes, but UNHCR put a different spin on these activities. "Assuming the truth of the allegation that intermediaries did solicit bribes, *the question is whether they did so as part of a scheme to influence refugee status determinations by bribing officials or whether they were simply defrauding asylum seekers*" (italics theirs).[18]

On separating adult and minor siblings, UNHCR, in the same publication, stated, "Occasionally siblings were given different decisions. Such cases required careful handling at the appeals stage. *UNHCR came to the difficult decision that unmeritorious positive decisions in the case of one sibling was not reason for UNHCR to support the case of another sibling on appeal*" (italics theirs).[19]

Most UNHCR officials went along with the official rationalizations of their organization, but a few, like Anne Wagley Gow, did not. She resigned her post, after which she launched her attacks on her former employer. Others who vehemently disagreed with the policies and practices of their agency tried to work within the system, often without success. Such a person was a young field officer whom we interviewed near the end of 1991 in Hong Kong's island camp of Chi Ma Wan. Unlike those in his agency who formulated policy, removed from the people they affected, this young man worked directly with children in the camp on a daily basis. Based on his firsthand experience and knowledge of the asylum seekers, he questioned the fairness of the screening system, the clarity of the decisions, the facile assumptions of interviewers that they understood the Vietnamese situation, the pushing for voluntary repatriation, and splitting of children from their relatives.

The field officer expressed his frustration with the unresponsiveness of his agency. "It is unforgivable to let children wait longer for a decision or to split them from their relatives. I'm an interventionist with the minors; I've gotten to know them well and their problems. I see them every day; I know their background and their cases. I try to help them. I write memos for them to help them, but it does little good. The kids are pretty cynical now about the UNHCR office; they don't expect much now. I apologize profusely and say how embarrassed I am. These kids are in terrible condition, and there's nothing I can do." Six months later, he was no longer at Chi Ma Wan.

"The Slow Buffalo Always Drinks the Dirty Water"

DESPITE THE elaborate assurances of UNHCR that its policies and decisions were fair, asylum seekers continued to dispute its claims. We found widespread mistrust and misunderstanding between asylum seekers and the officials who determined their destinies. In the eighteen camps that we visited in six countries, we spoke with children and adults who claimed they had been intimidated by interviewers who called them liars when the interpreters mistranslated what they had said. We interviewed ex-military officers of the South Vietnamese army who, despite suffering grievous persecution, having ample documentation to prove it and thus qualifying for resettlement in the United States, nevertheless were initially denied refugee status, and only after appeal were recognized as refugees. Several of these cases were given worldwide publicity by human rights organizations, including our own.

One highly celebrated case was that of a former major in the South Vietnamese army who, after the war, had been under house arrest for fifteen years and had not been allowed to hold any job. He was denied refugee status because he had not been in a reeducation camp for three years and his lack of employment was interpreted as an "economic," not a refugee, issue. His situation, however, was not so easily dismissed. Because he had lost a leg, he had remained only twenty-one days in a reeducation camp, but then, without being released, was sent to another camp for hard labor, where he made five hundred bricks a day. After twenty-two months, he became quite ill and was sent home but still was not officially released. Because of this, he could never leave his village nor hold a job. He escaped to the Philippines in 1989.

The major was a well-educated man who was not anti-UNHCR but whose observations of the status determination process differed significantly from the UNHCR version. He criticized UNHCR for not living up to its own principles. His remarks show the difficulties asylum seekers had in trying to present a convincing and credible case for refugee status. For children, the difficulties were far greater.

In Vietnam, he had never heard of the Comprehensive Plan of Action, even though he lived in an area convenient for escape. Upon arrival in the Philippines, he was given a brief biographical interview. One year later, a Filipino lawyer representing UNHCR conducted a preliminary interview, forcing the major to sign a blank piece of paper. The major received no guidance or documents that explained screening or what the interviewer was looking for, and the major misinterpreted the questions. The interviewer wrote an evaluation, not shown to the major and not checked for accuracy, which was used later at the screening interview, conducted by a Philippine immigration official.

The woman who conducted the screening interview was hostile to former South Vietnamese military men. The major reported that "people thought this was to show that the only way to get screened in was to pay a bribe."[20] She interviewed twenty-two officers in his unit and rejected twelve of them; eight of these were screened in on appeal. He told her he had been denied a family registration card, which meant he was unable to find a job. In his village, he was forced to attend political indoctrination sessions at which he was accused of being "one who sells his country." She wrote that he had a family registration card and had returned to his village to start a stable life; therefore he had not been persecuted.

He said, "Many people told me as they left for resettlement that they had been screened in because they had paid bribes. Corruption is big; everyone knows it. Of the four thousand screened-in people I knew, one-third made it through bribery. But there is no actual proof. We just knew it because the person had no background to justify approval of refugee status. They had money in the camp, sent by their relatives. Bribery was easy at screening interviews because one person made the decision." However, "Just because you paid a bribe, you were not always screened in. At the appeal stage, it was more difficult because it involved many people." After he was denied refugee status, he received a book about screening.[21] He appealed, showing that he had endured fifteen years of house arrest, been denied a residence permit, and denied employment, as was his wife. The appeals committee overturned the original decision.

The major believed that UNHCR deliberately slowed down the interviewing of unaccompanied minors in the camps, so their delay in being resettled would deter others still in Vietnam from escaping. No evidence exists to support this view. Despite the controversies over corruption, and some mistakes, the major thought that screening was basically fair. The biggest problem was that pre-cutoff and post-cutoff asylum seekers with the same situation were treated differently, with one screened in and the other denied. "People were disappointed. The only difference was their date of arrival. They are like the buffalo at the end of the herd when they go to the river for a drink. We have an adage for those who arrive late, "The slow buffalo always drinks the dirty water."[22]

We met children who had been separated from elder brothers and sisters and forced to live with strangers on the grounds that their relatives were not their parents, and therefore did not fit the definition of family in use by UNHCR. A child in Palawan, in the Philippines, showed us his denial notice, which predated the interview in which his best interests determination was to be made. As with the major, many children in Palawan First Asylum Camp and in Galang Camp, Indonesia, told us that their friends had bought their way out of the camps. Ten minutes after we arrived in Indonesia, a man offered, for a fee, to buy the release of any asylum seeker in the Galang Camp. We could not tell if this was a scam to defraud us, or a genuine offer. However, in Galang, we gave $1,000 directly to an asylum seeker. His brother in the United States had sent him the money through us. A few months later, we ran into this asylum seeker at a Vietnamese New Year (Tet) festival in San Jose, California.

Several children in Palawan told us they were repeating rumors about bribery, but one unaccompanied minor gave us a specific description. "I have been rejected, so when I hear about people like myself who have been accepted, I feel sad. I know several children who were accepted. Unlike me, they had money. Unqualified people with money replace qualified people without money. My friend, an unaccompanied minor, went to her interview. She gave money to the intermediary. She was given a very quick positive result and sent to Bataan transit camp for resettlement. Before leaving, she said to me, 'If you have money, you can get through. I gave the intermediary five hundred U.S. dollars. If you have money, I'll introduce you to him; he's a Filipino man who works inside the camp.' But I had no money. I felt desperate, denied, sad, but what could I do?"

UNHCR firmly denied that asylum seekers were not informed of the screening procedures in the Palawan Camp. "The claim of inadequate UNHCR counseling is baseless." To support their response, they quoted from a 1991 report by the U.S. Lawyers Committee for Human Rights that confirmed the UNHCR view. The Committee wrote that compared with applicants in other first asylum countries, *"the enhanced prescreening counseling opportunity appear [sic] to result in asylum seekers who are better prepared for their interviews"* (emphasis theirs). UNHCR concluded, *"it has always been UNHCR's impression that the RSD [Refugee Status Determination] process was and is very clearly understood"* (emphasis theirs).[23]

When we talked to the unaccompanied minors in Palawan in December 1991, they emphatically disputed the claims of UNHCR. Several screened-out youngsters insisted that before they had left Vietnam, they had never heard about screening or the CPA, and that in the camp, they had received no information.

A fourteen-year-old in the same camp related a different experience that departs from the official UNHCR version. "I never saw the Vietnamese-language document that explains the process, and no UNHCR person ever spoke with me about it. However, I did receive adequate information about screening. A Vietnamese volunteer working for the Center for Assistance to Displaced Persons [CADP] informed me in detail. I knew that screening was done to qualify people for refugee status. I knew that I would not be screened as an adult but evaluated by a Special Committee for children, and they would determine if I was qualified or not. I had no warning, suddenly the volunteer told me to go to the interview, and I went. I was really worried, and I was afraid during the interview. I did not know how to answer the questions in order to let me be accepted."

Another boy, fifteen, told of being intimidated at his interview and at his appeal. "My father was in a reeducation camp, then released. Two months after I escaped, my father was put in jail, where he died. I received a letter and a copy of the death certificate, but the Filipino interviewer would not believe me. In the first interview, I said that my family had *planned* to escape twice, but the interpreter wrote down that they had twice *attempted* to escape. Because of this discrepancy, she did not believe me. I tried to correct this after the interview, but she said, 'No, the interview is over.' I told her that the interpreter had wrote it down wrong, that I had said 'planned,' not 'attempted' to escape. She replied, 'No, you don't tell the truth, and I don't believe you.' So I am scared; she won't believe my father died and she will recommend against me."

An American volunteer in the camp said, "The UNHCR official who deals with the children never talked to this boy, and the boy is scared of UNHCR. He has had no legal counsel. He can turn for help to the Center for Assistance to Displaced Persons, but they don't have the resources or knowledge to proceed with cases like this. The intentions of UNHCR are good, but people generally distrust them. From time to time, they call kids to tell them about the 'best interests of the child.' Some go, some don't. This boy does not know where to go. He feels hopeless and in despair, not knowing where to turn."

Blaming the Children

UNHCR OFFICIALS were hardly indifferent to the plight of the children. They expressed dismay at what was happening, especially to the vulnerable unaccompanied minors, yet they were unable to reach these children and convey their concerns. This was because the premises from which they began were not universally shared by others.

The frustration of UNHCR is reflected in a memo, "Social Services Mission to the Philippines," written in December 1992 by the UNHCR Senior Regional Social Services Officer.[24] From October 19 to 28, 1992, she visited Palawan with the program manager for Nordic Assistance to Repatriated Vietnamese (NARV), an organization contracted by UNHCR to provide assistance for people who returned to Vietnam. The UNHCR officer wrote that she found a camp that was the most open in Southeast Asia but also the most resistant to repatriation. The detainees would not tolerate even a mention of returning to Vietnam. They acted as if the CPA did not exist and they would never have to return.

The Philippines became a bitter battleground over conflicting interests, and a peculiarly vexing and frustrating embarrassment for UNHCR. Upon advocating voluntary repatriation for screened-out asylum seekers, UNHCR found itself portrayed as violating their rights. Detainees, despite humane treatment and relatively easy living conditions, strongly resisted repatriation. The CADP, a nonprofit Catholic welfare agency founded by the Catholic Bishops Conference of the Philippines to provide humane treatment and assistance to Vietnamese boat people, became a harsh critic of UNHCR measures aimed at persuading the asylum seekers to choose voluntary repatriation.

The UNHCR Senior Regional Social Services Officer and the NARV program manager tried to persuade the NGOs of the benefits for repatriates of NARV activities in Vietnam. They encountered hostility and silence. Similarly, the Women's Association of Palawan refused to listen to them once they mentioned the word "repatriation." The memo's author reports that the unaccompanied minors, some six hundred persons or fifteen percent of the total camp population, were the most resistant group the author had ever encountered.

The UNHCR officer had no doubt where to place the blame for this situation. She wrote that a high percentage of detainees had close relatives in the United States, prompting unrealistic expectations of resettlement. A group of former soldiers and their families staunchly resisted repatriation and influenced others to do the same. An overly lenient Special Committee screened in too many people and was willing to review appeals over and over, creating false hopes of resettlement. CADP and the Catholic Church obstructed repatriation.

Significantly, this officer's harshest criticism was directed at the unaccompanied minors themselves. The children fabricated family disasters to persuade the Special Committee to reopen and prolong their cases, hoping for the miracle that their cases would be reversed and they would be resettled.

Her solution was to present a clear message to the detainees. Their only choice was repatriation to Vietnam. To accomplish this, she recommended that the Philippine government articulate this clear message. To shatter the detainees' sense of permanence, she recommended reduction of their extensive medical programs. For the same reason, she also recommended limiting the remittances to detainees from their relatives, restricting their movements, reducing education to the primary grades 1 through 5, and having the Philippine government persuade CADP to curtail their English instruction and skills training. To address the problems of the minors, she recommended that they be denied repeated reviews of their cases, that NARV develop projects in Vietnam to prompt minors to return, and that local schools and training in Vietnam be improved for these children and youth. Finally, she recommended that minors from the same town or village should be returned in groups so that they would not be stigmatized for having "failed" their parents.

One can understand and sympathize with this official's frustration. As an employee of UNHCR, she was obligated to follow the directives of her agency and the guidelines of the CPA as interpreted by UNHCR. But she had also been assigned to design and implement procedures for the treatment of unaccompanied minors within the framework of the CPA. Her problem was that the detainees didn't buy her argument; neither did the CADP or the Philippine government. They had a different view of what was humane, permanent, permissible, and realistic. The Philippine government, for example, was extremely reluctant to repatriate people who didn't want to return, and eventually, the government decided to let them stay, a position which was well within the guidelines of the CPA but which this officer and other UNHCR officers did not accept at that time.

The CADP adamantly maintained that humane treatment consisted in providing all possible assistance to asylum seekers until they made their decision to repatriate or not. The CADP's statement on this, written in English, leaves no doubt of their commitment. "At all times, CADP has always brought to the refugees the loving concerns of the Philippine Church whose Migration and Refugee Mission has never ceased to show its solicitude to the distressed refugees who landed battered and broken. . . . CADP facilitates the fulfillment of the refugees' educational and cultural needs which are not available from public funds . . . CADP was born with the needs of the refugees on the first days of their exodus. CADP also hopes and pledges to see them all off safely to their whatever destinations with their feelings of being ushered through the painful journey."[25] Thus, the CADP openly opposed the notion that voluntary repatriation was freely chosen when people were coerced or given vague promises of help in Vietnam. From their point of view, the position and recommendations of the Senior Regional Social Services Officer were neither realistic nor humane.

This officer's remarks, based on a regional Southeast Asian outlook, were far removed from the context in which screening and Special Committee decisions had been made in the Philippines. She appears to have realized this, but was a prisoner of her agency's regulations and guidelines. It was her job to defend those guidelines and come up with justifications for them. Most asylum seekers were convinced that screening was inconsistent and rigged in favor of applicants who could buy their way out. In their view, people who deserved refugee status were turned down when they told the truth. Asylum seekers, including minors, believed that they had been lied to and that the screening was unfair. It seemed to them that persons who had a clear record of being persecuted were denied for reasons that appeared to be contrived. A persistent complaint was that many had been required to sign a blank sheet attesting to the accuracy of their interview before the interview was held. As previously mentioned, a minor showed us his denial notice, which was dated prior to the date of his Special Committee interview. In these circumstances, as many minors told us, it did no good to tell the truth. The Senior Regional Social Services Officer was outraged that the children had lied in their interviews, but if the children were correct in their perceptions, she had held them to a standard of truth that was higher than that of their interviewers. She also failed to consider the climate of fear, disillusion, and distrust that pervaded the camp because of the way the interviews were held. From the minors' point of view, the primary consideration was not the truth, which might be twisted and used against them, but survival.

Most UNHCR officials whom we met, seasoned as well as newer employees, seemed to have internalized the United Nations jargon of humanitarian concepts. They spoke earnestly about "best interests," "durable solutions," and "voluntary repatriation." We listened as they distinguished between "refugee" and "economic migrant" as if they were utterly separate, despite the lack of clarity in this distinction, and the fact that some controversial status-determination decisions based on that distinction had been overturned on appeal. We heard their contradictory justifications for separating unaccompanied minors from adult relatives in the camps, but repatriating minors with adult relatives in Vietnam. The officials were truly convinced of the rightness and rationality of their views, their official publications supported them, and some of them wrote for or were quoted in these publications. They saw themselves as humane, protecting asylum seekers, properly determining the "best interests" of children, both morally and within their mandate, and justifying their evaluations on the basis of reports which they believed to be reliable—some of which, as described in Chapter 6, we now know to have been false. Understandably, high level officials in UNHCR, far removed from the children whose lives they were affecting, depended on these reports.

They had gone well beyond their mandate by trying to protect and assist nonrefugees, helping them to return to Vietnam and monitoring their reception. They expressed bewilderment and sometimes impatience when critics vilified them for their alleged lack of sensitivity, concern, and understanding about the asylum seekers. They looked for rationalizations to support their views. One official tried to convince us that the excessive delay in completing "best interest" determinations for children was actually humane because it extended protection for the children. Another resolved the contradictions he faced by telling us, "If you can sleep at night, don't worry about your decision."

Accounting for Discrepancies

HOW DO we account for the discrepancies between UNHCR and children's views? The differences stem not only from vested interests, but also from knowledge of policy and procedure, and knowing how policies actually are implemented. The impressions created by people and the environment in which they are heard also influence how their words are judged.

In December 1991, we interviewed the UNHCR Field Officer in her office at the Palawan First Asylum Camp, right opposite the food distribution depot. With her was the Durable Solutions Officer, who managed the voluntary return to Vietnam of rejected asylum seekers. Both were clearly sympathetic about the situation of the children in the camp, and they discussed with particular

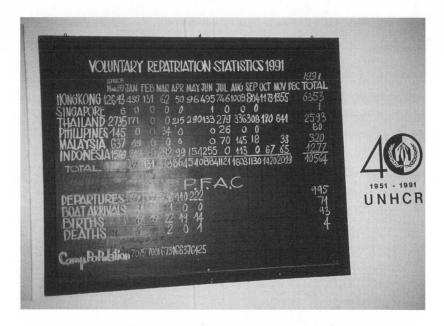

Sign inside the entrance of the UNHCR office, Palawan First Asylum Camp, the Philippines. The sign announces the number of people who voluntarily chose repatriation and indicates to asylum seekers that UNHCR favors repatriation, not resettlement. *Photo: James M. Freeman.*

concern the unaccompanied minors. But it was evident why children were terrified of stepping into the UNHCR field office. On a wall facing them as they entered was a large blackboard which announced the numbers of asylum seekers who had been repatriated to Vietnam, but nowhere were there figures of those who had been resettled. Children and adults understandably interpreted this as meaning that UNHCR favored repatriation over resettlement. That this was not always the case became evident when a worker in the UNHCR office interrupted our interview with the news that a particular person had just won his appeal and had been granted refugee status. The work in the office stopped, the Field Officer handed soft drinks to everyone, and for several minutes the office staff celebrated. But this is not what the children of the camp saw, heard, or believed. Cuc, whose story appears in Chapter 3, described the Field Officer as "mean. People [said], 'She wants to send us back to Vietnam.'"

The Field Officer seemed to be sincerely concerned about the children but quite unaware of the negative impression she made on them. She described to us in detail what she and her staff had done to prepare the minors for their interview. "Our Durable Solutions counselor briefs the minors for their interviews. This is done in a group. They are told what kinds of questions will be asked, why they are given the opportunity to appear before the Special Committee, and that they can then ask questions. This briefing is followed up by a case-worker, who calls each minor. The caseworker documents the information, which is sent to Manila. The Special Committee consists of three representatives— an officer of the Bureau of Immigration of the Philippine government, a representative of Community and Family Services International, a voluntary organization that has experience in psychology and child welfare, and the UNHCR Deputy Representative, who gives advice. These three people meet each week, discuss the cases, and decide what is in the best interest of the child. Children age sixteen and seventeen, those who have aged out, are treated somewhat differently. If the Bureau of Immigration rejects them for refugee status, the Special Committee can still evaluate them in terms of 'best interest.' We call for the collection of more information by the UNHCR caseworker, then the Special Committee evaluates the applicant. Sometimes the children are recommended for resettlement, even though they are not refugees. Our priority criteria for these decisions are, first, family unity, second, if the minor has a claim for refugee status, and finally, a cumulative assessment, including evaluation whether or not the child's family in Vietnam is capable of taking care of the child if the child is returned."

In our second interview with the Durable Solutions Officer, he informed us that the general procedures for screening were published in October 1990, and the one for unaccompanied minors was published in January 1990.[26] Regarding the procedures for minors, he noted that "on occasion there have been some problems with the accuracy of translations. They are never perfect; the connotations are sometimes difficult to determine. We find out about these problems when a Bureau of Immigration official says that the applicant said one thing and the applicant says he didn't. Then we check into it, and we give the benefit of the doubt to the applicant."

Information on the CPA and voluntary repatriation was distributed to the asylum seekers; we have copies of the pamphlet for unaccompanied minors and children. It is possible that some children, particularly those who arrived soon after the CPA came into force in 1989, did not receive the pamphlet before their prescreening interview, since the pamphlet was first published in January 1990. But the Durable Solutions Officer did talk to some children.

The problem was not that the children didn't receive the information, but that they didn't understand what they heard or read. The legalistic process of being interviewed, offering consistent answers, and preparing answers according to criteria that were foreign to the children caused considerable confusion. Even when informed about them, the children remained terrified of these interviews conducted in a situation of dominance and subordination, where they were on occasion intimidated by interviewers who put them down, called them liars, and dismissed their statements. Some children may have lied, but the conditions of the interviews clearly intimidated them and made it difficult for them to answer clearly. On the other hand, intimidation of the children was largely unintentional—and perhaps it was unavoidable, given what was at stake: resettlement if they succeeded, and repatriation if they didn't.

Furthermore, the pamphlet the unaccompanied minors received did more harm than good. By portraying a happy future for them when they returned to Vietnam, it created panic and caused the children to believe that UNHCR was against them and was lying to them. Some children told us that they felt insulted, that the pamphlet was simply "propaganda for the communists in Vietnam." A cartoon near the end showed a map of Vietnam and parents saying they would be happy when their children returned. This may have applied to some children, but for others, this created terrible dilemmas; their parents had written them telling them not to return, that their best hope for the future was to remain in the camp.

CHAPTER SIX

REPATRIATION

Nowhere to Return

UNHCR'S DIFFICULTIES with Vietnamese asylum seekers increased when UNHCR expanded beyond its role as protector to include the contradictory one of advocating the repatriation of many of these same people.[1] Asylum seekers, feeling betrayed by the organization that was supposed to protect them, and disillusioned by what they considered to be inconsistent and unfair decisions on their refugee status, refused to be repatriated. Since at first Vietnam would not accept forcible repatriation, tens of thousands of screened-out adults, as well as children recommended for repatriation, remained in the camps, despite terrible living conditions. As the situation of unaccompanied minors in these camps became known, international criticism centered on UNHCR's failure to provide them with adequate protection and the long delays in establishing Special Committees for their evaluation.

Desperate to show positive results, UNHCR intensified its efforts to persuade unaccompanied minors to repatriate, reducing their food rations, curtailing their schooling, badgering them to repatriate, and offering them money if they did so. In Hong Kong, with UNHCR approval, children as well as adults were frequently relocated from one camp to another so that they would have no feeling of permanence. The consequence of these actions was to increase rather than reduce opposition in the camps. Internees, including children, became militantly hostile to UNHCR. However, some children did volunteer to return.

Some of the children who repatriated simply gave in to the constant pressure, but others no doubt were influenced by extravagant promises of assistance to returnees. Nordic Assistance to Repatriated Vietnamese (NARV) published a colorful brochure with bright assurances that all would be well if the unaccompanied minors returned. The brochure, written in Vietnamese, was titled, "Returning Home is Not the End of Everything But is Only the Beginning." The brochure contained photographs of smiling repatriated minors and answered typical questions of returnees. The children were informed that NARV would help them with repatriation. "We will visit you at home, talk with you and your family, and help you if you run into any difficulties." NARV would help them go back to school. If they had any difficulties, NARV would "meet school officials to find the way to help you." This included extra tutoring, if necessary. The European Community International Program (ECIP) would open free vocational training programs for them. NARV would help the returnees contact ECIP and would provide transportation or boarding costs for those who lived far from the training center. If possible, NARV would "make every effort to help you to get a job or apprenticeship near your home." The returnees would receive a UNHCR repatriation allowance, and in special instances NARV could give a fixed amount of financial assistance. NARV assured unaccompanied minors worried about harassment by local authorities that nothing had happened to those who had already returned, except for occasional delays of a few weeks in the start of their repatriation allowances. Furthermore, UNHCR would "help to resolve all difficulties concerning education, lodging, as well as other activities for you and your families." The children worried that their families would not welcome them back; NARV assured them that very few parents would act like that, but if they had concerns, a NARV staff member would visit them and their families immediately after they had returned. For those who could not return to their families, had any health problems, or needed any kind of special assistance, NARV would prepare appropriate solutions. If a returnee could not stay with his or her family, NARV would work out a long-term plan for good treatment in a foster home, and arrange for education or vocational training.[2]

Supplementing this brochure were other publications, including those intended to reach the international community and elites in Vietnam. An example is the *Science Information Review* of the National Institute for Educational Sciences of Vietnam, which devoted a special issue to "Education and Returning Children." Most of the articles were published both in English and Vietnamese. Nguyen Dinh Bin, Assistant to the Minister of Foreign Affairs, presented the Vietnamese government view that unaccompanied minors had no future in the Hong Kong and Southeast Asian detention camps. "Their fate is a humanitarian issue to which the Government of Vietnam has been doing its utmost

Hunger strike, Whitehead Detention Center, Hong Kong.
Photo: Nguyen H. Duyen.

to reach a good solution." Children whose parents were living in Vietnam would "be accepted on repatriation by the Government with necessary financial support from the international community so that they can continue normal life until the age of maturity." The government was prepared to accept orphans and keep them in childcare institutions until they reached the age of eighteen. The government was trying to help these returnees. "Children are the future of a nation. That's why the central government and the local authorities as well, in spite of tremendous socio-economic difficulties, have been doing their best in creating favorable conditions for repatriated children to reintegrate themselves into the social environment of their friends."[3]

In the same issue, UNHCR officer Christine Mougne, the author of the anchor theory of child asylum seekers, expressed her concerns that the detention camps had disrupted the education of the children: there were declining standards of teaching, a poor environment for learning, and an incomplete curriculum. By this she meant that, for political reasons, the detainees refused to accept the national Vietnamese curriculum. For these reasons, children in the camps lagged educationally behind their age-mates in Vietnam and would need special remedial support when they repatriated.[4]

Jon Liden, NARV Information Officer, wrote a piece in *Science Information Review* pushing repatriation of minors. It begins, "Would you send your son or daughter to prison?" He goes on to note that thousands of Vietnamese parents had, effectively, done so, sending their children to spend years in Hong Kong and Southeast Asian detention centers where they had suffered terribly. But NARV would help these minors when they repatriated. Liden cites the case of a girl who returned to an area near Haiphong only to find that her parents had divorced and remarried; the girl was no longer welcome in either household. But, luckily for the girl, someone in the Hong Kong detention camp had told her about NARV. When she returned to Vietnam, NARV, with the help of local Vietnamese officials and agencies, found her a nice place to stay and helped her get vocational training. Liden closes on a high note. "The Program always works together with the local People's Committees and DELISAs. Without the co-operation and assistance of these offices, no work could be done. . . . The boat people problem is soon a closed chapter in Vietnam's history. The NARV/UNAM Program assists Vietnam in closing it faster and making it a happy ending for as many unaccompanied minors as possible."[5]

Could UNHCR-backed NARV really deliver on these promises of happy endings? Given the damage done to unaccompanied minors in the camps, could these repatriated youths reintegrate easily and successfully? It was exceedingly difficult to monitor and evaluate specific cases of repatriated unaccompanied minors, even when there were indications that all was not right with them. The Special Committees in countries of first asylum and UNHCR wrote reports claiming that the repatriation of the children was in their "best interests," and NARV supported repatriation with its own glowing reports of conditions among returnees. The only way to question this was to have outside or additional observers on the scene, in the detention camps or in Vietnam, to discover whether the reports reflected the actual state of affairs. But many camps were closed to most outsiders and permission to visit them was difficult if not impossible to obtain. In Vietnam, repatriated unaccompanied minors were dispersed widely from distant villages in the north to remote locales in the Mekong Delta. To visit one child might involve two days of travel or more. Furthermore, permission to visit them was not automatic; it had to be secured first from the local provincial officials of the Department of Labor, War Invalids, and Social Affairs (DELISA) and from NARV. But officials in many provinces were quite uneasy about inquiries in their areas, while NARV was concerned with protecting its public image as a care provider. The cases we describe are unusual, not in what they represent, but in that we visited the camps where the children were detained, we had neutral observers there who contradicted the officials' statements, and (in 1993, 1994, 1995, 1999, and 2000) we visited the children after they had been repatriated.

One such returnee was Chi Lan, mentioned in Chapter 2, whom we had interviewed in Sikhiu Camp. By a lucky coincidence we located Chi Lan living not in her village but on the floor of a coffee shop in Cho Lon, Ho Chi Minh City's teeming, dusty Chinatown. Spilling from the doorways of nearby shops were racks of clothes, pots and pans, gleaming statues of Quan Am (Kuan Yin), the Buddhist figure of compassion and mercy, and household furniture. The crush of pedestrians made it almost impossible to push our way into the coffee shop. The raucous noise on the street was deafening. Idling Honda scooters with loud mufflers were locked in a two-block-long traffic jam. Chi Lan recognized us, smiled broadly, ran to greet us, and invited us inside. We sat at a table and she described her new life. "I live on the floor of this coffee shop. At night, after the customers leave, I sweep aside the food strewn on the floor and lie down to sleep."

This was not what we or she had expected. An official of the UNHCR had told her that her adoptive mother was waiting for her at home. The repatriation of children was based on the principle of family reunification. If there were no relatives, in their best interests unaccompanied minors were supposed to be resettled to countries other than Vietnam. The official promised her that she would receive cash assistance if she repatriated: US $50 upon her return and $30 a month for a year, as well as job training. She would be looked after by NARV. Since the average salary at that time in Vietnam was $15–20 a month, her repatriation grant should have enabled her to live well and still save something for the future.

Chi Lan's adoptive mother was nowhere to be found, and all of her monthly allowance was taken by the coffee shop owner. "I returned to my home village, but no one was there. I did not know where my mother was, and no one else knew. I went and lived in the house of a neighbor for a couple of months. Then I moved to Cho Lon, bought a bicycle, and took a sewing class. This is the job training promised me and paid for by the ECIP. But I'm scared. All of the money I receive each month goes for room and board, and next month the coffee shop will close. I have no friends and no relatives. All of my money is spent each month. What will I do when the money runs out and when the shop is no longer here? I'll be on the street, and I have nowhere to go!" With tears streaming down her face, she said, "If I had known what I was returning to, I would have stayed in Sikhiu; if I had the choice again, I'd never return!" We alerted the NARV officials of Chi Lan's predicament; they expressed shock and assured us that they would see to it that she would not end up on the street. They seemed to be genuinely concerned as well as embarrassed at our discovery.

At the conclusion of our trip, we wrote a report about our findings.[6] We had asked NARV officials to introduce us to typical unaccompanied minors who had repatriated. Throughout Vietnam, we found cases like Chi Lan's. Although we saw no evidence of political persecution, we heard complaints about the neglect of the children and observed children who had been abandoned even though officially they were being looked after. We found children without parents being returned to other relatives who could not possibly afford to feed them, and we found relatives who took the children's repatriation money for themselves.

Based on our report, Beryl Cook of Hong Kong's *South China Morning Post* wrote an article, "Homeless Viet children spark refugee inquiry." In it, a UNHCR official confronted with our findings of child neglect responded that, "the cases were probably exceptional because the UNHCR used elaborate screening to determine what was in the child's best interest . . . It would be highly unlikely that a child would return home to find no one waiting." A NARV spokesman in north Vietnam, who had unknowingly taken us to visit a boy who had just experienced what the UNHCR official had claimed was highly unlikely, now also echoed that the cases were "exceptional."[7]

On June 19, 1993, we interviewed a twelve-year-old boy from Haiphong. NARV's Jon Liden had claimed to have helped a girl from this area; in contrast, the NARV official who took us to meet the boy did not realize that he faced serious difficulties. He sat stiffly on his bed of wooden planks, his voice quavering as he tried to keep from crying. "If I had realized that I had no place to return to, I would not have left Whitehead. Even though Whitehead was horrible, I would have never come back to Vietnam."

UNHCR claimed that they located relatives in Vietnam who could receive the children before they were repatriated. The boy had been led to believe that his mother was waiting for him, so he volunteered to return, happy to leave the crowded, violent steel cages of Whitehead. When he returned home, he was told that his mother had moved to the south, but nobody knew where she was. He wandered the streets until he located a half-brother, who lived in one small room behind an appliance store and gave him temporary lodging. At the time of our interview, however, the half-brother planned to marry, and soon his sibling would have no place to stay. The boy was several years behind in school and did not know what he would do.

NARV had a UNHCR contract to look after repatriated unaccompanied minors. NARV had not realized that the boy in Haiphong was on his own. After our interview, they searched out and found his mother in Ho Chi Minh City. They now claim that this case was an exception.

In August 1994, we returned to Vietnam with the intention of visiting this boy as well as other children whom we had interviewed the previous year. At the NARV office in Hanoi we were informed that, because their contract was only for temporary assistance, NARV kept records on a child for only six months after the file was closed on the child. After that time, the regional office sent the file to the NARV office in Hanoi, which then sent it to UNHCR. NARV officials referred to this as "clearing out the files." The only information remaining was the name and last known address of the child. As a consequence, once a file was closed and sent away, there was no way to follow up on a case unless the child or the child's relatives went to the NARV office and asked for additional assistance. Even if they did so, their earlier file was no longer available. NARV claimed that many people came to their office for help, but the twelve-year-old boy from Haiphong was not one of them. Despite our efforts, we were never able to discover his whereabouts. At his last known address, people said he had simply disappeared.[8]

UNHCR and NARV claimed that most repatriated unaccompanied minors reintegrated well over time. But this conclusion masked the problem. We found that while children returned to their biological parents seemed to have adjusted well, those sent back to stepparents, other relatives, or to no one were suffering grievously.

Because many children refused to repatriate, in late June 1993, UNHCR, in cooperation with the Socialist Republic of Vietnam, began repatriating unaccompanied minors, often against their will, if a relative in Vietnam would accept them in return for cash. This action was called Operation Family Reunion, later renamed as the softer-sounding Family Reunion Program. NARV workers, accompanied by a Vietnamese official of DELISA, asked parents or relatives of the children to accept them. Because some children had no parents, UNHCR reversed its previous practice of repatriating only to a parent and sent unaccompanied minors to any relative who agreed to take them.[9]

One of the first children returned was a ten-year-old girl from Haiphong. The girl's father was in prison and her mother had run away. In 1993, we spoke to her elderly grandparents prior to her repatriation. They lived in a one-room bamboo shack next to the river; they had barely enough to eat. "We love our granddaughter," said the grandmother, "but we cannot feed her. We don't know what we will do. An official came and told us that she would be returning, so what choice did we have? We could not say no to the official; we had no other choice."

Because of our 1993 report, NARV gave this girl and her grandparents special attention. In 1994, we found her at home with her grandparents. UNHCR gave her U.S. $360, as promised. NARV gave the grandparents $300 to upgrade their dwelling and $200 for the grandmother to improve her tea shop. NARV had helped to place the girl in school, where she was about to begin the fifth grade.

The grandfather said, "It's very difficult to bring her up properly because we are so poor, but we try to do the best we can, and she is happy to be back in Vietnam. When our granddaughter returned, she was at first shy, but now she feels more at home. It was the right decision to get her to come home in time. Now she is healthy and is growing up. She dreams of becoming a tailor."

We were not allowed to talk with the girl alone. In the presence of her grandparents and NARV staff, she answered shyly, "It is not hard for me now. I enjoy myself. I go to school." She said nothing else. She sat solemnly on a large wooden bed in the back of the shack. Three feet away, also on the bed, sat her younger sister, while their grandmother sat behind them. They did not appear to be a close family. NARV considered this case a "happy ending," and they made a video of the family to persuade other children who still remained in the Hong Kong camps to repatriate.

UNHCR expected NARV to close cases quickly and call them successes. UNHCR was concerned that if they recommended resettlement for some asylum seekers, they would give false hope to those recommended for repatriation, and this would encourage them not to return. But by recommending repatriation "in the best interests of the child" when it was clearly inhumane and harmful to the child, they accomplished precisely what they hoped to avoid: they hardened the resistance of asylum seekers, and on occasion provoked mass protests.

In a highly publicized incident, on January 15, 1994, sixteen-year-old Ngo Van Ha was removed from Hong Kong's Tai A Chau Detention Center to the Whitehead Detention Center in preparation for his repatriation to Vietnam. Over two thousand Vietnamese detainees of Tai A Chau staged a mass demonstration, sit-in, and hunger strike that lasted three-and-a-half days.

Ngo Van Ha had fled Vietnam in 1990, but immigration officials in Hong Kong had denied him refugee status and his appeal had been rejected. Although his cousin in California applied to sponsor him to come to the United States, the Hong Kong High Court turned them down, and the Special Committee of UNHCR determined that Ngo Van Ha's best interests would be served by returning him to an uncle in Vietnam under the Family Reunion Program.

Ngo Van Ha's parents had been killed when he was ten years old. UNHCR wanted to send him back to an uncle who the youth said had abused him. As a rule, a child is sent to the "closest relative," but the Special Committee has the discretion to choose otherwise and is supposed to take into account the child's own wishes. One of Ha's relatives in the U.S. had visited the uncle in Vietnam and found that Ha's younger brother and sister had been thrown out of the house and were living with and working as servants for families who were not related to them. When asked by UNHCR, Ha's uncle in Vietnam refused to take him back. He said he had no money to feed another person.

Newspapers throughout the world featured Ha's story in articles critical of the Hong Kong government and UNHCR. Human rights organizations wrote letters to Hong Kong and UNHCR officials urging humane treatment for Ha. Representatives of both Hong Kong and UNHCR admitted to us unofficially that the Ha case got out of hand, caused them much embarrassment, heightened the detainees' distrust of officials, and set back voluntary repatriation by several months. Faced with a continuous barrage of negative publicity, the Special Committee in Hong Kong recommended that Ha be resettled in the United States, where Ha now lives.[10]

Because his case provoked international attention, Ha was given a decision that is an exception to the rule, though within the UNHCR mandate. But what about other children who have not come to the attention of the public? A tragic example is that of an orphaned girl from Thua Thien Hue Province who was lured back to Vietnam with the promise of assistance, only to be denied it once she returned. In 1993, Nguyen Dinh Huu was present when a NARV staff worker made that promise to her uncle. In 1994, when we asked to visit the girl, NARV staff in Hue said curtly that the girl did not qualify for assistance. After she had returned, an interviewer in Hanoi determined that she was over eighteen and therefore aged out. The interviewer found a discrepancy between the girl's statement of her date of birth and the birth date listed in her case profile, and NARV in Hanoi instructed its Hue office not to provide any assistance.

The problem for the girl was that she would not have returned—and her uncle would not have agreed to accept her—had they not been promised support. The NARV staff denied any responsibility for what happened to the girl. They were evasive and seemed uninterested in doing anything except the minimum to close the files and send them off to Hanoi. "These children lie all the time. They don't deserve help," one staff member said to us. We said we would like to see the youngster anyway. The NARV staff in Hue replied that Vietnamese officials would not allow us to visit her village, which was in a remote area, since people had been fleeing Vietnam from that area. This was an unverified rumor. Furthermore, there was no prohibition on the girl visiting us, but the NARV staff refused to arrange this.

We were perplexed by their inconsistency in refusing to lift a finger to help one aged-out minor but intervening to assist another, even though the latter didn't qualify for NARV attention either. This twenty-year-old mother had given birth to a child while in Tai A Chau Detention Center, Hong Kong. NARV had persuaded her husband's family to accept her in their house, despite their initial refusal, and had convinced the European Community International Program (ECIP), which helps repatriated adults, to loan her husband U.S. $1,500 for his failing shoe repair business, which, despite the low interest loan, was continuing its downward spiral.

Once a child returns to Vietnam, the responsibility for that child rests with Vietnamese authorities. If a child complains about not receiving the assistance promised, UNHCR points out that the children are no longer its problem, but that of NARV (through 1994) and Vietnamese officials. Unaccompanied minors are not the only children at risk in Vietnam, and Vietnamese authorities show more sympathy to needy children who have remained in Vietnam than to those who have tried to escape.

Because NARV worked in Vietnam under a UNHCR contract, it was dependent on the directives and good will of UNHCR. When it was asked to help UNHCR persuade unaccompanied minors to repatriate, its credibility plummeted in the detention camps. Officials and staff in many organizations, including UNHCR, told us that UNHCR did not want to hear about cases that failed in Vietnam; it wanted them settled as quickly as possible. Whether true or not, this belief had a chilling effect on NARV field staff, who filed positive reports that were unwarranted by the situations.

In addition, some NARV staff told us they hadn't agreed with certain home assessments that were conducted before unaccompanied minors were repatriated, but that UNHCR did not want to hear about failures. Therefore, these NARV employees filed unjustifiably positive reports. One worker pointedly blamed UNHCR for this. "Children have been returned to relatives who said they could not take care of them, and to families where a parent is a drug addict. Those children should not have been brought back. But my superior said, 'Do not recommend. Just follow the orders of UNHCR.'"

Almost everywhere we went, NARV officials trumpeted their successes and showed visitors preselected cases that confirmed their claims. One notable exception was a Vietnamese-American consultant who was in charge of the NARV office in the Mekong Delta town of Can Tho. In July 1993, she arranged for Freeman to see what she said was a typical example of problems faced by children who are returned to relatives other than parents.[11]

A thirteen-year-old orphan had been returned to her sixty-eight-year-old grandmother and her two uncles, who were poor farmers. Their house, one large room that sheltered seven people, lay along a canal in a remote area of Kien Giang Province. To reach it required a full day's journey from Can Tho by car and boat.

The NARV consultant was especially worried about this girl, who had witnessed the killing of her parents and brother by Thai pirates. In her June 28, 1993, report to the UNHCR Working Group in Ho Chi Minh City, she wrote that the girl's grandmother loved her granddaughter but was unable to control what was happening to the girl. Neighbors said that the girl's uncles used her UNHCR allowance for their own business activities. (The uncles also admitted this to a NARV staff worker.) The girl did not have adequate hygienic care and had not bathed for several days when the consultant saw her. The girl's emotional state suggested that she had been traumatized; she was indifferent and passive, unable to answer complex questions, and reluctant to initiate conversations.

When Freeman visited the girl one month later with a NARV staff worker, the girl was dressed in clean clothes and was livelier than the earlier report indicated, but she was wearing white medicinal cloth patches on her temples. She said, "I now get headaches that last two or three days." Her grandmother said, "I can take care of her as long as I am alive. But I am old. Once I die, her uncles will abandon her. I am worried about her."

The staff worker turned to Freeman and expressed concern. "Who will take care of this child when her grandmother dies and NARV support ends? Once our office closes, it will be completely impossible to keep track of children like this. They live far away. There is no way for them to reach us even now, and once we leave, there will be no one who can help them."

While most of the NARV employees were dedicated and hard-working, the organization faced some basic structural problems which stemmed from its style of operation, and these seriously interfered with its ability to function effectively in Vietnam. One worker said to us, "In 1994, we have a budget of $800,000 for staff and other expenses, and only $500,000 for unaccompanied minors." High salaries and expensive benefits to foreign staff, and salaries to Vietnamese staff of from four to twelve times the salaries of ordinary Vietnamese workers, caused resentment among other Vietnamese. Some Vietnamese officials were said to have obstructed projects because of this. Vietnamese officials in Hanoi told us that they were deeply concerned about the possible disruption caused by nongovernmental organizations and foreign development projects which distributed large sums of money to families and communities.

The most serious concern expressed by the NARV staff was that the job training the unaccompanied minors received did not lead to employment. One staff member said, "I know of no placement in jobs after the completion of training programs and the acquisition of job skills. This is a consequence of the bad economy, in which jobs are not available."

In February 1994, the Fifth Steering Committee of the International Conference on Indochinese Refugees recommended that all unaccompanied minors be removed from the camps by the end of that year. The NARV project was expected to close, except for a possible skeleton crew.[12]

This deadline both created and perpetuated problems. First, to repatriate and thus get rid of them quickly, UNHCR continued to send unaccompanied minors to virtually any relative who was willing to take them. Given the financial inducements that were offered, some relatives accepted repatriated unaccompanied minors even if they had little capability of or interest in taking care of them. This problem was especially acute in the central Vietnamese province of Thua Thien Hue, which in 1994 was undergoing its third straight year of drought and facing famine, and whose officials were seeking assistance to avert disaster. Local Vietnamese officials were particularly worried about what would happen to the children, including repatriated unaccompanied minors, who were already being neglected. Despite these serious problems and the failure of NARV to contact a third of the children who had already been repatriated, UNHCR continued to return more children to this environment. Second, the NARV staff was clearly disturbed and distracted by the prospect of most of their jobs soon coming to an end. They told us that this was affecting their performance. Third, many NARV staff feared that difficult cases would remain unresolved. The staff could not address the serious long-lasting traumas suffered by children during their escapes or their lives in the camps. Fourth, as the closing date approached, unused funds were distributed with less concern for their effect than for simply getting rid of the money. Fifth, cases were closed with the claim that they were "happy endings," even though they did not reflect actual success. Finally, six months after a case was closed, the files were cleared and sent off, effectively preventing any follow-up or further assistance for those still in need.[13]

In August 1995, UNHCR published an upbeat report on repatriated boat people, claiming that they were being well cared for and were benefiting from the new Vietnamese economic reforms. "Returnees can hope to start a fresh life, with a substantial repatriation grant and the help of our offices and those of other institutions. . . . Thanks to a new climate in the countries of origin [Vietnam and Laos], these economies are now booming beyond the recognition of the desperate migrants of 1989 and 1990."[14]

UNHCR was correct in pointing out that Vietnam's economy was improving, a trend which has continued. Poverty, malnutrition, and hunger have been reduced, though the country remains desperately poor and economic growth is uneven.[15] But UNHCR's glowing accounts failed to mention that repatriated unaccompanied minors were suffering from neglect, hunger, and mistreatment. They had no future in the new Vietnamese economy.

We are not the only ones whose findings contradict the UNHCR spin on repatriation. NARV itself finally recognized that unaccompanied minors faced serious problems when they returned to Vietnam, and NARV's final report stated that many repatriated unaccompanied minors regretted returning. Those whom we interviewed confirmed these findings. Most preferred the detention camps, where at least they had friends and two or three meals a day.

"They Should Never Have Been Returned to Vietnam"

WHAT HAPPENED to two brothers and a sister illustrates how children at risk were hustled back to Vietnam, dumped, and forgotten. They were born in 1981, 1982, and 1985 in Binh Thuan Province, central Vietnam. On March 21, 1988, prior to the start of the CPA, they escaped from Vietnam with their parents and a nineteen-year-old cousin; the children were seven, six, and three years old. They traveled through Cambodia, hoping to reach Thailand. Their guide abandoned them and they became lost. A Cambodian led them to a village, where they remained for a year. In their second attempt to cross the border, they were stopped by bandits who killed the children's parents and abducted a couple of other children who had traveled with their group. When the survivors reached Thailand on May 5, 1989, two months after the CPA deadline, the three children and their cousin were placed in Ban Thad, one of the Thai border camps. They were moved from one camp to another, finally ending up in Sikhiu camp. They were interviewed and advised to return to Vietnam. They remained in Thai camps for five years.

Because as unaccompanied minors they were considered vulnerable, the three orphans were evaluated by a Thai Special Committee consisting of immigration officials, an expert on child development, and an advisor from UNHCR to determine whether it was in their best interests to be resettled in a third country or repatriated to Vietnam. The children asked to remain with their cousin, who had cared for them for more than five years in the camp. Instead, the Durable Solutions Counselor of the Special Committee ruled that the children should be separated from their cousin and repatriated to their grandmother and uncle, disregarding the fact that their grandmother was eighty-three, blind, frail, and dying, and that their uncle, in his forties, was an unmarried, disabled, unemployed alcoholic whom the children did not know. In her letter of request of November 29, 1993, the Durable Solutions Counselor wrote that their cousin did not take good care of the three children and that he didn't want custody of them.[16] Yet the cousin wrote to us twice that he and the children were close and they wanted to remain together.[17]

Nguyen Dinh Huu, concerned that the welfare of the children was being disregarded, wrote two letters to the Director of the UNHCR Regional Bureau for Asia and Oceania. Nguyen pointed out that in Vietnam there was "no adult relative who could take care of them," that the children did not want to leave their cousin, and that, based on our observations and interviews in Vietnam, we were convinced that "children returned to relatives other than parents are highly likely to be neglected and are likely to end up on the street. Sending back these three orphans is not in their best interests." Instead, he reminded the Director that UNHCR had several choices within its mandate in dealing with the orphans. One was to resettle them in a third country. A second was to allow the children to remain with their cousin in the camp. A Vietnamese-American woman, hearing of the plight of these children, offered, as a third choice, to adopt these children if permitted or to sponsor them as immigrants to the United States, also allowed within the mandate of UNHCR. Nguyen specifically requested that the Director "exercise the UNHCR mandate power to intervene on their behalf and find some humane way to resettle them."

In his second letter to this same UNHCR official, on December 4, 1993, Nguyen reminded him that "the children are to be returned to a distant relative whom the children do not know. The children do not wish to be separated from

their cousin who has reared and nurtured them since the age of 7, 4, and 3."
Speaking "as a professional knowledgeable about child development," he observed,
"it is not in their best interests to be separated from the person who has reared
them and to whom they are strongly bonded. These children have expressed
the wish that they remain with [the cousin] and he has expressed the wish to
take care of them."

Nguyen called attention to the United Nations Convention on the Rights
of the Child and to the preliminary draft of UNHCR's own *Refugee Children:
Guidelines on Protection and Care* (1993). Page 136 of that document reads,
"Depending on their degree of maturity, children over the age of 9 or 10 may
be able to make rational choices about durable solutions if provided with adequate information. Their preferences should, therefore, receive appropriate consideration. Children below 9 or 10 years of age may not be sufficiently mature
to make an independent judgment, but they should always be given the chance
to express their views and the competent decision-making authority must determine which durable solution is likely to be in the best interests of the child."
Nguyen noted that considering the wishes of the child is the central principle
of Article 12 of the Convention on the Rights of the Child. The unofficial summary of the Convention reads, "The child has the right to express his or her
opinion freely and to have that opinion taken into account in any matter or
procedure affecting the child." Nguyen again requested that the Director exercise the UNHCR mandate to intervene on behalf of the children.[18]

On December 20, 1993, the Director of the UNHCR Regional Bureau for
Asia and Oceania wrote a letter to us, basing his response on the finding of the
Special Committee in Thailand and the two pre-return home assessments by
UNHCR and by NARV. He affirmed their decisions. The Special Committee
had considered all the elements of the case and concluded that it was in the
best interests of the children to be sent back to Vietnam. The UNHCR office
in Thailand had asked a representative from the UNHCR office in Ho Chi
Minh City to visit the home, a detailed home assessment was conducted, and
the UNHCR office in Vietnam agreed that it was in the best interests of the
three children to be returned to their grandmother and uncle in Vietnam. To
further indicate the overwhelming evidence for repatriation, the UNHCR
Director added that a NARV representative also visited the grandmother's house
and confirmed the same findings.[19]

The UNHCR and NARV reports which determined the fate of these children show how bureaucratic commitment to a general rule which did not have
to be followed prevailed over expertise on child development as well as common

sense. Dumping children with relatives who are incapable of caring for them is an example not of best interests, but of child endangerment.

The reports themselves show how a clearly unacceptable family environment was rationalized so that the children could be returned no matter what. A UNHCR Repatriation Officer, of Vietnamese descent, visited the children's grandmother and uncle. In her report of October 15, 1993, she wrote that the children's grandmother wept on hearing about them and requested that the children's cousin bring the children back from the camp while she was still alive; that way they would get to know their ancestor. The officer also noted that the grandmother was, at the age of eighty-three, nearly blind, very frail, and near the end of her days. Nevertheless, the officer maintained that the grandmother still had control over the family and loved her grandchildren, and concluded that, as long as the grandmother lived, she would take care of the children.

The officer noted that the motives of the uncle were questionable, since he seemed to be eager to get hold of their food allowance (U.S. $360 for each child for one year). Then she contradicted herself, saying that the uncle did not care about the money: he just wanted to put it in the bank to earn interest to pay for the children's expenses. The uncle commented that some people with bad motives might try to convince the children that he loved their food allowance rather than them.

His remarks were revealing. In fact, he wanted a good deal more than their food allowance. As the Repatriation Officer wrote in her report, the uncle wanted 3 million Vietnamese Dong (U.S. $300 at that time). He claimed he would use it to renovate his workshop, improve his earnings, and support the children independently. The uncle was given a lump sum of $1,740 dollars, over six-and-a-half times the average annual income of a similarly sized family, which at that time was $260. This included the food and repatriation allowances of the children ($1,080), the money for the workshop ($300), given to him by the European Community International Program, which assists adults, $60 for the children's school supplies and fees, and $300 to jump-start a business: buying a fishing net and part interest in a boat.[20]

The NARV consultant who directed her agency's office in Ho Chi Minh City is a former social worker from Sweden. After conducting another home visit prior to the repatriation of these children, she was under the impression that the uncle would use some of his money to renovate the house in preparation for their return. She concluded, similarly, that this was a good home environment to which to send the children. Based on these two home visits, the children were repatriated against their will on April 28, 1994.[21]

On May 24, 1994, another NARV social worker, himself a Vietnamese citizen, visited the children at their home. He wrote that the three children were getting along well with their uncle and neighbors. He praised the uncle, calling him a good adoptive father, who spent a lot of time with the children and used the windfall of money he'd received to establish a cooperative business with other fishermen. His report made it sound as if everything was going well.

We wanted to see for ourselves that this case was as successful as these reports indicated. Three months later, we talked with the social worker in Ho Chi Minh City. He contradicted what he had written. "The uncle told me that he used to be an alcoholic, but he has improved since the children came back." We asked, "Why didn't you put this in the report?" He replied, "No one wants to hear it; they only want to hear about successes. These children are neglected. They should never have been returned to Vietnam."

Although the children lived in a remote village in central Vietnam, NARV officials far away in Ho Chi Minh City were responsible for assisting and monitoring their situation. When we asked to visit them, the NARV consultant said she would introduce us to the DELISA officials in Binh Thuan Province but could not promise that they would allow us to visit the children. On August 31, 1994, we made the journey, which took all day by car. In the provincial town of Phan Thiet, we met with the DELISA officials for about an hour and explained why we wanted to meet the children. The officials agreed, and they and the NARV consultant accompanied us the rest of the way. Both the NARV consultant and the officials wanted to be with us when we interviewed the children.

As we rode, the NARV consultant rationalized the repatriation of the children. "The most important thing is to return the children to their own culture. That is the best solution. Culture is very important. You must understand Vietnamese culture and the extended family. Then you would know that returning these children to their uncle and grandmother in Vietnam was the right and best decision."

We arrived on the outskirts of the village late in the afternoon. We met the uncle and the eldest child returning from watching a soccer match and gave them a ride home. The uncle had alcohol on his breath and he seemed to be drunk.

We left our vehicle and walked about two hundred yards down the dirt path that led to their house. Dozens of children and adults from the neighborhood accompanied us, shouting and laughing. The house was filthy and unswept; no improvements had been made to accommodate the children. The grandmother, now virtually blind, was lying on a wooden bed. She was too ill to sit up in her bed, so a neighbor lifted her up. Except for an inch of cold soup, no rice or other food was in the house. Cooking was done on an area of dirt and brick behind the house. The kitchen equipment consisted of two pots placed on a charcoal fire, five small bowls, and some chopsticks.

The house contained only two small wooden beds, so Nguyen asked the uncle where the children slept. He pointed to the dirty cement floor. To confirm this, Nguyen also asked the children. The youngest said, "Grandmother and Uncle sleep on the beds; we sleep on the floor." The middle child, the sister, hid in fear near one bed. The eldest brother was severely malnourished and ill. He said, "We are hungry. We do not have enough food to eat." Nguyen asked the uncle, "Where's the food?" He replied, "I'll start cooking soon." Nguyen asked, "Have you been drinking?" The uncle replied, "I've just had something to drink." A DELISA official added, "He drinks a local wine."

Through an interpreter, the NARV consultant asked the children how they were doing. "Fine, happy," said the oldest brother. He did not elaborate. He had a frightened look on his face. The NARV consultant asked, "Do you have friends?" The boy looked at the children outside and said, "Lots." The NARV

Two brothers and their sister, repatriated to their dying grandmother and their unemployed, disabled uncle, Binh Thuan Province, central Vietnam. Their parents were killed by bandits while escaping through Cambodia. *Photo: James M. Freeman.*

consultant then turned to the youngest brother, "Did you go to the soccer match?" The child replied, "No, I stayed home to guard the house." His orange T-shirt was torn and soiled. The NARV consultant asked the uncle, "Have you used the money we gave you to develop the fishing business? Are you working on the boat? How about repairs on the house?" The uncle replied, "I haven't done those yet."

Freeman asked the NARV consultant, "What do you think about this?" She replied, "This isn't working. I can see that without even asking anything. Something's got to be done. The uncle hasn't done what we had hoped he would do when we gave him all that money. I remember the grandmother. She was cheerful and energetic, not like now. She has changed. She cannot care for the children any more. But we must do something that fits within the culture. We've got to find another relative or people in the village who will take care of the children. But we should keep the children here; that's the best solution."

In Hanoi, we met with the NARV/UNAM Program Director in Vietnam. She saw no problems. "I know of no example of money given to an unaccompanied minor that was misused by a family." We reject her claim, since we found that families did misuse these funds.

The plight of these three children was predictable and was similar to that of other unaccompanied minors who were repatriated to relatives other than their parents. With no responsible person to care for them in Vietnam, these three orphans, aged nine to thirteen, should never have been repatriated. For five years their cousin in Sikhiu had cared for them. To be taken from him and returned to their dying grandmother and their middle-aged, unmarried, alcoholic uncle was hardly a suitable durable solution.

The principle of returning children to their own culture or extended family is a reasonable one, but adhering to it without exception is both inhumane and wrongheaded. It presupposes an idealized and static view of culture. It also assumes that a person's culture is inherently beneficial.

Both of these assumptions are unwarranted. Not all cultures are beneficial; some are clearly harmful, especially to children. Southeast Asian refugee and detention camps are one example. A second is the family culture into which these three children were placed, which constituted a clear example of child endangerment. The assumption that the Vietnamese extended family will automatically take care of a child fails to take into account the actual, desperate, economic circumstances that many families face. The temporary windfall of NARV and ECIP money does not alter this, as relatives have often taken these funds to benefit themselves, not the children who were returned to them. The extended family, not in its idealized nurturing aspects, but in its actual functioning, is on occasion exploitative, neglectful, and ultimately harmful to the child. In the Vietnamese family, situations involving stepparents or adoptive parents frequently lead to conflicts, especially during times of economic crisis, with some stepparents harassing and pushing out, if not simply neglecting, children other than their own.

Situations of neglect or abuse are very hard to monitor when, as was the case with the three children of Binh Thuan Province, they are in hinterland areas far removed from NARV offices. For the same reason, it is unlikely that these children would or could ask for help. Given what we saw, we believe the desperate situation of the two brothers and sister would have gone unnoticed and unreported had we not visited them.

In January 1994, the UNHCR Director visited the United States. After waiting several hours, the Vietnamese-American woman who had offered to adopt or sponsor the three children of Binh Thuan Province was given a moment to speak with him. She later said to us, "He promised me that he would look into this case carefully and inform me of the result, but he never did. I never heard from him again."

On February 16, 1994, responding to an inquiry about the three children of Binh Thuan Province, the Chief of Operations of the Joint Voluntary Agency in Thailand, which interviews people accepted for refugee status, wrote that she could do nothing for them since, as a family (with the cousin), they had been screened out and thus denied refugee status. Because they were not granted refugee status, they were not eligible for resettlement, and JVA could not interview them. Furthermore, she wrote that the UNHCR office had informed her on December 12, 1993, that the three children had decided voluntarily to go back to Vietnam.[22]

There was nothing voluntary about their return. A reliable source in Sikhiu Camp, who was unrelated to the children but knew them well, informed us that the children cried bitterly because they did not want to be separated from their cousin and repatriated. No doubt they were told they had no other choice, but, in fact, an alternative was available, and officials had been informed of it several times. The officials could have used the UNHCR mandate to intervene in favor of adoption and resettlement in the United States. They deliberately chose not to do so.

Instead, on April 20, 1994, another UNHCR officer, the Head of Desk, Regional Bureau for Asia and Oceania, wrote us reaffirming the UNHCR's commitment to repatriate unaccompanied minors without parents to their country of origin, and denying that there was a problem. He rejected Nguyen Dinh Huu's claim in one of his letters that the process of determining best interests for these children had been "patently unfair due to massive outright mistakes," dismissing it as opinion unsupported by any evidence.[23]

On January 19, 1995, we received a letter from a Vietnamese NARV field worker. He made no mention of the vow of the NARV consultant from Ho Chi Minh City on August 31 of the previous year to move the three children out of their destructive environment as soon as possible. Instead, he noted that the uncle had received $1,000 to set up a fishing business and assist the children. This was the money that had disappeared and could not be accounted for at the time of our visit. NARV did not even visit the three children again until December 21, 1994, nearly four months after we had discovered their actual condition. The grandmother had died in September, less than two weeks after we had seen her. The NARV field worker, however, wrote that the three children seemed to be happy and well cared for by their uncle, so NARV did not need to take further action. Case closed. In any case, NARV would cease to assist children at the end of April 1995; the office of this employee ceased operation on March 15, 1995.[24]

In December 1995, Nguyen Dinh Huu visited the children for a second time. Accompanying him was a DELISA official from Binh Thuan Province. The uncle had gained weight but the children were listless and emaciated. The house stood unrepaired and food consisted of one small bag of rice. As before, all of the money had disappeared.

Because of our previous visit, the DELISA official knew about these children and had expressed concern about their care. Since Binh Thuan Province, an impoverished area in the southern part of central Vietnam, has no orphanages, he had tried to place them elsewhere. Other provinces refused, since they had too many orphans of their own. Meanwhile, the Vietnamese-American woman from San Jose, California, who had offered to adopt them periodically sends them money, which is channeled through Aid to Children Without Parents (ACWP) so that the children don't end up on the street.

In Whose Best Interests?

WE HAVE dwelt on the single case of the three children of Binh Thuan Province for a reason. Our own investigations show why, despite the difficulty of conducting them, on-site investigations by trained, independent observers are absolutely necessary to uncover the true conditions under which children are living. The discrepancies between official reports and actual conditions could not have been discovered otherwise.

It would be a mistake to focus on the failings of individuals. The neglect of repatriated unaccompanied minors is a systemic problem. Given the initial constraints created by the reluctance of countries to accept Vietnamese asylum seekers, UNHCR responded with policies or guidelines that powerfully influenced nongovernmental organizations such as NARV, ultimately to the detriment of the children. UNHCR made the decisions, but NARV ended up taking most of the responsibility and blame. By attempting both to protect asylum seekers while at the same time returning them to their country of origin, UNHCR compromised itself and put itself in an untenable position.

The stated aims of UNHCR (to protect asylum seekers) and of NARV (to provide assistance to returnees) were thwarted by the pressure to produce successes and to maintain the careers of their employees, despite the harm done to unaccompanied minors. To return children to situations of abuse, endangerment, or neglect violated the U.N. Convention on the Rights of the Child, the UNHCR Comprehensive Plan of Action, and Vietnam's 1991 Law on the Protection, Care, and Education of Children.

It is worth noting that officials used terms and concepts that appeared to express humanitarian concern for policies which actually ruined the lives of children. "Durable solution" was used for solutions that created long-term harm. "Best interests" masked actual abuse and neglect. "Family reunion" was a justification for dumping children with relatives who had no interest in them, and whom the children often scarcely knew. "Voluntary repatriation" turned out to be high-pressure coercion or, as in the case of the three children of Binh Thuan Province, complete disregard of their wishes and repatriation against their will. "Orderly repatriation" actually referred to forced repatriation.

"Culture" was simplified into an idealized and static list of characteristics, overlooking that cultures, families, and individuals change. This concept of essential culture meant that returning children to their culture and country of origin gave the appearance of a policy and practice that was rational and humane. In reality, this not only harmed children but also obscured what actually went on from outside scrutiny. Changes in Hanoi's economic policy were used as an excuse to proclaim that the economic and cultural climate had changed, and that returnees benefited from it, disregarding the fact that unaccompanied minors were almost completely excluded from benefits. Of course, millions of poor children who had never left Vietnam were also excluded.

In recent years, anthropologists have come to critique essentialist definitions of culture as overemphasizing uniformity, structure, and stability. Ironically, as anthropologists have moved away from essentialist definitions, others have adopted them, claiming—as did the NARV consultant from Ho Chi Minh City, following the lead of UNHCR—the existence of a cohesive identity for "Vietnamese culture" or "the Vietnamese family," where in fact there is much variation, fluidity of boundaries, and change. Essentialist definitions can be used as a rationalization for actions that have political implications, as was done in the case of the three children of Binh Thuan Province, as well as others.[25]

The concept of culture is neutral, but its misuse devastated the lives of children, the most vulnerable victims of politics. Especially invidious was applying a general principle (repatriation to one's own culture) while disregarding its effects on particular persons. "Happy ending" and "success" were used for cases that were anything but happy, but which were quickly closed.

On March 16, 1995, UNHCR announced that it would help to send back Vietnamese asylum seekers, thus breaking with their long-standing tradition of opposing forced repatriation. Critics charged that UNHCR now was advocating openly what it actually had been doing indirectly for years. At the Sixth Meeting of the Steering Committee of the International Conference on Indochinese Refugees, with the international community firmly behind her, Sadako Ogata, the United Nations High Commissioner for Refugees, proclaimed that those who had been denied refugee status should not expect to be granted asylum. "To those who still linger in the camps in the false hope of being resettled," she said, "I wish to say to them again: Do not lose any more time; seize your opportunity now and return home as quickly as possible to take advantage of international assistance while it still lasts." In total, 3,782 unaccompanied minors were to be returned to Vietnam. By the end of 1994, all but 439 had repatriated. At the time Ogata made her remarks, some of these remaining children still had not left the camps. For them, her admonition was both irrelevant and misleading, since specific NARV assistance for them had already ceased. All that remained was the promise of economic and employment assistance, which was supposed to be extended to all repatriated asylum seekers but often was not implemented.[26]

A joint declaration by thirty countries, including the United States, supported the UNHCR about-face: "There is no option for these people other than repatriation." The U.S. State Department, which had long opposed forced repatriation, now said that rejected asylum seekers "have no option but to return to their country of origin."

The UNHCR Director of the Regional Bureau for Asia and Oceania, who had previously demonstrated his indifference to the plight of the three children of Binh Thuan Province, summed up the attitude of UNHCR and the international community concerning the Vietnamese asylum seekers. "We feel sure that it is now time for these people to go home. It's time to wrap this up." UNHCR's Chief of Mission in Hong Kong explained why. "These are illegal immigrants, not refugees. We've already gone beyond our traditional mandate. We've operated under a special license to exceptionally exercise our good offices in dealing with the voluntary repatriation of people who are not refugees." He then added, "We have nothing to apologize for in this part of the world. We've provided the solutions."[27]

With such remarks, UNHCR and its officers dismissed themselves from the wreckage of Vietnamese children's lives created in part by their own failure to implement their own high-sounding principles of human rights and children's rights.

What Really Happened to the Returnees?

OUR EARLY interviews were conducted in 1993 and 1994, when the initial problems of reintegration were acute. Subsequent visits confirmed our original findings. But not all people would agree with our assessment. A 1997 study by Australian psychologist Maryanne Loughry and Vietnamese sociologist Nguyen Xuan Nghia proclaims a happier ending. Loughry and Nguyen compare unaccompanied returnee children in Thua Thien Hue with local children. They find little difference between the returnees and local children in education level, marital status, or material well-being. They contend that many children returned to poor conditions that matched the situation of local children. Three to four years after their return, the repatriated children showed few mental health problems, though they appeared to be more passive than local children. These results are surprising, since, as we described in Chapter 4, the literature on traumatized children typically points to long-term residual effects, including post-traumatic stress for some children. Either these children weren't as traumatized as McCallin and other writers have suggested, or the Loughry and Nguyen study needs further explanation.

Although their economic condition was similar to the local children's, the returnees tended to believe that their own situation was worse. Loughry and Nguyen believe that this is because the children "possibly fared well in the camps because of the relatively better living conditions," a grim indicator of the extent of poverty in Vietnam. Their conclusions are based on the results of interviews and psychological tests similar to the ones McCallin used in Hong Kong and the Philippines. The children commented on the assistance given them by NARV and ECIP but not that given them by local authorities. However, the greatest assistance in reintegration back into Vietnamese society came from the families of the returnees. According to Loughry and Nguyen, "this assistance has been successful. The children have successfully repatriated and reintegrated."[28] While the study distinguishes among those who live with both parents, father, mother, relative, spouse, others, or alone, there is no specific discussion of relationships with stepparents or how they compare to those with biological parents, which we claim is the crucial distinction. Loughry and Nguyen report that the incidence of family conflict for the returnees was low, less than that found among local children. This is surprising, in light of their findings that the children were much more worldly and knew about alternative patterns of behavior as a result of their stay in the camps. (Loughry and Nguyen state that the children did not always understand the categories used by the investigators or the questions they asked, but discount this as affecting their results.)

Even if their findings of little conflict are accurate, they do not necessarily demonstrate successful reintegration. The children had failed their families; they had been sent out but had not been resettled. They had received extravagant promises from NARV of assistance in education and in getting jobs if they returned, but when repatriated found the promises to be empty. They felt enormous guilt over their failure, and this might well explain their not talking back or disputing issues in their families. Their parents were discouraged at the return of their children, as failures and as additional economic burdens on the household. As young adults, however, the children no longer fit easily under the authority of their parents, and were not close to their other siblings. Given this, the parents may simply have given up attempts at control over their repatriated children and let them do as they please. Thus, the lack of conflict may not indicate successful integration but quite the opposite: an uneasy distancing between parents and their repatriated children.

Indeed, this is what was found by Nguyen Thanh Ha, an ARCWP volunteer in Palawan, the Philippines, who visited a teenage girl named Dung after she was repatriated to Vietnam. She had been in Palawan for five years, after having been sent out of Vietnam because her parents could not feed her. They told Dung not to return, in the expectation that she might be resettled and have a better life. In the camp, food and services were cut back to force her to leave. UNHCR and NARV promised her schooling and job training if she returned, and she took them up on their offer. But as the author of this report observes, "the thing that concerned her most was how to explain so that her parents would understand. She had to face questions such as how could others resettle and she had to return after 5 long years."

Her reception was not as promised. "The family was bitterly disappointed. . . . Dung's younger siblings no longer knew who she was since she left Vietnam when they were still little. . . . The European Community have stopped their aid and so she no longer had tuition money. Her family had to worry about each meal for the day, and couldn't take on the costs of Dung's tuition." She had no one to complain to; she had to remain quiet and accept her fate.[29]

In the study by Loughry and Nguyen, 403 children were reported as returning to Thua Thien Hue. This is less than half the number (879) mentioned by NARV in their Final Report of 1995. What happened to the 476 missing children? Of the 403 returnees they cited, Loughry and Nguyen interviewed 208; the remaining 195 had "left Thua Thien Hue for work and study or had moved to a new location without a forwarding address." It may be that those who were having a particularly difficult time were among those who moved away and could not be found. The same may also apply to the additional 476 children recorded by NARV. Loughry and Nguyen conclude that reintegration was successful, but they do not define reintegration or success. They assume that success is indicated by the absence of mental health problems and few reported family conflicts. Loughry and Nguyen compare 208 returnees with 187 local children who were acquaintances of the returnees. Although the repatriated children reported that they were helped by NARV, ECIP, and other nongovernmental agencies, their economic and social situation was not significantly better than that of the local children, raising serious questions about the effects the assistance had in improving their lives. Most of the repatriated children lived in coastal areas where the primary employment was fishing. There was little evidence of the development of new skills. If they were well integrated, it was into an environment of poverty. The report lists single occupations for people. This is misleading, since people in dire straits often seek a variety of ways of earning money.

One of our volunteers who lived and worked with repatriated minors and other needy children in Hue in 1997–1998 reported that "improving the economic situation for the children is the most important and difficult task. The majority of disadvantaged families have no steady source of income. They either survive on odd labor jobs in the city or rely on the seasonal crops of the land. Most of them don't have the resources or the knowledge to improve their situation." There were children without families who needed shelter, education, and job training. For many children, major health care needs were unmet, especially in rural areas.

Successful reintegration involves more than the children's mental health situation as reported on questionnaires and in interviews. It involves a consideration of the wider environment in which they live and the realistic prospects they have to gain skills to improve their economic situation.

The study by Loughry and Nguyen was supported by Norwegian and Danish councils associated with NARV and published by a Vietnamese university. Not surprisingly, it recommends that future efforts to integrate children with families be made through repatriation programs such as NARV. The not-so-subtle political message and justification for further NARV projects emerges in the final paragraph. Organizations such as NARV can help children's families improve their standard of living. "The children are no longer leaving their country. The time is now ripe for intervention from non-Government agencies to help the families proactively so that the temptation to flee is not considered a solution to poverty and other difficulties."[30] Assistance is given in order to keep people from running away.

"Up to Now, Nothing in My Life Is Happy"

IN MARCH 1999, Nguyen Dinh Huu returned to Hue to interview some of these "successfully integrated" children; he returned again with Freeman in September 2000. Many of the returnees are now young adults. Their testimony calls into question Loughry and Nguyen's conclusion regarding successful integration. To begin with, from the moment of their arrival, local government employees systematically squeezed repatriation allowances out of these youngsters until they had nothing left—doing so indirectly, making the bribery virtually impossible to trace. For instance, when children traveled to local offices, asking to be reinstated on their household's registration card, nothing happened. They would then return two or three times, with each journey often involving an all-day trip, still without results. The government employees never asked for anything, but their delay and the way they talked to the children conveyed what they expected: "coffee money." The children had a choice: travel back and forth until they had no more money and the permits were finally granted, or pay off the authorities and get the permits quickly. These children spent all of their repatriation allowances regularizing their identity and household cards.

Those receiving assistance from the European Community through ECIP fared no better. Funds set aside for job training were not paid directly to the youths; instead, they went through DELISA—and the children were unable to use this money for training unless they divided it with local DELISA employees.

In any case, of the children who spoke with us, none found employment related to the job training they received. One youth said he rejected job training because he had to go right to work to take care of his family. He transported goods on a bicycle, an uncertain job that brought in just enough to feed his family.

A twenty-three-year-old expanded on these obstacles. He returned to Vietnam after six years of detention in Hong Kong; he'd left Vietnam at the age of fifteen and was repatriated at twenty. His difficulties began before he returned. "I wrote home, but I heard later that the mailman would not deliver the letter unless my family paid him. He kept letters three to four months. I was a minor, so I was sent home. I was supposed to have money for job training. I paid no bribes, so I was unable to get any classes for the money that was set aside for me. For the EC program, if you did not share your money with the person in charge, you could not get into the class. We were told that DELISA organized the training. But we found that if we wanted our allowance, we had to share it with DELISA employees or we would not get it. They would find an excuse not to give it. I missed one day, so they said I could not continue in the training. I had three friends who agreed to give some of their allowance to the teachers. One paid one-third of his money to get into an English class; another paid seventy-five U.S. dollars to get into a six-month jewelry training class, another paid ten dollars. None of them or I could find a job. There are three things I want: first, a job; second, to be resettled; third, for my family to have enough food, clothes, and an easy life. I have had none of those. Up to now, nothing in my life is happy."

These details come as no surprise to anyone familiar with local conditions in Vietnam. As mentioned earlier, in 1993, we visited a youth in Haiphong who was unable to get a household registration card despite the repeated efforts of a NARV social worker, who was a local resident. UNHCR, in checking on complaints of delayed permits, dismissed the problem as trivial and temporary, but to those who were affected, these delays were disruptive and stressful. Without a household registration card, returnees were barred from enrolling in school or job programs, taking employment, moving to a new residence, and many other activities. In Hue, a NARV worker said he knew of no one who had become employed through their job training.

Why didn't the children Loughry and Nguyen interviewed report similar experiences? Perhaps they did not encounter these same difficulties; however almost everyone we interviewed complained in detail of having their money taken away from them, with those in the rural areas being most vulnerable. It matters who conducts the interviews, and whom they represent. Respondents may lie; they may carefully select what they choose to disclose and offer information according to what they think the interviewer wants to hear. How they respond will depend on the extent to which they trust the interviewer. In Vietnam, with its turbulent recent past, people are understandably wary, especially with officials or others who might represent government agencies. The children may have spoken more forthrightly to Nguyen Dinh Huu than with the other interviewers. He is a child welfare social worker and well-known benefactor, experienced in talking with and assisting Vietnamese repatriated children.

A young woman told us an all-too-common tale of heartbreak, abandonment, and disappointment. The eldest of five children, her parents are farmers. In 1991, when she was fourteen, she escaped. Her voyage by boat was perilous and her detention camp life excruciating. Even so, her parents did not want her to return. In 1997, after giving birth to a child in the camp, she was forcibly repatriated. The father, a twenty-seven-year-old man, was repatriated in 1996, and she has not heard from him since. "At the time I gave birth, the camp was almost closed, and nobody cared about my situation. No one gave me any help. That's the way it was in the camp. Even earlier, since I had no relatives, I received no assistance and life was very miserable. I did not have enough to eat. Ten days after the birth of my child, the officials forced me to go home to Vietnam. I had resisted going back as long as possible. If I had been without a child, I could have been some help to my family, but with a child I am a very heavy burden. When I returned, my father met me at the bus station. He did not know I had given birth to a baby. He was sad when he learned that I had a baby without a husband at home. Not only do I bring shame, but I am also an economic burden. Our situation here is worse than in the camp. There I worried about the future but I had some food every day, even though it was not enough. Here my concern is where I am going to find food. I am obsessed about my family. My parents are poor and my younger brothers and sisters are too small to work. Since I have a child, my future is dark. I have no solution. At the present time, I am like a dead body."

Rachel Burr claims that it is easy to underestimate or overlook the extent to which the returnees are viewed and treated as outsiders, both by neighbors and their own families. While working with children in Vietnam in 1997, Burr interviewed several repatriated unaccompanied minors. They expressed feelings of isolation and alienation, as well as shame at having failed their families. They described how they were shunned in Vietnamese society because they had become contaminated by outside, Western influences.

One returnee had spent seven years in a Hong Kong camp. Her family had sent her out when she was twelve years old; she returned in 1996 at the age of nineteen. Her family had sent her out so that, if life became too difficult in Vietnam, she could help them all escape to start a new life in America. She told Burr that while growing up alone in the camp was difficult, she felt proud because she was doing something for her family. She had been sent out rather than her brother because he was said to be more important to the family. Burr interprets this as indicating that the young woman was more expendable than her brother. Her return to Vietnam "was something which she spoke of with shame. . . . Her life had been a waste. . . . She had failed her family." She found readjustment difficult. She now lived with her uncle. "Relations with her immediate family were strained and . . . she was treated as a stranger who was viewed with some suspicion. . . . She did not think that anyone would want to marry her because she was now viewed as not pure Vietnamese." Burr comments that this young woman "left a lasting impression on me because she seemed to view her own life as so futile and because she knew that returning to Vietnam was viewed as failing on her part. She said that her family knew nothing of what had happened to her in the camps and were not interested in hearing about why she had not been able to get abroad. Her resentment and alienation were palpable, and seemed to be exacerbated by there being no real support available to her. . . . [A]lthough she was with her family, her feeling of isolation was intense." Although she lived in an urban area and would have been easy to reach, "she had not been interviewed by anyone since she had returned to Vietnam and was not aware (as neither was I at the time) that any help might be on offer. When I later found out that some support might be available to her I tried to find her but could not."

Other returnees also expressed a sense of loneliness and helplessness. A youth told Burr that his family had told him to leave Vietnam because "as a second son he was not so important. Having been promised a good homecoming he had returned to find his hopes and dreams quickly vanishing. . . . In a hushed and fragile voice he told me that . . . he was never ever going to be trusted by people . . . because they knew where he had come from" (that is, he was tainted by the camp experience and Western influence). Another youth had run away from home at the age of sixteen after an argument with his father, an act of rebellion and a "big adventure." After five years in the camp he had been repatriated, only to find that he no longer fit in. Burr observed him at work and found that his peers viewed him as a "social and political outcast." He was disliked; he was unfamiliar with aspects of Vietnamese daily life, and he was eventually fired from his job. Burr concludes that "he was viewed and treated as an outsider by his Vietnamese contemporaries." His camp experiences had "shaped his life in a way that left him feeling alienated and isolated."[31]

These are the real stories of at least some of the returnees: stripped of their repatriation allowances and their dignity, unable to find or keep employment, often hungry, rejected by their own families and peers, feeling deeply ashamed of their failure to resettle, isolated, out of place, clearly disaffected. The repatriation of these young people may have been inevitable. But to claim that these returnees were "successfully reintegrated" is to demand our gullibility beyond reason and twist conventional notions of "successful" or "reintegrated" far beyond recognition. It trivializes the physical suffering and mental anguish that they have endured and continue to endure. It insults the memory of their extraordinary dream to have a better life, and their desperate and risky attempts to achieve it.

CHAPTER SEVEN

RESETTLEMENT

Challenges of Resettlement

UNACCOMPANIED MINORS have been resettled in the United States since 1975. Prior to the Comprehensive Plan of Action, they stayed as a matter of routine in refugee camps for six months to a year and then were resettled. After the CPA was implemented, they spent three to five years in refugee and detention camps. Some children and "aged-out" minors continued to be resettled, but most were repatriated.

Unlike their counterparts repatriated to Vietnam, the primary crisis of unaccompanied minors in America is not one of economic survival, but loneliness. Vietnamese psychiatrist Tran Minh Tung writes of the apprehension that refugees feel when they arrive in a new land. For instance, they experience an overwhelming despair when they become ill in unfamiliar surroundings. Because of language and cultural differences, refugees cannot make their distress known. They are used to counting on their family, but no family is available. Yet, though their anguish may be great, they may not look desperate or depressed; they cover their anxiety, as expected in their culture. "Patients cannot or do not want to acknowledge the extent of their misery, lest the distress become overwhelming and the façade that they put on crumbles when they cannot bear it any more."[1]

The most vulnerable of the "first wave" Vietnamese, those who arrived in the United States in 1975, were the unaccompanied minors. They were hit particularly hard by separation from family and friends. Even in the first days of their arrival in America, while waiting in refugee camps to be resettled, some of these children showed symptoms of psychological distress, and within three months several were "depressed enough to be suicidal." In a study of refugees at Camp Pendleton, California, Liu, Mamanna, and Murata found that children in families fared reasonably well; unaccompanied children did not. The unaccompanied minors were ridiculed by other children, who called them "bastards." The unaccompanied children suffered from insomnia and "vague somatic complaints . . . the prevailing mood was one of lethargy and hopelessness." Three of the eighteen children in the group manifested marked signs of depression: "they lay in bed both day and night, with little or no sound sleep." American officials did not fully comprehend how vulnerable these children were because of their separation from family. They contributed to the distress of these children by removing them from the custodial Vietnamese families who were caring for them.[2]

Despite their initial difficulties, most first-wave unaccompanied minors were able to make it through school and find employment. They have selectively adopted American values and customs. Some of them are financially successful, although without family or relatives, their paths to success were difficult.

Subsequent unaccompanied minors, who came to the United States as "boat people" in the late 1970s and throughout the 1980s, have had a much more difficult time than those who preceded them. They suffered for years under Communist rule in Vietnam and during their perilous escapes. Those who escaped through the early 1980s remained up to one year in refugee camps before being resettled; later arrivals often were stuck for several years. These children have had to cope with the memories of their ordeals of escape and their life in the detention camps. Difficulties with English have affected their ability to communicate, especially if they came to America as teenagers rather than small children. Their cultural expectations have often led to conflicts with their foster parents. Many of these children have never considered themselves to be members of the foster families in which they were placed; they have seen themselves as outsiders.[3]

Mortland and Egan, citing several studies and their own research conducted in the middle 1980s, conclude that unaccompanied minors have had enormous difficulties in adjusting to America, especially in the first year of their arrival. The stages of adjustment are similar to those of bereavement: shock, disorganization, pain and despair, and finally some kind of reorganization that integrates old and new ways. A major problem has been the placement of unaccompanied minors in foster homes. Mortland and Egan cite an earlier study by Walter and Cox of unaccompanied children between 1975 and 1978 that describes the process as "tumultuous and traumatic." The youth find it difficult to accept new parental figures, particularly the foster mother. Sometimes the children cooperate; at other times they are aggressive, angry, and sullen. From the point of view of foster parents, these children seem ungracious, ungrateful, and unpredictable. Walter and Cox describe common negative responses to placement in foster homes. These include "fear, a sense of helplessness, anger to be in such a situation, despair, feelings of identity loss and lack of self-worth, and frequent experiences of loneliness and guilt."[4]

Mortland and Egan focus on the adjustment strategies that unaccompanied children use to deal with resettlement. The children say they have come to the United States to acquire education, a good job, material possessions, and help for their families in Vietnam until they can bring them to America. As a result, they look to acquire money and material possessions quickly. They assume that their foster parents are wealthy, and that the monthly foster care stipend belongs to them. This has led to misunderstandings and conflicts among children, foster parents, and caseworkers. The children assume that their foster parents should buy them certain expensive and prized possessions. Foster parents resent the children as excessively greedy, while the children view their foster parents as stingy. The children solicit information from many different sources, such as peers, foster parents, and caseworkers, which often contradict one another. The children prefer to maintain greater independence than is generally allowed in the foster homes. This leads to resentment of family regulations, including assigned chores and restrictions on personal appearance. The children say they came to America to be free; they find themselves constrained more than they had expected. Mortland and Egan describe the resultant conflicts as examples of incongruities between the expectations of foster parents and children, especially regarding the values, traditions, and structures of the family, the nature of foster care, and attitudes towards money. They predict that "unaccompanied minors in American foster homes would not easily accept American families as substitute families. Not only have they been raised in a society that views the natural family as the source of one's strongest ties and obligations, they come from a society that has no formal counterpart to the American foster care system."[5]

A Success Story

THE LIFE stories in this chapter illustrate the varying responses of Vietnamese unaccompanied minors to living in foster homes, group homes, and with relatives in the United States. Hoang, the first narrator, describes the long process by which he gradually overcame his feelings of low self-worth, as he grew more comfortable in American society.

Hoang came to the United States in 1982 as an unaccompanied minor. He related his recollections of childhood to us in 1999. Hoang was born in 1967 in a small town in central Vietnam, the fifth of six children. When he was four years old, his mother passed away. His father, a policeman for the Republic of Vietnam (South Vietnam), remarried, and his new wife had another child. The Vietnamese have a proverb, "Never does the rice cake have bone; never does the stepmother love the husband's child." Many children in this book encountered hostile stepmothers, but Hoang's experience was different. His stepmother treated him well, and to this day he retains contact with her, speaking with her by phone every month. "Still," says Hoang, "she is not my real mother. It is not the same. I wonder, how would my real mother treat me?" With these words, Hoang introduces the central themes of his life story: his feeling of not quite belonging, his quest to develop confidence in himself, and his gratitude for what he does have. A loving stepmother is better than one who is hostile or no parent at all.

The Communist victory in 1975 brought profound changes to Hoang and his family. His father was sent to a reeducation camp for eighteen months; his family moved to a village in the south, not far from the seaside town of Vung Tau. Hoang dropped out of school. He explains, "We did not have anything. We lived in a house of mud and straw, with a roof of coconut leaves. After my father came back from reeducation camp, he became a farmer, the only job he was allowed to hold. We had to live far from the village, so I couldn't go to school. It was a half-hour walk to school over muddy roads, and besides, I had to work all day to help support the family. I stopped going to school in 1977; I had just started the third grade."

Hoang describes his daily routine. "Every morning, I would go to catch small crabs. I would put them in a basket, cut them in half, mix them with banana tree, slice them up small, and feed the mixture to the ducks. It was amazing, but when the ducks ate this, they gave large eggs, ten to fifteen each day. We would take the eggs and sell them in the market. That took up half the day. Then I would collect grass for my cow. Later in the evening, I would go fishing. I would put worms on hooks that were attached to poles. When the sun was about to set, I would set them in the water and leave them overnight. I would pick them up the next morning. That was my routine when I was small. When I was a little older, I started to help my dad plow the fields. So I was a very important member of the family. It was a hard life, we did not have much food."

Despite their desperate circumstances, Hoang's father told him to return to school, but Hoang, who could hardly read or write, felt discouraged. The school was far away, over muddy roads, and Hoang felt ashamed to be so far behind in school. "I continued to help my father in the fields."

Hoang left Vietnam in 1982, when he was fifteen. He recalls his departure vividly. "It was in late June, and I was plowing. My stepmother rode to the fields on her bicycle. She said, 'Go home right now; Daddy wants to see you.' I kind of suspected because my family secretly talked about it all the time at home. The authorities would punish us if they knew we were trying to escape. Now my mother gave me the call. I was excited. I dropped everything and ran home as hard as I could. My dad took me close to him, hugged me and said, 'You go with your younger brother. We pray that you make it, and then when you get there and are happy, always remember God. And when you are sad, always hold on to God, your source of rescue.' We are Catholics, and he had always instilled in me the love of God. At that moment, every sort of emotion passed through me. I felt happy and sad at the same time. I was leaving my life of hardship and hunger, but also my family. I knew why my father had selected my brother and me to escape. I was almost old enough to be drafted into the army to be sent to Cambodia to fight. My younger brother would follow soon after that. We had to be sent out. Even so, I was stunned. I just looked at my dad and my sister. Little did I know that this was the last time I would see them for many years."

Hoang and his eleven-year-old brother escaped from Vung Tau on a boat that held forty-nine people. The journey was difficult. "We had food and water for five days. At the end of the fifth day, there was no land in sight. We continued without food and water. I was scared. I remembered my father telling me to believe in God. If you have as much faith as there is sand, you can walk on water. I thought, I have faith; this water is not salty. I dipped a cup over the side of the boat, drew up a cup and drank it. The water was salty. I had lived through a hard childhood in Vietnam, but our journey across the ocean is the worst memory of my life. Even now, when I go to the ocean and see the water, it brings back the memories of the boat going up and down, day after day. On the fourteenth day, a Thai fishing boat came alongside. They gave us supplies and directed us to the Malaysian shore. We landed soon after that. We had survived the journey."

Hoang and his brother were taken to Pulau Bidong Camp, where they remained for almost a year. At first the two boys were very homesick. "We would cry a lot at night, but I got through this by thinking I am lucky to be alive and lucky to be in the camp." During the day, the brothers played soccer and watched for boats bringing new refugees, hoping to find people they knew. Three of Hoang's friends from the village arrived; all were resettled in America, and they still visit one another. After a few months, Hoang began to study English in preparation for living in another country.

Hoang and his brother were interviewed three times while in Pulau Bidong Camp. The interviews scared them, as did rumors that all unaccompanied minors would be repatriated. UNHCR did recommend this in 1982, but at that time Vietnam refused to allow repatriation. "I lost sleep worrying about this," says Hoang. "I thought about how much I had sacrificed, and now I might be sent back to Vietnam where life was so hard, with not enough food, and then I would be drafted to fight the war in Cambodia. I could not sleep, worrying about this." Finally, because they were the children of a South Vietnamese policeman, they were selected to resettle in the United States.

Hoang recalls his early days in the United States. "In October 1983, we boarded a plane and landed in Seattle. From there, we were sent to a city in California, and I have remained there ever since. I was placed in a foster home with a Vietnamese foster parent. His own family was still in a refugee camp in Thailand. There were six other adults in the house. Our foster father treated us like his own children, and what really touched me is that he even contacted our parents in Vietnam. He took us to church, shopping, and he kept us with him when he washed the car. He showed us how to do things and he took us everywhere. We even shared the bedroom with him, so I felt very special at that time. After a couple of months, his wife and child arrived from Thailand. After that, the relationship became a little more distant. But I have always been grateful to him and his family, and I still visit them quite often."

Many new Vietnamese arrivals say that their initial school experiences were unpleasant, and Hoang explains why. "I started school two weeks after I arrived in the United States. I was scared. The school had other Vietnamese kids who had been in the United States for several years. These kids were unfriendly. Non-Vietnamese students tried to be friendly, but I could not communicate with them, and I was very scared. Every time they approached, I knew I would not understand them, so I would look to hide; I would avoid them. The teachers were helpful, but I was pretty much by myself. At that time there were no Vietnamese-speaking teacher-aides. I learned English by writing down the words I saw on banners. Then at night I would look up the words in an English-Vietnamese dictionary. I have never been able to speak English very well, but I can communicate. I began speaking in physical education class, using simple words: 'Throw me the ball.' I would answer 'yes' or 'no' or give number answers to questions in math class. But I don't remember the feeling of being comfortable in communicating until I went to college. I remember in my senior year that there was a Cambodian or Filipino girl I was interested in, but I couldn't approach her because of my limited English. In middle school I had no friends except a Chinese boy who also had limited English. We felt we belonged together."

Although Hoang got along well with his Vietnamese foster parents, he felt that he was not learning English in that household. He requested to be transferred to an American family. For nine months he remained with this family, but unlike the Vietnamese, they were not Catholic. They would drive him back and forth to church. Eventually this became too difficult for them, and Hoang returned to his Vietnamese foster parents. These days, he retains close contact with both families, attending their family reunions and talking to them frequently.

Hoang attended high school but saw no point to it. "I come from a farming family, so I did not see its usefulness. I only went to school because I was forced to go. I met a social worker who paid attention to my well-being. The social worker told me about the value of education, but I didn't see it. What I saw was that I could earn money if I took a job, and I did this during my senior year in high school. I thought that was more practical. I did just what was necessary to get a passing grade. Not until college did I change. What caused me to change my mind was that all my friends were going to college. I found that I could get financial aid. Along with work-study money, I could earn as much as when I worked in a store. And all I had to do was go to school."

Hoang attended a community college, where he found that to get financial aid, he had to earn higher than C grades. The social worker persuaded him to study social work. Hoang transferred to a four-year university and began to do better. "I found it easier than high school. I go in the morning, stay until ten in the evening, and have all day to study just one or two classes. And the friends I made in college [they were all Vietnamese], I stayed with them all day; we socialized and studied together in the library. We'd hang around together at lunch, and when we had leisure time, we'd go to coffee shops, picnics, the beach, and play games together. So I began to have a sense that I belong. Still, it was not until I did my graduate work that I had a mentor who assisted me and encouraged me to raise my level of confidence. I started to feel better about myself."

The more he accomplished, the more Hoang's self-esteem rose. "When I finished my two-year and four-year degrees, I did not attend the graduation because I felt too ashamed. I felt that they were not worth celebrating, they were not accomplishments worth celebrating. When I completed my masters, I celebrated. At that time I also had been hired by a private agency for my first job as a social worker. Within the next two years, I took jobs at two other agencies, and finally with the county. I bought a mobile home. Later I married a young woman who was a relative of my Vietnamese foster parents. We now have a fifteen-month-old son and have just bought a new house. My mother-in-law, who lives a couple of miles away, takes care of our son while we go to work. My brother still lives with us."

Hoang comments on the directions his life has taken. "I am very grateful for the opportunity to be here and to have the life I have right now. I appreciate what I have and am blessed with my wife, my son, my job, and myself. I am satisfied with the progress I have made and my goal of trying to become a better individual, professionally and individually. I think of what my life would have been like had I remained in Vietnam. It crosses my mind frequently. I'd have a bigger family. Even though I would be the same age, I would be an older man because of more worries and less food. I am happy with every aspect of my life. Compared with everything I got into and then was saved [from], I am very fortunate. In Vietnam I had a hard childhood and then was saved from it. Then I was on the boat and did not know if I would live, and I was saved. Then I was saved from the refugee camp and the worries about being returned to Vietnam. Even in school, when I was in a corner, something bailed me out; then the marriage, the job, and the new house. So when I think back, every day I appreciate my life so much, the opportunity. Even if something is bad, I have learned to see it as a blessing. My son wakes me up at night. I could frown and yell, but then I remember, I have a son to wake me up; others don't have a son. I can smile because I have a son and am still breathing."

Like many Vietnamese in America, Hoang describes himself as having two identities, American in the office and Vietnamese at home. It is a relationship that is changing in emphasis. In 1994, Hoang returned to Vietnam for six weeks to visit his family. He feels close to them but distant from Vietnam. He has become increasingly comfortable with his life in America. As an unaccompanied refugee minor, he started with the feeling of being out of place, not part of the family, school, or society in which he lived. That feeling has given way to a sense of belonging. "I went to Seattle, where I met one of my village friends and his group of friends. I felt they treated me as an educated individual. They treated me with respect. When they had concerns, they came to me and asked me for advice. Everyone knew I was in my masters program. So I feel like I am special."

Hoang believes that his harsh childhood has profoundly influenced his attitude toward life and what he wishes to teach his son and the foster children he supervises as a social worker. "I hope my son will learn to appreciate everything and not take things for granted. I want him to know that life and its opportunities are not to be wasted. I want him to take school seriously, but whatever area it is, I will honor his wish. I have a feeling of belonging now that I didn't have before. With Vietnamese kids in foster homes, I tell them my own story, that I was a foster child and I understand the foster child mentality, the feeling that you are not being treated the same as a biological child. I tell them that those feelings will be gone once you graduate and have a job, when you are on the same level as so many other people. I tell them I now feel I belong. At first when you go to college, you may not be sure because you do not have that feeling yet. That's how I felt. But once I graduated and got the job, then I felt I belonged. Now I am part of the whole society, and you will be, too."

Overcoming Tragedy

QUE AND her older brother came to the United States as unaccompanied minors in 1986. She was eleven years old and he was sixteen. Unlike Hoang, they were placed with relatives. Their boat experience was far harsher than Hoang's, and Que has had long-lasting symptoms of post-traumatic stress, including crying almost every night for five years. At times she still feels disconnected, and she distances herself from the people around her. Que and Hoang both were brought up in the United States without parents. Hoang attributes his lack of self-esteem to this, but Que says she is not ashamed that she has no family (parents) in this country. She refers to herself as a free spirit. She dismisses what some Vietnamese might think of her, emphasizing instead that there are many ways to define what it means to be truly Vietnamese. Que reveals an extraordinary drive to succeed, prompted in part by her memories of the tragedy at sea that took the lives of her mother and two siblings and nearly led to her own death. She told us her story in April 2002.

Que, the fifth of eight children, was born on February 15, 1975, in a village near Danang in central Vietnam. Ten weeks later, the Communists defeated South Vietnam, and Que's father, who was a soldier in the South Vietnamese army, was imprisoned for four years. After his release, he tried to escape from Vietnam, was caught twice, and was put in jail until Que's mother bribed officials to secure his release.

During the first seven years of her life, Que lived in the village, where three of her four older siblings had died before the age of three. By the age of five, she worked in the house, carrying water and cooking, and started school. At that time her father moved to Saigon, and about a year later the rest of the family followed. They lived in a house with about ten other people, including her father's nieces and nephews and her mother's siblings. Que recalls that her mother tried to earn money by selling bicycle parts, but it failed. "There were days that I would go with her," says Que. "We squatted all day long next to the bicycle parts that we displayed on the ground. We waited and waited but no one would buy. Many of those days, we would bike home in the rain without selling a single bicycle part. Finally, my dad decided that my mom should give up. My family was quite poor. We kids had no extra money for candy, but being typical kids, my brothers and I would sometimes skip breakfast so we could use our breakfast money to buy candy instead. I did not mind being poor since this was, and still is, the happiest period of my life."

One day, Que's father took his family to a coastal area. The family told their neighbors in Saigon that they were leaving to hold a memorial service for their ancestors, but in reality, Que's father had planned his family's escape from Vietnam. He intended to stay behind so that, if the others were caught, someone could pay to get them out of jail. Que recalls their escape, which occurred on August 15, 1985.

"We hid in the house until night. Then really late at night we went to the beach. We couldn't wear shoes for fear they would make too much noise when we walk. There were a lot of mud holes, thorns, and prickly plants on the path toward the beach. My mother sank into one of the mud holes and people had to pull her out. My younger brother, who was four years old, started crying a lot. We gave him all kinds of sedatives, but he didn't stop crying. At the boat, we decided to leave him behind with one of the villagers." Que left Vietnam with her mother, who was forty-two, her older brother, fifteen, her younger brother, eight, and her youngest sister, who was one. Also going with them was her aunt, who was eighteen. Que was ten years old.

Que was surprised that the boat was so small. Thirty-one people crowded into the boat. Que's father paid a lot of money to the captain to buy a good boat, but the captain "kind of ripped us off and he kept the money. We didn't think he would do that because he and his son were also on the boat."

For the first three days, most of the people stayed hidden at the bottom of the boat so that they would not attract attention and be caught. The waves were high, and everyone became seasick. On the third day, the engine died. They were stranded with a little bit of food, some rice and jicama. By the fourth day, the food was gone. Que recalls, "We were starving and dehydrated. We did not have enough food or water. Our skin cracked with exposure to the sun and seawater in the boat. I got really sick. I developed infections and sores all over my body, and pus oozed out. I still have scars on my body and legs from those sores."

On the fourth day, the first person died, a girl who was sitting on the bow. A wave came up, the boat lurched, and she fell into the sea. She could not swim. The waves were too high, and the people in the boat could not rescue her. "We watched as she drowned, crying for help. Then on the seventh day, my sister passed away, due to thirst, starvation, and lacerations on her skin. We cried a lot. The next to go was my younger brother. He died on the tenth night. Someone pushed him from the deck, and my older brother and I discovered him dead. We did not want to tell Mom for fear that this would emotionally weaken her. This was her fifth child to die. I was sleeping next to her and holding on to her that night, which was something I always did when I slept next to her. Her body felt very cold and stiff to me. In the morning, I tried waking her up but, after several attempts, I realized that she was dead. I had cried so much when my sister died. Now, with the deaths of my brother and mother, I was so shocked, I ran out of tears. At that time, I thought I was so emotionally callused for not being able to shed a single tear over the death of my own mother. I was upset at myself for a long time for this. All the dead bodies were tossed into the sea. I never imagined this would happen. I refused to look. I was too scared."

Que recalls that her mother died with her eyes open, which was not a good sign. "People were scared. They said she was not at peace with herself when she died. People on the boat told me, though I still don't know what to make of it since I am not very superstitious, that while I was unconscious, my mom came into my body. She told the people to open the boat's windows so bad spirits from unjust deaths could leave. She said this was the only way we would be rescued. My mom had been religious. Before leaving Vietnam, she went to a temple to ask for advice. The Buddhist monk told her that she should not go, or she would die at the age of forty-two. If she remained, she would live until sixty-two. My mom told the family, and my dad brushed it off. He was not superstitious. But Mom's family never forgave my dad for this. Some blamed him for killing her, saying he sent his wife and kids off to die."

On that journey, ten of the thirty-one people died. Que was the youngest person to survive. One day, they saw a cruise ship. Que says that the people on the ship tried to rescue them, but the waves were too high. "Two guys from our boat tried to swim to them. They drowned."

Que and the other survivors were on the seas for almost a month. She says she doesn't remember much because she floated in and out of consciousness, but she does recall that it rained. Her aunt caught some of the rainwater in a raincoat, and that helped them to survive. Finally, a Filipino fishing boat stopped them. "They made all of the females undress. The fishermen searched for jewelry, and they took all of our possessions. They were going to leave us to die. But the owner of the fishing boat looked at my aunt and felt compassion for her. He announced that they would save all the women, but not the men. My aunt begged him to take along the men, and, finally, they rescued everybody."

The fishermen took them to an island in the Philippines. Que says, "I don't remember much of this. I was very weak and was mostly unconscious. I had lost a lot of weight. The pus was running out of the sores on my body and legs. I had a constant high fever. My aunt tells me that they saw only the whites of my eyes, and thought I might die. When I woke up, I was incoherent, and I had memory loss, especially of relatives in Vietnam. Many years later, when I returned to Vietnam, I still could not remember their names or recognize them. My brother and I are very close, but we have never since talked about what happened on the trip."

The survivors were sent to the Philippine First Asylum Camp on the island of Palawan. During the day, Que roamed around, went to English classes, hung around the beach, and read a lot. She remembers that the ration of food consisted mostly of canned sardines, cabbage, and rice. She describes the food as "enough but not very good." Que and her brother had an uncle in the United States. Que's brother wrote to him, and he sent them some money.

Several months after their arrival in the camp, Que's aunt married, became pregnant, and moved to another dwelling. Later the aunt, her husband, and their child were resettled to the United States. Que and her brother were left to fend for themselves. "My brother and I took care of each other, taking turns getting the food that was distributed and sharing it, but he was five years older than me and often he was off with his friends. In the daytime, I was a happy kid, but each night I found myself crying before going to sleep. I roamed and explored every possible territory with my best friend from the camp during the day. But at night, I was too young to go around. That was when I felt a lack of supervision. I would go to the library and read. When the library closed, I would sit on the cement wall by the sea and wait for my mom to appear. I was naive. I did not really understand that my mom would never come back. When it became very dark, I would return back to my room and would wait more. It took me a long time to realize that dead people don't come back. I then thought the best way to get through this was to forget everything about the past. I began actively forcing myself to forget and this went on for a long time."

Que and her brother remained in the camp from September 1985 until December 1986. Then they were authorized to resettle in the United States. They were brought to a small town in southern California, where their mother's younger brother lived. Que did not feel at ease in the house. "I was excited to finally meet and live with the uncle that my mom had always spoken so highly about, but I didn't feel like it was home. My dad had written a letter to us, telling us to 'be as little burden as possible. Don't cause your uncle and aunt too much trouble.' At dinner several days after my brother and I arrived in America, my uncle talked about our escape. He said, 'Your dad is a stupid man for sending your mom off to sea and killed her.' This statement pierced my heart. I thought it was very inappropriate for him to say such mean things about Dad, the only parent I have left. I instantly felt distant to my uncle. There were other situations in the house that made me become very unhappy, though I never complained since my dad had advised us not to be a burden. At age sixteen, I decided that I would go and live with my brother, who was in a different city attending college by that time."

In Vietnam, Que had been a top student. She also did well initially in the United States. She remained in an English as a Second Language class for only three months, then entered sixth grade, and skipped seventh grade. Her uncle and his family were the only Vietnamese family in town, so Que learned English fast, made friends easily, and quickly adapted to American customs. Through ninth grade, she excelled, winning academic awards and being selected citizen of the year. In tenth grade, she started working to save money to go and live with her brother. She also started questioning many things about life. "There were many things, most related to my relationship with my aunt and uncle, that made me very unhappy during this period of my life. I became a B student as a result. I spent all my weekends flipping burgers and making snow cones to save enough money and move in with my brother."

Since the ninth grade, Que has moved many times, not remaining in any one place for more than one-and-a-half years. At the age of sixteen, she went to live with her brother. He shared a house with two young men near a university where he was earning his engineering degree. "I worked while attending eleventh and twelfth grades. I did okay. I got As and Bs but I felt like I wasn't passionate and did not excel in anything. This pattern continued during my freshman year in college. My brother said that I should not work in college and should concentrate in school. I decided not to work during my freshman year at the university but my grades got worse. Actually, for the first time in my life, I failed a class. The problem wasn't because I didn't have time to study. Every time that I sat down to study, I just couldn't concentrate."

Not until 1995, ten years after her escape from Vietnam, did she pick up the pace of her studies. "There were a swath of credit card companies that flooded college students with credit, I signed up for a card and charged a plane ticket to Vietnam. After ten years, I returned home for the first time to visit my father and my younger brother who had been left behind. I saw my old neighbors and relatives. Seeing the people and places that made up my past made me very sad. It reminded me of the family I have lost and it was also a stabbing reminder that I will never be able to have a normal family life again. At the same time, I also realized that in order to move on with my life, I had to face my past head-on and not just try to forget the sad memories. This helped me find direction in my life. I realized the reason why I came to the United States. This was what my mom, younger brother, and sister died for. I see my younger brother in Vietnam and realize that I want to take care of him. The sheer thought of him roaming around by himself if something happens to my father brings tears to my eyes. That trip made me realize that I wanted to be passionate about life and what I do again. I owe this much to myself, my mom, and, most importantly, to the family that I do have left."

Back in the United States, Que worked at three jobs while taking five classes. "One of the classes I took was an honors genetics course. The professor of this class asked me to apply for a grant. At first I thought he was joking. I didn't expect to get it, since my grades were not on a par with other applicants. Some of their professors also wrote the grant for them. My professor didn't do that. He left me to do everything myself. I went to the library, researched everything, and wrote the grant. I was shocked when the grant committee announced that I won. My trip to Vietnam had a major impact on me. I started doing very well in my classes again and won several honors and awards as a result."

Que then entered a doctoral program in pharmacology at another university, funded by a National Institutes of Health Fellowship. During that period, she developed a cancerous tumor, which was removed by surgery. She remarks, "This made me reevaluate what's important to me. I found I was not passionate about my research. It was too narrow, and I wanted something with a broader vision. I preferred reading about other topics than doing my research. I informed my professors that I wanted to complete a master's degree and leave. My professors didn't want me to leave. They thought I was depressed due to my tumor and should take a leave of absence. But by this time my tumor was completely removed. I insisted on leaving with a master's degree. They finally agreed but said that my fellowship was for doctoral studies only. I completed my masters at my own expense and went to work. In April 2001, I moved to northern California and lived with my brother. My father was coming soon to live permanently in the States and I wanted to be near him and my brother. I found a position with a small start-up company, where my workday is usually ten to twelve hours. Everyone at the company is very nice, happy, and hardworking. I don't have to work all the hours I do. I do it because I like my job."

Despite the adversities she has faced, Que expresses a persistent optimism. "I believe we can do anything if we put our mind to it and work hard. If a challenge is hard, I work harder. I use my passion, hard work, and the values my family instilled in me to achieve my goals."

Que has many friends from a variety of ethnic groups. She is involved in many social activities and sports, and she works as a volunteer for a nonprofit organization. But a dark shadow remains in her life, the long-term consequence of her traumatic experience in childhood and her unusual upbringing in the United States. "I am very friendly and sociable but sometimes I feel a disconnection, which makes me become sad and aloof. I usually go for a walk alone to feel better. None of my friends went through what I did, and many don't realize what has happened in my past. I remember in sixth grade, my English teacher asked us to write a short book, consisting of only twelve pages, about what we dream to have and why. I wrote about wanting to be with my family again. The teacher liked my story and got other students to read it out loud in all her classes. My friends were shocked. They didn't realize I didn't have my parents. I never told them, not because I was ashamed or I was trying to hide something. It was not in the context of what we talked about. We played sports and gossiped about classmates and teachers, but never talked about family. While living with my older brother and his friends, I became conscious of the fact that I had no female guidance, no mother, aunt, or older sister. I had to solve my own puzzles regarding many issues, including puberty, through trial and error. Some people asked me if I get jealous of my friends or envy the lifestyles of other people. I can honestly say that I never have. I sincerely believe things happen for a reason. There were times when I struggled in finding the reasons behind some of the things I had to go through, but I never envied my friends for what they have. We all have our own adversities in life. Mine just came a lot sooner than most people. I never made a conscious evaluation of low esteem due to growing up without the typical nuclear family. My family might be a lot smaller now, but they have always been my strongest supporters behind everything that I do. I also have many friends, who have always been like an extended family. When my friends don't get along well with their brothers or sisters, I tell them that they should feel lucky and appreciate what they have, since it may be gone tomorrow. I had to learn a lot of things early in life due to my circumstances, but I take it like a blessing in disguise. Through it, I learned to appreciate many things that people might take for granted. My life has been tough but I have no regrets. I also realize that my past is an integral part of my present and my future. It shaped who I am today. I didn't realize this when I first left Vietnam, since recalling the past was too painful. Then I realized that if I forget my past, I forget who I am. I don't feel angry about what happened. I sometimes think about the captain of the boat, but I don't feel anger toward him. I just think he was stupid and greedy, holding onto the money my dad gave him instead of buying a better boat. He died on that trip and his son has no father due to his father's greed."

Que explains why at times she has felt removed from others. "There was a stretch of time in eleventh grade when I felt very disconnected, that I did not fit in. My friends did a lot of things that I didn't do. They would go on vacations with their family or would go somewhere on Christmas or Thanksgiving. My brother and I would rent Kung Fu movies and eat noodles all vacation long. My brother and I had an odd life. No one else I knew lived with their brother at the age of sixteen. In college, during Thanksgiving, other holidays, and summer, all the students left for home. I was left with no home to go to. Most of the time I sauntered around the college town by myself since my friends were gone and my brother was doing his graduate work elsewhere."

Que does not fit the stereotype that some Vietnamese people expect of a young Vietnamese woman. Que challenges their view of what it means to be Vietnamese. "Some Vietnamese people don't like the fact that I date 'white guys.' One Vietnamese guy in my class asked me, 'Don't you ever date Vietnamese guys?' Actually, I have, for two years. I have also dated guys from Chinese, Russian, German and other ethnic groups. By his tone of voice I felt like what he actually asked me was, 'Why are you losing your culture?' Before college, I was not around many Vietnamese since there weren't many in the town I lived. But the more I learned about what this guy considered to be Vietnamese—to lower your car, dye your hair, wear baggy pants and carry a cell phone—I realized I do not want to be part of that Vietnamese culture. I know more about Vietnamese history than most Vietnamese people I have met. I still know how to read and write Vietnamese and I love Vietnamese music, art, and theatre. My dad has always told me that it doesn't matter if I marry a Vietnamese or non-Vietnamese, as long as my husband and I love and respect each other. I would like to have a bond such as I have with my brother. Money has never been an issue between us. I can take a hundred dollars from him, and he from me. We never worry about it since we always trust and take care of each other. We also want to be with people who are supportive of us. We want our dad to live with us when he comes to America."

Que concludes by saying, "I still have a shrine of my mom in my room, even though I live in a house with an Italian, a Japanese, and an American. I know I will never forget my culture or where I come from. I don't think I need to be surrounded by Vietnamese to be Vietnamese. I carry Vietnamese character within me. I don't make claims about what it means to be Vietnamese. People can see the passion I put into helping kids in Vietnam and the amazement I feel toward the tenacity of Vietnamese people. I think from looking at that, they can realize by themselves how much I love Vietnamese people and my culture. I also love many other cultures around the world. I am always astounded by all the diversity we have around us. If I could, I would help kids everywhere, not just in Vietnam."

Que and her brother were pre-CPA unaccompanied minors, automatically considered refugees and resettled to the United States. Had they arrived after the CPA was in force, they would most likely have been considered non-refugees. As ten- and fifteen-year-old unaccompanied minors with a parent in Vietnam, they would have been repatriated. Que and her brother spent a little over a year in a refugee camp. Even though they had suffered the devastating loss of their mother and two siblings during their escape from Vietnam, their relatively short period in camp, and the fact that they had each other to depend on both in the camp and in the United States, enabled both of them to adjust fairly rapidly to their new land.

Amerasian Unaccompanied Minors

HOANG HAS come to terms with being a stepchild, foster child, and refugee. Que and her brother have adjusted to their losses and are comfortable with who they are. Many unaccompanied minors have failed to do this. Vietnamese Amerasian unaccompanied minors face an exceptionally difficult crisis of identity and adjustment. These children were born in Vietnam of Vietnamese mothers and American fathers. Because American fathers were involved, the American press has lavished much attention on the plight of Vietnamese Amerasians. Most Amerasians do not know who their fathers are, and, even if they do, they do not expect to be reunited with them. Nevertheless, these children have been coming to the United States for years. Most of them did not flee Vietnam as refugees and did not spend long periods of time in refugee camps. They came in as immigrants whose fathers were American. Beginning in 1982, under the provisions of the Amerasian Immigration Act, Vietnamese Amerasians were allowed to come to the United States, provided they had sponsors. At first, their mothers and other relatives were not permitted to resettle with them. In late 1982, under the Orderly Departure Program (ODP), Amerasians whose American fathers had filed papers for them were admitted to the United States. Later, Amerasians without such firm documentation were brought in. Because of bureaucratic delays by both Vietnam and the United States, many children waited for years to be brought to the United States. In 1988, the Amerasian Homecoming Act paved the way to bringing Amerasian children and their immediate relatives to the United States. By September 1994, nearly 20,300 Amerasians and 56,700 of their relatives had emigrated to America.

In Vietnam, some Amerasian children have been insulted and ridiculed at school by teachers or students who call them "half-Americans" or "half-breeds." But many others have been treated reasonably well. Discrimination occurs most often if the child lives in an area controlled by Northerners, or if the child's mother is considered of lower class.[6] Some Amerasians have become street children at the margins of society, scrounging for whatever scraps of food they can. The American press has highlighted their stories. When he was nine years old, Duong Ngoc Nhuan sold coffee at the zoo in Ho Chi Minh City, then worked as a fisherman at the port town of Vung Tau and sang in a circus act. Other Vietnamese discriminated against him. He came to America, but returned for a month to Vietnam, only to encounter harassment from officials and his former friends. After two weeks, he said he wanted to return to America.[7]

In the United States, Amerasian children have had a hard time adjusting. Felsman et al. note that, compared with their Vietnamese peers, Amerasian children are more likely to have difficulties in American schools. A higher percentage have had little or no school in Vietnam; this results less from discrimination than poverty, which forces them to earn money rather than attend school. They list several "at risk" factors which they say are predictors of school failure: female, Afro-Amerasian, low scores on oral and reading tests, completion of less than nine years in school, not raised by mother, not accompanied by mother, not accompanied by siblings, history of illness and/or hospitalization, and history of missing school. They caution, however, that the presence of one or more factors does not automatically mean that a child will encounter problems.[8]

While it's not a typical outcome, some Amerasians have been abandoned in America. One Vietnamese family adopted an eighteen-year-old youth in order to qualify to come to the United States as his relatives; once here, they left him. The adoptive family of another young man, twenty-one years of age, disappeared during a church service. An orphan, he had been sold for the price of his immigration paperwork so that his adoptive family could come to the United States. A third youngster described how he had been sold for two rings, a watch, and a radio. When his adoptive family came to the United States, they ignored him. In Vietnam, the adoptive family of another youth yelled at him until he left them. He was six years old at the time. Twelve years later, they sought him out as their passport to America. He agreed to go with them to the United States. One day, he returned to the house they rented: it was empty and cleaned out; his adoptive family had disappeared.

These and other abandoned Amerasians, who typically speak little or no English, fear deeply about the future. One has said to a journalist, "I don't have a future to talk about." Another: "Life has always been hard, and now it will only get harder." For several years, Mary Payne Nguyen of the St. Anselm's Immigrant and Refugee Community Center in Garden Grove, California, has assisted these Amerasians. She has stated, "All their lives, they have been denied their birthrights, yet through their pain, they have an incredible ability to forgive." But the road to adjustment for these twice-abused youths is formidable. As Mary Payne Nguyen observed, "They have no peace of mind. How can they study, how can they concentrate after all they have gone through?"[9]

"I Had No Intention to Leave Vietnam"

IN 1995, Freeman interviewed Ngo Van Hai, a black Amerasian born in 1975. He came to the United States as an unaccompanied minor. While less than 10 percent of the Vietnamese Amerasians in the United States are unaccompanied minors, this small group has had greater discipline and adjustment problems than the others. This includes Hai, who has struggled with how people treat him in America.

Hai knows nothing about his biological parents, though his physical appearance indicates that his father was black. He was born in Saigon, but at the age of three months was brought to a coastal town in central Vietnam by his foster parents. He bears their name and he loves them as his parents. He refers to them as Father and Mother, corresponds with them, and frequently sends them money.

Hai's childhood in Vietnam was mostly happy. He had friends at school, he had enough food to eat, such as rice, fish, and various soups, and he loved his parents and his brother and sister, the biological children of his adoptive parents. Unlike the great majority of Amerasians, who came to the United States as ODP immigrants, Hai arrived as a "boat people" refugee.[10] He never intended to come to America. His "escape" was an accident.

One night, Hai and his friend decided to sleep on the roof of a boat owned by his friend's father. They fell asleep looking at the stars. They awoke the next morning when thirty-two people climbed aboard and told them they were going to a picnic at a nearby island. They did stop, but only to pull up some containers of oil hidden in the sea. Hai said he wanted to swim to shore, but a man said, "If you jump overboard, I'll shoot you."

Hai recalls, "I felt terrible. I missed Mom. I was crying. I didn't know where we were going, and I was panicked." After six days, they landed in the Philippines, and after six months he was brought to the United States. Hai was ten years old. After ten years in America, Hai comments, "I had no intention to leave Vietnam. If someone had asked me then, I would have said I want to return. Now, my home is the United States. I'd like to visit Vietnam but live in the United States."

Since in America he was a minor without parents, he was placed with a cousin who had been appointed his foster parent, but she treated him badly. "She would send me to the store to buy something. When I couldn't find it, she would call me stupid. Her brother, who was my age, would call me names and threaten to beat me. I told a social worker about this and he moved me to another Vietnamese foster home. This was worse. I fought with one of their children who wouldn't let me eat. He threatened to kill me. When their father died, they blamed me, saying I was black, so I brought misfortune to them. I almost believed it. I wasn't angry; I didn't know any better."

Hai fought with other foster children. Because of this, and the fact that he talked back to his foster parents when he felt wronged, he was moved from one foster home to another. He didn't like this because it was difficult to make new friends each time. Children in elementary and middle school were friendly, but in the higher grades, students treated him badly. In his first year of high school, he studied enough to earn a B average. He excelled in math but had a harder time with English. In this school, the students were friendly. Then he went to another foster home and another school. He played football, hung around with friends, and his grades dropped. The only person who gave him any advice was his foster care social worker. He transferred to a third high school, where he also played football. The school fragmented along hostile racial and ethnic lines: black, white, Hispanic, and Vietnamese.

Hai comments, "In sports, the groups all worked together as a team. But after the game, they split into their own groups. But where did I fit in? When the Vietnamese first saw me, they were unfriendly; they thought I was black. But when I spoke Vietnamese, they were surprised. 'I thought you were black,' they would say. After that they were friendly. Not all were like that. Some kids accepted me for who I am. Still, I was not really accepted by either the Vietnamese or the blacks. I wasn't really black or Vietnamese. I am in between. I appear black, but my behavior inside is Vietnamese. I don't feel I belong with either of them. I get along better with other groups."

Like two-thirds of the Amerasian unaccompanied minors who came to the United States between 1983 and 1985, Hai had problems adjusting to family situations, various foster parents, and other children.[11] He was strong-willed, and this led to conflicts. Near the end of high school, he responded to the guidance of his foster care social worker and to a Caucasian foster family, who offered him both trust and firm discipline. He credits their efforts with the fact that he turned his life around.

Hai now attends college, where he is enrolled as a computer science major. He sees the school and the students as racist. "I enrolled in an English class. On the first day, I talked to a couple of guys in front of me and a couple of gals sitting next to me. They were white. They seemed nice at first, until they heard my name, Ngo Van Hai. After that, they wouldn't have anything to do with me. They avoided me because of my name. It bothers me, but I'm not angry. I hear Hispanic students say the school is racist. But people don't show color discrimination. They are not overt; they don't call you names. They are too smart for that. They show it in their body language. I have been at the college for two years; not one person has come up to befriend me. I am presentable, I'm well dressed, I'm not a troublemaker."

Hai's one close friend is black. Hai wishes to be accepted as a person, not a type. "On the outside I am black, but Vietnamese culture is trapped deep inside me. But I'm also glad I am an American. I prefer to be described as American. In college, I don't want people to know I'm Vietnamese. I feel vulnerable. If I meet Vietnamese people, I don't mind them finding out I'm Vietnamese, but I prefer not telling them. When they know I'm Vietnamese, they accept me right away and are really friendly. 'He can speak Vietnamese.' They accept me automatically. I'd rather that they first find out about me as a person, who

I am. I'd like to see how they would treat me if I were not Vietnamese. If they treat me well, not knowing I'm Vietnamese, then I know for sure they are good."

"All I Know Is, I Can Take Care of Myself"

MANY VIETNAMESE children in America have had the good fortune to live in households in which parental figures exert guidance and control, either direct or indirect. Studies show that academic achievements and successful adjustments in America occur most often in such households.[12] Despite early difficulties, both Hoang and Hai succeeded thanks to their foster parents. Many Vietnamese foster children are not so fortunate. They struggle both with the challenges of adjusting to new ways, and in coming to terms with the memories of what they have endured to reach America.

Unaccompanied minors who arrived in the 1990s after the Comprehensive Plan of Action was instituted have encountered greater obstacles than the earlier arrivals. They have endured many years of abuse and hardship in postwar Vietnam. They are often undernourished and have little or no education. They have lived in households torn apart by the removal of relatives to reeducation camps and the denial to their families of regular employment and education. These families have had to survive at the margins of society. To make ends meet, the children have often had to scrounge for odd jobs rather than attend school. Their outlook is much like Hoang's was at first, focusing on immediate, practical gains. But, unlike Hoang, many have been betrayed by stepparents and relatives, and they have learned not to trust people. They avoid authorities and lie to them.

Like the earlier boat people arrivals, the unaccompanied minors of the 1990s have endured dangerous escapes from Vietnam. In contrast to the asylum seekers who preceded them, they have spent not months, but years sitting in the camps, wholly dependent on the camp or perhaps receiving some money sent to them by relatives in other countries. The camp environment has made adjustments to America far more difficult. The inconsistencies of camp rules have bred disillusion and resentment; the political atmosphere has encouraged distrust of and resistance to authority, and strong anti-Communist attitudes. Ironically, these attitudes are less accepted by the Vietnamese who have been in the United States for several years, who wish to do business in Vietnam or go back and visit their relatives. The camps have interrupted schooling, and the lack of parental guidance or discipline has allowed unaccompanied minors to run wild in the camps and resist control.

Coming to the United States, these children need special guidance and counseling. Their self-esteem has been shattered. They bear the stigma of being foster children. Vietnamese children born in or resident in the United States for several years have little in common with the newcomers and typically reject them, following their parents, who typically assume that all unaccompanied minors are delinquent troublemakers and a bad influence. The parents tell their children not to associate with unaccompanied minors. The new arrivals are several years behind in school and have a hard time catching up. They have trouble with English, American customs, and an unfamiliar school setting. In the camps, they learned that lying to authorities was a basic survival technique. In America, this creates problems with foster parents, teachers, and social workers. Many of these children become discouraged, and some are drawn into youth gangs.

Vi, born in central Vietnam in 1977, and her brother Quang, one year older, are marginalized, at-risk unaccompanied minors. In Vietnam, they lived with their parents and two younger siblings. The family was desperately poor, though apparently stable. At the ages of eleven and twelve their parents sent them out of Vietnam alone, telling them that they would have a better future elsewhere. Vi wanted to leave but her brother didn't. They landed in Hong Kong and for two years were moved into and out of five detention centers, overcrowded, steel-encased hotbeds of violence, degradation, and social disruption. Recalling those days, Vi says, "I had no schooling. The Hong Kong camps were horrible. I remember riots and killing, boredom and loneliness." Although neither they nor their parents had ever been persecuted, Vi and Quang were granted refugee status. The reason, says Vi, was that "the interviewer liked us and told us that he would recommend our resettlement." Then they were transferred to a transit camp in the Philippines while they awaited resettlement in the United States. Here, too, they received no schooling or parental guidance. This camp was even worse than those in Hong Kong. "I lived in constant fear of being beaten, kidnapped, and raped by the guards or by the people of the area. For an entire year, I did not venture out after 6 P.M. I don't want to think about those camps." Here, too, though, Vi and Quang were lucky. The interpreter for the agency that interviewed them coached them how to answer the questions from INS, and they were accepted to come to America.

In America, because they were unaccompanied minors, they were placed in a foster home. Quang, however, soon got himself in trouble, and he and his sister had to move to another foster home, and then a third. Quang became involved with a Vietnamese gang. He was in a car when there was a shooting, and he ended up in juvenile detention. The authorities recognized that Quang, a lonely target who could easily be manipulated, had not been directly involved in the shooting. They knew that he was not yet a hard-core gang member and that he felt sorry and scared about what had happened, so they offered to release him if he gave them information about the gang. Since his life would then be in danger, they sent him and his sister to their aunt, who had recently arrived in the United States and lived in a town far removed from Vietnamese gangs. It was a place where the two youths had a chance to start over.

We interviewed Vi and Quang in January 1993, one-and-a-half years after they had come to the United States. In June 1995, we spoke with Vi a second time, five days before she and her brother left for their aunt's house. In the first interview, Vi, though younger, did most of the talking. Her English was better. She was in a higher math class than her brother and was doing pretty well in school, even though she found it difficult. Her brother was having a harder time in school and in their foster home.

Vi's school experience was discouraging. "When I came to America, I was placed in the eighth grade, even though I had missed three years of school and had completed only the fourth grade in Vietnam. I felt old and stupid. I didn't know anything or understand what the teachers said. I tried really hard, but it did no good. I couldn't speak; I couldn't communicate. The teachers did not like me because I was shy and could not speak to them. They acted like I ought to understand them, but I couldn't. I felt so bad, because a person cannot live without communication. I wanted to go back to Hong Kong, even though there was no hope or future there."

Vi also found herself in a hostile and destructive social environment. "People in America were not friendly, including the Vietnamese who had come earlier. They did not want to mix with new arrivals. So I felt sad. I found that kids only cared for me if I was 'cool.' To be cool, you have to wear nice clothes—no one cares how you get them—and some girls turn to shoplifting. Or you have to hang out all night with the guys, and then sleep with this guy or that, or smoke what they give you. They tell you to steal. And when you don't do what they want, they hit you, or drop you, or call you 'bitch.' I don't want to be cool. I don't want to be manipulated."

The following year, Quang was at a juvenile ranch and Vi was in a group home. Mostly she was on her own. "I eat out most of the time, at fast-food places. I like America. In Vietnam, my parents told me what to do and controlled me. Here in America, I am free. I can come and go any time of the day or night. I like that."

Vi lives in a low-income neighborhood of a city dominated by Mexican-American and Vietnamese gangs. In dress, mannerisms, body language, speech, and values, she and her older brother have taken on the culture in which they have found themselves. She now has a steady boyfriend, also a Vietnamese unaccompanied minor, with whom she can share her loneliness. They live right on the edge of delinquency. "Last year, a friend of my boyfriend gave me a lift; he had borrowed my boyfriend's car. The police stopped us, searched the car and found a gun, so they handcuffed us and said we had to tell whose gun it was or they'd book us. I was really scared. When the high school found out, they threw us out. My boyfriend felt sorry about messing up my school. His friend hadn't told him about the gun. Now I go to another high school."

Vi's account of her new high school gives a chilling picture of student-teacher relations. "Some teachers are nice, but many are mean, like my history teacher. He gives us homework but doesn't ask if we understand. 'Write one page. Did England have the right to regulate commerce in the American colonies?' I have a hard time; I don't know what this means. When I ask, the teacher says, 'What have you been doing in school? Read the book.' But I have read it, all three hundred pages, and the answer is not in there. I want to learn, but I don't understand. I don't see how the reading connects with the assignment. The teacher has no time to see students; he has two jobs. So I ask my friends for help. All are Vietnamese boys."

Vi's only ties are to her older brother and to her boyfriend. She expresses no interest in or concern about her family in Vietnam. About her brother, she says, "He cares about me a lot, and he respects me. And I care for him. He's not a strong character. His friends made him get in trouble. I worry about him. And he worries about me. He calls and checks to see how I am doing." Concerning her boyfriend, she says, "He and I don't have parents in America. I live in a foster home and he lives with a relative. I will be moving to another town. When he's old enough, he plans to move to that town to be with me. As for the future, I don't know. I want to get out of high school and be with my boyfriend. All I know is, I can take care of myself."

The lives of Quang and Vi have been disrupted by three years in refugee camps and another three years in American foster and group homes. They have experienced loneliness, fear, abandonment, and helplessness. They have been torn from their cultural roots, which have been replaced with life at the bottom of urban America. Would they have been better off if they had been repatriated to Vietnam? They don't think so. They say they value their freedom and don't care about their family in Vietnam. Hai, the black Amerasian, maintains ties with his stepparents in Vietnam but states that his home is America. Hoang the social worker, who retains a strong attachment to his family in Vietnam, rejects Vietnam even more emphatically. He speculates that if he had remained in Vietnam, he would have aged faster because of more worries and less food.[13]

We certainly do not endorse what has been done to many of these youngsters in the United States, but it is self-evident that educational and occupational opportunities in the U.S., whatever difficulties they present, far exceed those in Vietnam, especially for the unaccompanied minors. More controversial is the issue of the cultural rights of children who are removed from their homeland. Although all of the unaccompanied minors we interviewed in America lived for some period of time with Vietnamese foster parents, these children became distanced in varying degrees from Vietnamese traditions and their own families and relatives. We discuss the cultural rights of children in the final chapter.

CHAPTER EIGHT

INTERVENTIONS

To Intervene or Not? Cultural and Moral Dilemmas

WE HAVE called attention to the shortcomings of individuals and agencies entrusted with the care of unaccompanied minors. The children were short-changed; that is why we intervened to assist them. Were we justified?

Nancy Scheper-Hughes has noted that anthropologists are changing their attitudes towards intervention. Earlier, many pushed an ethically rela-tivist view of child rearing practices in different societies, defending them as adaptive, and thus not to be tampered with. Children were said to be resilient to practices ranging from harsh initiation rites to child swapping to multiple mothering. What might be considered "abuse" in one society might be the acceptable norm for another and make sense in the larger ecological, social, and cultural context in which those practices were embedded. Recently, anthropologists have challenged the appropriateness of relativism; they have questioned "the 'goodness' and 'just rightness' of such normative practices for the child, although their adaptiveness for the parents and other adults remains undisputed."[1]

But this does not automatically justify intervention when children are per-ceived as being "at risk." Scheper-Hughes cautions that what is considered harm-ful, what causes harm, and the wider context in which harm occurs remain controversial.[2] "The reluctance to prescribe, along with a tendency to criticize well-intentioned but misguided interventions, is not born of the scholar's nat-ural disinclination to action, but rather from an informed understanding of the complexities of social life and of the sociogenic side-effects of a sometimes self-serving altruism."[3] In other words, intervention in the face of perceived abuse or neglect is neither self-evident nor a universal imperative. To be justified, it requires a thorough understanding of the wider ecological, economic, and social setting in which the intervention occurs. It also requires a consideration of the ethical and moral implications of such action, an awareness of whether or not such interventions mesh with the thinking and practices of the people whom interventionists purport to help, and, finally, consideration of the cultural and social assumptions interventionists bring with them, as well as the impact that their values and style of operation have on those who are influenced by their actions.

For Scheper-Hughes, one of the "greatest lies and self-deceptions" in examining the abuse and neglect of children worldwide is "the denial of collective social responsibility for the welfare of parents and their children." She argues that infanticide, selective neglect, and child battering cannot simply be explained away as a problem of "demented" or defective parents. These issues also involve institutional and social matters. Specifically, she points to "structural inequalities in the world economic order. . . . The greatest threat to child survival in the world today is the poverty of Third World mothers."[4] The primary cause of the neglect of children, says Scheper-Hughes, is poverty, whether in America or elsewhere.[5]

The warnings of Scheper-Hughes apply to the controversies surrounding unaccompanied minors. Vietnamese parents and relatives removed sons and daughters from their families and sent them on perilous journeys into Cambodia or across the South China Sea. These desperate acts, which contradicted normative childcare practices in Vietnam, resulted in the deaths and grievous suffering of thousands of children. But exposing children to these risks reflected not a lack of concern about their fate, but such excessive conditions of hunger, poverty, and political oppression that parents saw no alternative but to send their children away. The selective neglect of repatriated children by their relatives also reflects conditions of poverty, not indifference or moral decay. So, too, the neglect of children in refugee camps is not so much the fault of their immediate caretakers in the camps. Rather, it is the collective social responsibility of those who, for political reasons, set up and maintained the camps with insufficient resources to protect these children and allowed them to remain there for years on end. These wider political and economic considerations played an important role in our decision to intervene on behalf of these children, and the ways in which we chose to do so.

Assisting Unaccompanied Minors in Detention Camps

PRIOR TO the CPA, the problems of the unaccompanied minors were not so acute, since they were resettled, usually within a few months of arriving in a camp. After the CPA was put in force, especially because of the long delays on decisions that followed, the situation of the unaccompanied minors became desperate.

Aid to Refugee Children Without Parents (ARCWP) was formed to call attention to the plight of Vietnamese unaccompanied minors in refugee camps and give them some assistance. It was not easy to gain access to the camps. The mass exodus of Vietnamese asylum seekers had produced a contentious political atmosphere. Some journalists and Vietnamese anti-Communist activists had publicized harrowing conditions in the camps. In response, officials had closed many of the camps to outside observers, while defending their treatment of the detainees.

Because he was a child-welfare expert, officials gave Nguyen Dinh Huu and the members of ARCWP permission to visit children in every camp he requested. In the highly charged atmosphere of the camps, outside observers were looked upon with uneasiness and suspicion. ARCWP adopted a nonconfrontational approach. ARCWP would offer to provide humanitarian assistance but remain politically neutral. Furthermore, the assistance would be given only in scrupulous conformity with the laws of the country and the policies of the camp in which the detainees were found. In the event of gross violations of the Comprehensive Plan of Action or evidence of clear-cut abuse or child endangerment, ARCWP would first work behind the scenes in informal ways to call attention to the abuses without creating public embarrassment. One effective, nonconfrontational way was to ask officials, "How would you treat these children if they were your own?" Only as a last resort, when all other avenues had been exhausted and children remained at risk, would the organization take a public advocacy position. Even so, ARCWP expressed its concerns only on humanitarian, not political grounds, and only when the evidence, supported by firsthand observation, was incontrovertible.

At this point, our aim, dictated by the conditions in which we had to operate, was to provide temporary, emergency relief for unaccompanied minors in the camps, helping them to meet basic needs and education. In those circumstances in which their legal rights were overlooked or denied, we advocated for them by calling attention to the noncompliance of agencies and organizations with their own regulations concerning the protection of these children. The key to our success was that we made regular visits to the camps to check on the condition of the children, and we worked closely with nongovernmental organizations that provided services for children in the camps.

How did our view of children affect our assistance activities, and how did our views mesh with those of the Vietnamese who sent their children out as asylum seekers? Scheper-Hughes suggests that parental attitudes towards children have changed as societies industrialize. In traditional societies, children are viewed in terms of their increasing economic worth as they grow up. In contemporary industrialized societies, children are seen as an economic liability but are valued for their expressive or psychological worth: the pleasure and satisfaction they bring. Many traditional societies have high population densities, scarce resources, short intervals between births, and expectations that many infants and small children will die. Under these conditions, parents "invest selectively in each, depending on their sex, health, birth order, temperament, or other culturally significant attributes, and . . . trust that at least a few of the 'best bets' will survive infancy."[6]

Traditional Vietnamese society holds values and parental attitudes that highlight the selective investment in some children over others. These include the preference for males over females, greater attention to the eldest child, who is expected to set the example for succeeding children, and favoring of the youngest child, who should support the parents when they are old.[7] The disruption of Vietnamese society during the war and postwar period has prompted families to invest selectively in their children in a nontraditional way—sending them out of the country as their best chance of survival. But families also reworked traditional patterns in a new context, when caregivers, often relatives other than biological parents, sent unwanted children out of the country.

Our position was that each child who made it to the camps deserved a chance to survive and to have the opportunity for a productive and fulfilling life. Some anthropologists claim that this view reflects "sentimentalization and sacralization of childlife."[8] If that fits us, so be it. What motivated us was that, with a very modest investment of time and effort, substantial improvements could be made for large numbers of children in the camps. True, we have represented these children as "vulnerable" and as "victims," though they were much more than that. Many of them developed powerful means of resistance to authority, and eloquent protests against the situation in which they were put. But the battle was unequal: children versus overwhelmingly powerful governments and agencies. Furthermore, the children clearly were being victimized, though not always broken, by those who attempted to control their destinies. We portray

Unaccompanied minors baking bread, Palawan First Asylum Camp, the Philippines. This activity was sponsored by Aid to Refugee Children Without Parents so that unaccompanied minors would have breakfast. *Photo: James M. Freeman.*

these children quite differently when we discuss their resettlement to America or repatriation to Vietnam: here we highlight the creative ways in which they attempt to remake their lives in new situations and environments.

In Palawan Camp, the Philippines, teachers discovered that unaccompanied minors were coming to school hungry because they received no breakfast. With CADP, ARCWP constructed a bread-baking facility; a group of unaccompanied minors baked and sold bread and provided bread for other unaccompanied minors. ARCWP sent several volunteers to work for one year as counselors and teachers in Palawan. In Sikhiu Camp, and in Section 19, Site 2, Thailand, ARCWP financed the education of children, paying the salaries of teachers and supplying books, uniforms, lunch, and supplies for the students. ARCWP built the school and donated all school expenses in Ban Thad Camp on the Thailand-Cambodia border. In Galang, Indonesia, ARCWP supplied milk for infants and malnourished children. In camps in Malaysia, Indonesia, the Philippines, and Hong Kong, ARCWP financed education, sent books and supplies, paid for small gifts for the children, and sponsored New Year and Christmas celebrations, as well as traditional Vietnamese festivals such as Mid-Autumn

(Trung Thu), the Lunar New Year (Tet), and festivals for the founder of Vietnam (Hung Vuong) and the Trung Sisters, who are Vietnamese heroines.

ARCWP worked closely in the camps with many nongovernmental organizations that gave material, legal, educational, social, and sometimes spiritual assistance to the detainees. For example, International Social Service, Hong Kong Branch, headed by Stephen Yau, offered education, vocational training, and recreation for children and adults in detention centers, and we coordinated our educational assistance with this organization. International Social Service was especially effective in working in tense, politicized atmospheres, like those of the highly volatile detention centers, without being pulled into political controversies. As mentioned previously, in Palawan, the Philippines, we worked with the Center for Assistance to Displaced Persons, headed by Sister Pascale Le Thi Triu. This Catholic agency established assistance for unaccompanied minors and advocated for them, often in opposition to UNHCR policies. They ran English language training, secondary education, job skills training, recreation, sports, festivals, and personal and religious counseling for camp residents.

ARCWP advocated for the protection of the children, closer monitoring of the activities of adult caregivers, and the use of a humane and common-sense approach to be used in "best interest" determinations regarding children. For example, ARCWP cautioned against separating adult siblings in the camps, who served as significant caregivers, from their minor siblings, because this traumatized the minors. For similar reasons, ARCWP also criticized the policy of resettling older siblings while leaving younger siblings behind in the camps. We coordinated our advocacy efforts with several nongovernmental organizations and individuals. One was Sister Pascale, mentioned above. In Hong Kong, Pam Baker, a lawyer who headed Refugee Concern Hong Kong, informed us of legal issues and conditions affecting unaccompanied minors. She effectively used media publicity and confrontation in the courts to inform people about alleged violations of the human rights of the detainees. Pam Baker first became aware of the situation of the detainees when she worked in the Hong Kong government's Legal Aid Department. She took up their cause as a lawyer, winning several celebrated cases, including that of Nguyen Ngoc Toan, mentioned in Chapter 5, overturning Hong Kong government and UNHCR decisions to deny refugee status to people. She was removed from the Legal Aid Department and banned from visiting the camps, but she continued to represent detainees in court, often at her own expense.

We heard of the abuses at Section 19 on the Thailand-Cambodia border through the tireless efforts of Father Pierre Ceyrac. When we met him in 1992,

School in one of the camps that housed the Platform Vietnamese, Site 2, Thailand. *Photo: Nguyen Dinh Huu.*

Classroom in Whitehead Detention Center, Hong Kong. The school was built in a large shipping container. *Photo: James M. Freeman.*

this seventy-eight-year-old Jesuit priest had been assisting the people at that camp for ten years. For years he had been a lone voice calling attention to a bureaucratic mistake of UNHCR that had resulted in denying refugee status to nearly 1,000 pre-CPA arrivals. We investigated their situation and published accounts of their plight.[9]

With the assistance of these and many other people, ARCWP called attention to the many problems that had occurred in the interviewing of unaccompanied minors. UNHCR and countries of first asylum either denied that these problems existed or claimed that improvements had been made, but not before thousands of children had been recommended for repatriation and sent back, eliminating any possibility of correcting whatever injustice may have been done to them.

The camps are now closed, and for the children who were victimized, it is too late to rectify the mistakes that were made. But the issues raised as a result of this experience might be taken into account in the future to provide better protection and care for other children who seek asylum.

Meeting the Needs of Repatriated Unaccompanied Minors

IN 1991, UNHCR organized a trip to Vietnam for representatives of non-governmental organizations to observe how repatriated asylum seekers were being treated. Nguyen Dinh Huu went to observe what was happening to unaccompanied minors. The group found no persecution on political grounds, but some evidence of economic harassment. An unaccompanied minor in the transit center in Hanoi told Nguyen that an official had threatened to detain him until he agreed to hand over his repatriation allowance and the jeans he was wearing. This incident was included in the group's report.[10]

Nguyen sensed that the problem for unaccompanied minors was not primarily one of persecution; it was more that Vietnam, while willing, was unable to accommodate large numbers of repatriates all at once. At the time, Nordic Assistance to Repatriated Vietnamese (NARV) was setting up a project of temporary assistance for unaccompanied minors to run through 1995; they did this under contract to UNHCR. Nguyen was convinced that repatriated unaccompanied minors would need more than this, including help that would extend beyond 1995, so he expanded ARCWP to include special assistance for them.

In 1992, we met a high-ranking Vietnamese official during his visit to the United States. We showed him our assistance plan, which he liked. He invited us to visit Vietnam to set up the project. In June 1993 and August 1994, we went to Hanoi and met with Vietnamese officials and academics concerned with social welfare. We proposed a small-scale project to assist orphans, street children, and repatriated unaccompanied minors, and they accepted it.

We explored several sites throughout the country and were well received in Hue. The president of the People's Committee of Hue City and the director of the Foreign Affairs Office endorsed our project, and other officials and groups then accepted it. In August 1994, the Mackintosh Foundation funded the start-up and we opened our office and formally began operation in 1995.

We chose Thua Thien Hue, central Vietnam, because this is a poor area with the second largest number of repatriated unaccompanied minors (after Ho Chi Minh City). Unlike Hanoi and Ho Chi Minh City, it receives very little child welfare assistance from foreign nongovernmental organizations.

Aid to Refugee Children Without Parents dropped the word "refugee" from its name, and is now known as Aid to Children Without Parents (ACWP), since the children in Vietnam are not considered refugees. The UNHCR Chief of Mission, Hong Kong, wrote a letter wishing us success and asked us for information materials to give to the remaining unaccompanied minors in Hong Kong.[11]

Government officials in Hue were especially responsive to our project for several reasons. It was small-scale by design and minimally intrusive. We were sensitive to the disruption that our presence and activities might create; we went out of our way to minimize this and monitor our impacts. We did not bring in or display large amounts of money, and we were especially careful to introduce projects in ways that were endorsed by local residents. Our paid staff was comprised exclusively of local Vietnamese citizens, who were both highly trained professionals, including physicians, and respected in their community. (ACWP staff members in the United States were volunteers.) Before setting up the project, we met with officials and local organizations to determine what needs were most pressing and neglected, and our projects addressed those needs and were updated to meet new ones. Our projects were realistic; we did not promise what we could not deliver. Local officials have become skeptical of outside assistance, since some NGOs have promised to bring in large amounts of money and new projects and then failed to do so.[12] In contrast, we demonstrated our ability to formulate and implement a diverse range of sustainable projects. Finally, because of the history of colonialism and other foreign interventions in Vietnam, some officials are understandably uneasy about foreigners exploiting them. We showed by our actions that our intent was humanitarian, without hidden agendas. Because of our cordial relationship with local authorities, we were the only

Children in the shelter built by Aid to Children Without Parents, Hue, Vietnam. *Photo: Nguyen Dinh Huu.*

Vietnamese-American NGO allowed to operate an office independently, and provide services directly, without working through local organizations.

Our activities consisted of several small projects that changed over the years, depending on need, staffed by three local employees. For the first three years, we constructed and operated one wing of a children's shelter for orphans and repatriated unaccompanied minors. Our wing housed forty children and operated continuously at full capacity. The cost for maintenance of each child, including food, clothing, education, care, and supervision, was U.S. $18 a month. In 1997, we handed over operation of that wing to a local nongovernmental organization and in 1999 planned construction of a larger shelter, scheduled for completion in 2002. Another project, started in Hue and later moved to a nearby urban ward, was a children's clinic offering free medical examinations, treatment, and medicine to repatriated children, orphans, and other impoverished children, some of them living in river boats. A third project, the "compassion classroom," was a one-room school constructed and financed by ACWP and providing education to over fifty children aged five years and up. At night, the school was used for the illiteracy eradication project, providing schooling for older repatriated and poor children who had to help their families by working during the day. This was an intensive elementary education program set up with local educational authorities. Instead of following the usual five-year cycle of education, a student attended for one hundred weeks and earned an elementary school certificate. A cattle-raising project operated in three wards of the city of Hue. While one aim was to foster economic self-sufficiency, its primary intent was to provide an incentive to keep children in school. To qualify for the project, repatriated unaccompanied minors or orphans were required to attend school and maintain satisfactory grades. If they did this, they were given five U.S. dollars a month and calves, which they took care of after school hours. They were allowed to keep the cows when they were full-grown. Each participating child gave the first calf born under his or her care to another child for rearing and kept subsequent calves. They were monitored and guided by adults in the community, who received a small remuneration for their assistance. They paid attention not only to proper animal husbandry techniques, but also to any wider impact that raising these animals might have in their community. Our reconstructive surgery project served children with cleft palate, clubfoot, polio, and disfigurements which, if left uncorrected, would seriously affect how they were viewed and treated in Vietnamese society for the rest of their lives. We gave small loans to the parents of repatriated unaccompanied minors. For our computer training and English language project, we shipped to Hue state-of-the-art computers, set up in Vietnam by our unpaid expert volunteers from the United States. The project was intended to prepare students for employment in Vietnam's new economic enterprises.

Despite our efforts to be minimally intrusive, might our presence have altered aspects of Vietnamese society? Anthropologists have long been aware that the introduction of even a single new item may profoundly change a society. But Vietnam is hardly unaffected by outside influence. Vietnam was under Chinese domination for more than one thousand years. It has been in continuous contact with Europeans since the seventeenth century and fell under French colonial rule for nearly one hundred years. It was occupied by the Japanese, who caused two million deaths by famine in 1945. Vietnam then entered its wars of independence against the French, followed by a war between North and South.

Virtually everything we introduced was already known and specifically desired in Vietnam. The introduction of computers and English came as the result of specific requests. The value of self-sufficiency through raising calves was an extension of already existing values. The counseling of children coincided with the activities of Vietnamese social workers. In summary, rather than introducing something entirely new, we built on values and structures already existing in Hue and among the persons whom we assisted.

In recent years, critics have claimed that aid to vulnerable groups or nations leads to dependency on outside aid givers. This creates and perpetuates a situation of unequal power at best, and manipulation, intimidation, coercion, and exploitation at worst. Inequality is reinforced by the threat, potential or actual, that aid givers can withdraw their support at any time. Even if aid givers are well-intentioned, there is the danger that the inequality of power will dominate their relationship with recipients.

We are sensitive to these issues, though we suspect that the greatest abuses

Free clinic funded by Aid to Children Without Parents, Hue, Vietnam. *Photo: Nguyen Dinh Huu.*

are likely to occur when the aid is massive. The fact is, all aid is intrusive and may create situations of unequal power. This is especially the case when recipients are vulnerable persons such as children without parents. Given clear and mounting evidence of the neglect of unaccompanied minors repatriated to Vietnam, what should we have done? We could have let them languish; we decided to do something to help them. In making this decision, we approached our assistance activities, not with an attitude of arrogance, but of extreme caution, recognizing that even well-intentioned actions might harm rather than help the children, and that our presence might have negative impact in the communities in which they lived. We knew full well that we could not help all children or even all repatriated unaccompanied minors. We had neither the funds nor the contacts to do so, especially since we felt a responsibility to follow through with assistance until the children we helped would be able to survive and thrive on their own. Our decision to work initially only in Hue, for reasons previously mentioned, enabled us to maximize the impact of our limited funds.

Except for emergency assistance in refugee camps and Vietnam, our projects were structured to be minimally intrusive, to foster self-sufficiency, and to be modified as circumstances dictated. We monitored closely the activities and the funds that went into these projects; the relationship between the aid giver and the youths receiving aid was not one of equals. But the imbalance characterized by dependency and inequality, which was found at the start of the project, shifted toward a more balanced relationship affording greater independence and equality as the project moved towards completion. Youths were given the chance to make it on their own, knowing full well from the start that the assistance was temporary, and intended to enable them to develop economic self-sufficiency as adults.

In summary, we approached the necessary inequality between aid giver and recipient by treating the community receiving our assistance with respect and dignity. This included the children, staff, local residents, and officials who participated in our project. Crucial to our success was that we met their expressed needs, and we helped a segment of this community to achieve economic self-sufficiency. We opened up new possibilities, such as computer training with advanced equipment, which were of great interest to them but which ordinarily would not have been available. Our project was small-scale but also cost-effective; our care and training of the children were accomplished at a fraction of the cost of other programs, because all our paid staff members were local citizens. We were welcome in the community because we provided jobs for adults as well as assistance to children in need, and the training we provided was designed to provide practical, usable skills that the children could take with them anywhere.

As mentioned in the Preface, we shifted the administration of ACWP in 1999 to other volunteers in America and started the Friends of Hue Foundation to assist impoverished families and provide emergency relief in central Vietnam. From the start, our aim at ACWP was to fulfill the promise we made to children in the camps who came from central Vietnam: if they repatriated, we would do what we could to help them until they became adults. Most of them have been back in Vietnam for five years or more, and most are now adults. In 2001, ACWP, under new leadership, moved its operations to south Vietnam, where it focuses on assistance to orphans and street children. Friends of Hue Foundation is completing the construction of the children's shelter in Hue started by ACWP and will take over its operation once it is completed.

——

CHAPTER NINE

CONTINUING CONCERNS

Childhood Abuse and Neglect: A Contested World Problem

THE TERRIBLE abuse and neglect suffered by millions of children through-out the world are seemingly endless. In war zones, children are witnesses to and often the victims of horrible atrocities. With the threat of execution if they refuse, they are recruited to fight in armies and forced to kill adults and one another. In cities throughout the world, violence on the streets claims the lives of some children and brutalizes countless others. Among those who flee as refugees from the terrors of war and persecution, half are children. Adding to the list worldwide are the victims of economic and sexual exploitation, those who go to bed hungry at night, whose diseases go untreated. The abused are not only the poor. Abuse and neglect occur in families from all economic lev-els, as well as in schools and other institutions, including some in the United States.[1] Despite their differences, each of these instances of abuse deeply trau-matizes children. They are harmed physically, psychologically, and in the dis-ruption of their social worlds.

In *No Place to Be a Child: Growing Up in a War Zone*, which deals with the most extreme cases of the abuse of children, Garbarino, Kostelny, and Dubrow discuss these three forms of harm to children: physical, psychological, and social. In respect of the last, they observe that "some of the worst consequences of today's wars are not physical and psychological, but social. Wars produce social dislo-cation, of which one consequence is a breakdown in the basic 'infrastructure of life.' All too often this includes food, health care, and education."[2] They dis-cuss Palestinian and Cambodian refugees, children from Mozambique and Nica-ragua, and inner-city children of the south side of Chicago. Regarding refugees, these authors write that "the problems of refugees are intrinsically political," that "governments and other political actors use refugees as pawns in their power struggles." Because of insufficient resources, "many young refugee children are suffering from malnutrition even though they are officially in the 'care' of the international community. The international refugee problem parallels the situation of the homeless in America, who often find the public resources available to them meager at best." Their general recommendations are to "increase the resources available for aiding refugee children, whatever their politics." Children with parents or supporting families should be relocated or repatriated to safety. Those without parents require "new homes and families for them as soon as possible." If deeply traumatized, they need long-term "emotional and behavioral rehabilitation," and, in some cases, psychiatric intervention.[3] The authors advocate following the letter and the spirit of the United Nations Convention on the Rights of the Child, and they have specific recommendations particular to each of the regions they discuss.

While the treatment of most Vietnamese unaccompanied minors in detention and refugee camps does not compare with the horrors recounted by Garbarino, Kostelny, and Dubrow, many Vietnamese children were deeply harmed nonetheless. The most damaging environments were Site 2, Thailand, and Whitehead and Shek Kong, Hong Kong, during their times of greatest turmoil and violence. In these camps, children rightly feared for their lives. But other camps also disrupted the fabric of social life. Most children said they were hungry all of the time, though officials claimed they got enough food. Most complained of suffering from untreated minor ailments. Most described the psychological torture of the best-interests status interviews. Many described their fears not only of being physically assaulted in the camps but of the unknown. Many cried when they recalled the loss of family and relatives. Some children were illiterate, and almost all others were several years behind in school, even if schooling existed in the camps. Because of the disruption of their lives, they could not concentrate on their studies or attend school. Taken together, these conditions show the true character of the camps: deeply abusive environments.

Not all abuse is the same; the cultural context of abuse is quite different in traditional and in industrial societies. Nancy Scheper-Hughes observes that "the emerging new threat to child survival and well-being in industrialized societies is posed by intentional child abuse." She contrasts situations of selective neglect and infanticide, characteristic of some traditional societies, and often caused by economic and environmental threats, with the contemporary deliberate mistreatment of children, including psychological abuse. "In terms of the relative damage, death is only rarely the outcome for abused and battered children. The abused child in contemporary society grows up and lives, often carrying within the scars of that early experience."[4]

The Vietnamese unaccompanied minors of the camps represent a situation that seems to include elements of both traditional and contemporary neglect. Faced with years of food scarcity and hunger, and seeing no possibility of change for the foreseeable future, families resorted to extreme measures, selectively sending children away as refugees. This was the first time in Vietnam's turbulent history that families resorted to such desperate acts. The escapes from Vietnam were perilous, and thousands of children did not survive. Many families tried to prevent their children from repatriating until the children were forced back, hoping that at the last moment the children might be resettled. The families would take these children back if there was no other choice. But given the precarious circumstances in which they lived, the families feared they could not feed the returnees, and they also were concerned that after years away from the family, the children would have difficulties fitting in. The family, already desperately poor, would have additional pressures put on it. The actions of these families were born of concern for the children, not indifference.

The actual condition of the children contrasts with Vietnam's ideal view of the child. Vietnam proclaims concern for the rights and welfare of children as part of its historic tradition. French colonialism, with Western concepts of the individual and of human rights, also profoundly influenced Vietnam. Vietnam was the second country in the world and the first in Asia to ratify the United Nations Convention on the Rights of the Child. In doing so, the Socialist Republic of Vietnam stated that implementation of these rights was its current goal. "In Vietnam, where children have always been the object of special protection and care, what better guarantee could there be that child-oriented policies will be more fully implemented than that national wealth and democratic rights are irreversibly advancing?"[5] In its official publication on implementation of the United Nations Convention on the Rights of the Child, the Socialist Republic of Vietnam spells out a Westernized notion of children and their rights, including rights to protection from economic and sexual exploitation, rights to food, medical care, and education, "respect for the views of the child," and protection of children "deprived of a family environment." The civil rights of children include preservation of their identity, freedom of expression, protection of privacy, and freedom of thought, belief, and religion. Special mention is made of protecting children from abuse and neglect. Vietnam's Law on the Protection, Care, and Education of Children (Article 8), passed on August

12, 1991, stipulates that "the State and society shall respect and protect the life, physical safety, dignity and honor of children."[6]

It is the industrialized version of abuse we found among Vietnamese unaccompanied minors in detention and refugee camps. It was not based on economic or environmental necessity; these children were not being sacrificed so that others in the family or society might survive. The abuse they suffered was intentional, or at least permitted to continue. Officials were well aware of the violent and disintegrative environment into which these children had been placed. Indeed, the officials were responsible for creating the long delays in setting up the Special Procedures. Of course, a child could end the waiting, abuse, and pain; all a child needed to do was offer to repatriate. Later, the intentional nature of this abuse became transparent. If children refused to do as they were told, namely, comply with a best-interest decision to repatriate them, then they would be punished by the removal of any remaining elements of a normal childhood, such as schooling. When this did not work, officials withdrew basic necessities for survival, including sufficient food and health services, and in some camps deliberately relocated children in order to disrupt their lives. Abuse became the punishment for noncompliance. The collective responsibility for this abuse rests with UNHCR and officials of all the countries that signed the CPA. They knew full well that the children were being mistreated, and they allowed the abuse to continue.

Nonrefugee children are not the responsibility of UNHCR—except for the fact that UNHCR deliberately used its "good offices" to go beyond its mandate and offer protection and care for Vietnamese nonrefugees, including unaccompanied minors. UNHCR therefore bears some responsibility for what happened to them.

Anuradha Vittachi uses the United Nations Convention on the Rights of the Child as the standard by which to evaluate the treatment of children worldwide. In doing this, she blurs the distinction between traditional and industrialized nations set forth by Scheper-Hughes. Vittachi accuses adults around the world of knowing that children are starving to death and "allow[ing] them to do so." She states that "more than a million children each month die unnecessarily from hunger-exacerbated diseases," and that "we allow it to happen." At the same time, we value children. "That adults see children as very precious is taken for granted."[7] She documents the abuse and neglect of children, claiming that it is preventable in many cases. As an example, she recommends that poor countries shift from Western-style curative care for elites to less expensive, primary health care that is simple, self-reliant, and preventative.[8] Vittachi's charges of collective adult responsibility for the death of children worldwide are controversial, as are her suggested solutions to complex issues, which may be theoretically plausible but actually hard to implement.[9] Nevertheless, she calls attention to two issues of concern to us. The first is the need for solutions that are less expensive, simpler, feasible, and acceptable in the societies where they are attempted. The second is the discrepancy between ideals of protection and care for children, as expressed in particular cultural settings, and actual implementation of these ideals.

Unlike Vittachi, some critics do not accept the United Nations Convention on the Rights of the Child as a universal standard. The distinction made by Scheper-Hughes between abuse in traditional and contemporary societies is one example. Another, along similar lines, comes from Rachel Burr, who has worked in Vietnam in a children's center and with street children. She questions the appropriateness of the Convention for Vietnam, since it tends to "overlook Vietnamese notions of childhood and therefore introduce working practices that fail to meet local needs." Burr proposes a more realistic standard, connected to actual local conditions, that Vietnam can live up to.[10] Only two nations, Somalia and the United States, have not ratified the Convention because it conflicts with their laws. For example, in opposition to the Convention, the United States wishes to retain a death penalty for minors who commit certain crimes.

In any case, UNHCR and the countries that signed the Comprehensive Plan of Action agreed to protect Vietnamese unaccompanied minors on the basis of the United Nations Convention Relating to the Status of Refugees, the Comprehensive Plan of Action, and the special provisions pertaining to the protection of unaccompanied minors. Given these accepted guidelines, we need not claim that in discussing the children of the camps there are or should be universal standards for the protection and treatment of children everywhere. Similarly, we need not debate whether or not "every child is precious," and whether or not we are collectively responsible for every child. Its signatories agreed to follow the CPA and the special provisions; whether by design or oversight, they did not. That failure was preventable and correctable.

Cultural Rights versus Children's Rights and Development

A MAJOR controversy concerning children in abusive environments is what to do when the rights of the child conflict with cultural rights. We have documented numerous cases of Vietnamese asylum seekers in which such conflicts ended up harming the children. In his article on cultural rights versus best interests of the child, D. Michael Hughes calls attention to cases in the United States in which the notion of best interest was given precedence over the child's right to a cultural identity. He claims that in the United States, with its emphasis on psychological considerations, "the larger social, cultural, and economic context that impinges on these families is rarely examined or discussed as relevant." He concludes that each child has a "right to grow up in and belong to a community of kinship and meaning—i.e., a child's right to culture—as well as the right to live free from physical harm, neglect, and the deprivation of necessities," and that these are affirmed in the U.N. Declaration of the Rights of the Child. "It is most unfortunate, as well as contradictory for child protective social workers to deny a child's right to culture in the name of acting in his or her 'best interests.'"[11]

The situation of Vietnamese unaccompanied minors is different. Harm came from assuming that children's rights and cultural rights automatically coincided. Following the guidelines for the treatment of refugee children, officials claimed that "best interests" were served by returning children to their culture. No attention was given to what that culture consisted of, or to the fact that many were returned to the streets, to hunger, to extreme poverty, and, often, to no support system whatsoever. Far from paying adequate attention to the wider social and economic world of these children, officials disregarded it entirely. No consideration was given to the physical, psychological, and social harm that came from preserving their cultural identity. We have seen that children were even repatriated to Vietnam when they had no family there. The rationalization for their return was cultural identity; the actual ruling principle was convenience.

When it suited them, officials overlooked the right to a cultural identity while still proclaiming they were acting in the best interests of the children. This is what occurred when children in the camps were separated from caregiving relatives because the relatives were not their parents. The justification was the need to ultimately return them to their parents; the actual effect was to remove them from any kind of family life.

Best interests and cultural rights do not automatically fit together; nor are they inevitably contradictory. Harm comes to children when decisions are blindly based on such principles and followed no matter what. A much more careful assessment needs to be made of the benefits and costs in the case of individual children. But cultural rights and best interests had little to do with what happened, anyway. The decisions made on behalf of the children of the camps were clearly influenced by political considerations. Ideally, decisions like these should be made free of politics. In the highly charged situation of the Vietnamese refugee exodus, this was not done.

Protecting Unaccompanied Minors

THE FIRST thing that needs to be done for children seeking asylum is to remove or protect them from immediate physical danger. As we found in the Vietnamese refugee camps, and as many others have found in far more violent environments, protection of children is not always feasible. Often, the only thing one can do is to negotiate behind the scenes, and, when that fails, call public attention to these terrible abuses, as we did in a situation that occurred at Section 19, Site 2, Thailand.[12]

We have shown that at various times numerous gaps existed in the protection and care of Vietnamese unaccompanied minors seeking asylum. The children were kept far too long in destructive camp environments, where they were often treated as criminals. They experienced or feared physical and sexual abuse. They had inadequate food and clothing, suffered neglect of minor medical problems, and received deficient or no education and skills training. They endured an emotionally starved environment that promoted anxiety, loneliness, and depression, especially when they were removed from relatives who acted as caretakers. They were given inadequate information about the CPA and screening interviews. They were subjected to flawed status evaluations, and possibly to corruption in the decisions, followed by coercion to convince them to repatriate. Officials and others in charge of them reduced their food supply, stopped their education, and in some camps moved them around so that they would have no feeling of permanence. Their preparation for returning to Vietnam was insufficient; once repatriated, they found that the promises made to them were not kept. Low-level government employees squeezed repatriation allowances out of them. The job training promised them was hard to get, inadequate, and did not lead to employment. The most vulnerable children were those who were repatriated to adults other than their biological parents.

Many persons and organizations called attention to abuses in the camps. Over time, government officials and UNHCR responded and improved or attempted to improve some of these conditions. Sometimes, they publicly defended their actions in official publications, claiming that they had made rational and humane choices. On occasion, they admitted error publicly. UNHCR officer Christine Mougne observed that her organization's most serious oversight was the length of time they let unaccompanied minors, indeed all children, spend in the camps. In private interviews many officials told us that they did the best they could under trying political circumstances, limited budgets, and severe time constraints that restricted their effectiveness.

We have questioned many of the actions and assumptions of these officers, but we also agree with some of their views. One example is that children should be removed from the camps as quickly as possible. We recognize that officials charged with the care and protection of these children operated under very difficult constraints. In pointing to their shortcomings, and to alternatives within their mandate that they did not pursue, our purpose is not to lay blame, but to call attention to some ways to protect and care for children seeking asylum in future.

The specific events and conditions we have discussed occurred in a unique historical context that may not be duplicated elsewhere. Nevertheless, the experience of Vietnamese unaccompanied minors raises some questions that might apply to other times and places where children are at risk. The primary question is to what extent persons in charge of children put the safety of the children first and foremost. In this instance, UNHCR, while well-intentioned, failed to pursue this goal as vigorously as it might have. To be sure, it expressed concern numerous times about the harmful consequences of life in the camps, but it did not make avoidance of these consequences its first priority.

An example of misplaced priorities can be seen in a March 15, 1993, memo by Robert Van Leeuwen, then UNHCR Chief of Mission in Hong Kong. The memo outlines a framework for implementation of the Comprehensive Plan of Action in 1993 and 1994. The order of the action items listed reveals the writer's priorities. Van Leeuwen starts, "There can be only one humanitarian objective: to identify those persons who qualify for refugee status as quickly as possible and to limit to an absolute minimum the length of time spent in detention." The second item covers persons whose cases are reviewed and who are determined not to be refugees. Third is dealing with the harmful environment of detention, with vulnerable groups, including children, being mentioned.[13] The memo was written during a turbulent period in the saga of Hong Kong's treatment of Vietnamese asylum seekers. Many children had been in the camps for three to five years and were being seriously harmed. Yet Van Leeuwen's first priority was not their protection or stabilization of their condition, but determining who was or was not a refugee. This may have been mandated by his organization, but need not be our priority, since we are neither members of that organization nor controlled by them.

The concern both here and elsewhere is clear: protect the children first;

stabilize their lives while they are waiting for a solution, and then determine their best-interests status. Only when unaccompanied minors seeking asylum are shielded from harm should their protectors turn to other considerations. Some of these are obvious and widely accepted, even by those who disagree about other issues. Severely limit the period of time that children remain in the camps. Make quick determinations of what is in their best interests, and repatriate or resettle them quickly. Some conclusions are not as widely shared, but we consider them important. Provide sufficient food while children are in the camps. Maintain educational and vocational training so that the children are able to adjust more easily to life outside the camps. Do not use coercion to force children to repatriate. If children are separated from their parents, they need special care until they are resettled or returned to their parents. Many people agree that such children need to be cared for by appropriate specialists in child-care and child development who know something about the cultures of the children. Care providers also need to recognize variations from the mainstream values and practices of these cultures.

This latter point is often overlooked. In dealing with Vietnamese children, as only one example, it is important to understand the special nature of the Vietnamese family unit, but also to realize that one pattern does not fit all children or all circumstances. One does not have to be Vietnamese to recognize this, and, indeed, being Vietnamese does not automatically ensure sensitivity to cultural variation among the Vietnamese. We have seen that officials in Thailand broke up the group homes of older unaccompanied minors so that the children would not reinforce each other's desire not to repatriate and that Vietnamese adults entrusted with the care of unaccompanied minors followed these orders. They attempted to impose foster parents on the unaccompanied minors when the children rightly preferred a group home. The adults rationalized that foster parents more closely corresponded to an idealized Vietnamese family. They failed to consider that the people called "foster parents" were given little responsibility for the care of the children. Also overlooked were the disruptive social and psychological effects on the children every time foster parents were relocated, leaving the children behind. This arrangement failed to provide any kind of stability or emotional support for these children.

Neither should children be separated from relatives in refugee camps who have taken care of them for several years. In such cases, granting refugee status to the adult caregivers but not the children is not justified, in light of the damage done to the children left behind. We have seen how UNHCR and other officials routinely disregarded the psychological needs of children in this respect, separating children from their caregiver relatives without concern for the consequences. Bureaucratic efficiency took precedence over child development. Many nongovernmental organizations concerned with childcare opposed these actions. Had culturally sensitive childcare professionals been allowed to determine both the best interests of these children and the best way to preserve their cultural identity, the children would not have been ripped away from their only source of emotional and family support. We share the concerns that writers such as Don Handelman raise concerning the ways in which social-welfare officials might construct a case of "abuse," justifying the removal of a child from a parent. Handelman's own conclusion is apt. "There likely are no panaceas. Perhaps the best one can hold out for is an informed critical awareness, on a number of levels, that might avert some tragedies."[14]

Both UNHCR and nongovernmental organizations (NGOs) are needed for the protection and care of unaccompanied minors. UNHCR operates most effectively in protecting refugees, negotiating with host countries for the rights of asylum seekers, and negotiating with other countries to develop resettlement agreements. But NGO workers provide the most effective care of asylum seekers. They know and understand their needs and concerns because they deal with them on a daily basis. UNHCR is unable to do this.

Some NGOs work well with UNHCR; others do not. In the Vietnamese refugee saga, acrimonious conflicts erupted regarding the control UNHCR exerted over some NGOs working in the camps. Some NGOs were under contract to UNHCR. UNHCR determined the access of others to the camps or granted them permission to provide services to Vietnamese detainees. UNHCR views on the amount and variety of services to be offered to Vietnamese detainees were often at odds with those of the NGOs. These conflicts affected the quality of services given to unaccompanied minors, a situation that we consider unacceptable and avoidable if the primary concern is the interests of the children and not those of the organizations.

NARV's experience in Vietnam raises concerns about the financial dependence of NGOs on UNHCR. NGOs benefit from this association, but sometimes at a heavy cost. NARV entered Vietnam because of its contract through UNHCR, but then could not negotiate effectively with Vietnamese officials, especially at local levels, to provide services. UNHCR set unrealistic time constraints for completion of these services, dooming NARV to failure in some of its efforts. The big losers were the repatriated unaccompanied minors, many of whom were neglected, abandoned, and forgotten.

An important question is what types of assistance projects are most helpful for children seeking asylum. We agree with Neil Boothby, who emphasizes the support of groups rather than the individual child per se. In his study of children displaced by war, Boothby concludes that, whether it is a matter of understanding, investigation, or action, it is not enough to focus on the individual traumatized child and how that child copes with trauma. It is necessary to consider the wider context. "The nature of the conflict, how children understand it, and how they perceive their roles in it, all affect psychological processes and mental health outcomes." He argues for "a two-dimensional model which considers the context of the crisis itself and children's coping in relation to that context, rather than solely in abstract, individualistic terms." Boothby points out that children exposed to violence also often experience other traumas. "They lose their homes, their possessions, their friends, and frequently their parents or siblings or other kin. For most children, the loss of a parent is an overwhelming event, and normal grieving and effective coping—difficult for any child whose parent or sibling has died—are particularly problematic for war and refugee children." For those who suffer severe deprivation such as insufficient food or lack of medical care, the effects are not only physical, but mental. "While physical development is stunted and survival questionable, cognitive and emotional impairments also occur." Boothby notes that uprooted children living within uprooted social groups "are often forced to alter their existing world views in order to make sense out of their new realities. The longer they live in the midst of danger and adversity, the more likely it is that their personalities, behavior, and moral sensibilities will become altered in the process." While individual approaches may be helpful for these children, Boothby's primary suggestion for assisting such children is to "mobilize human and financial resources to support community efforts to create a more positive social reality for children. Strengthening and reestablishing children's primary relationships with parents, families, communities, and in some cases, their larger ethnic groups, is a priority."[15]

Boothby focuses on refugee children who have been subjected to excessive violence and deprivation. The situation of Vietnamese detention camp children was not as extreme, but the traumatic effects on children of long-term incarceration in Southeast Asian and Hong Kong detention camps have been far-reaching. In varying degrees, many of the conditions described by Boothby apply to Vietnamese unaccompanied minors seeking asylum. Many were victims of violence while escaping Vietnam or in the camps. Many lost their parents, siblings, or friends. They were alone in the camps, and usually hungry, though not starving. Their social world was frequently disrupted by the breakup of households or groups in the camps and in some detention centers through frequent relocations. They were terrorized by gangs and intimidated by the interrogations of Special Committees. They endured months of mental anguish while awaiting the results of their interviews and, for those who were denied, years of uncertainty about when and how they would be repatriated. Meanwhile, they had learned how to survive in the camps. In Vietnam, they had to adjust to a changed social world, and those who received them had to learn to cope with children who had missed out on years of Vietnamese education and socialization.

To deal with this host of problems, attention must be given to the larger context of the return of such children. There is resentment, for instance, in many communities in Vietnam over the fact that these children who left the country now receive assistance, while others who never left are neglected. The repatriated children have to learn to conform to Vietnamese patterns of behavior, while those who care for them are confronted with children who may be much more worldly than other children. Community efforts are needed to bring about their reintegration into Vietnamese society. Our projects in Vietnam combine individual assistance, when appropriate, with community-based activities that benefit both the repatriated minors and others.

We have criticized the policy of housing children in camps with relatives other than their parents, and then, after several years, forcing the children to remain alone in the camps when their relatives were resettled. If the primary concern were for the children, the policy governing them would address their needs first, by focusing on interviewing them quickly and removing them from the camps as soon as possible.

Ideally, children should not be in detention or refugee camps for more than three months, but in any case no more than one year. A focus on children first would lead to treating unaccompanied minors quite differently from what these children actually experienced. Upon arriving in a country of first asylum, unaccompanied minors should be placed in a children's shelter apart from adult living quarters, though adults in the camp should supervise them. The children should be interviewed immediately, or as soon as possible, ideally within a few days of their arrival, to minimize the influence of the camp environment on their answers. If they are interviewed quickly, they will be more likely to tell the truth about their family situation and less likely to be coached, accurately or inaccurately, by camp detainees on how to answer questions or prompted to lie.

Attached minors also should be interviewed and resettled or repatriated quickly, but if they are left to reside in camp with relatives for more than three months, they should be resettled or repatriated with that family. All decisions should take into account exceptional circumstances that do not fit the general guidelines.

How could the children be repatriated more quickly? Again, this is a matter of the priority given to children. Vietnam was willing to take back unaccompanied minors after the CPA began. The predisposition of Special Committees in all countries of first asylum was clearly to send unaccompanied minors back to Vietnam. In light of this, there was simply no reason to keep the children in the camps for years while Special Committees dithered. The children may have suffered the effects of being in a family whose adult members had been persecuted, but, as a rule, persecution was not directed at the children. Certainly, they were desperately poor, hungry, and without opportunities for a better life, but if they had biological parents in Vietnam, they had some semblance of protection. Minors repatriated to relatives other than biological parents were more vulnerable, given the difficulties such children typically faced with these adults. Resettlement would have been a better choice for these children than repatriation.

The specific decisions that work for Vietnamese unaccompanied minors are not necessarily appropriate for children elsewhere, but the wider concern does apply: children seeking asylum should not be an afterthought, but the first priority. Our study calls attention to faults in the treatment of refugee children that can be corrected.

The events we have described show why it is imperative to act quickly to assist such children. The years of childhood are precious and short; they should not be spent behind the barbed wire of detention camps.

We also believe that people outside official government organizations and UNHCR can help in the protection of such children. They can pay attention to how they are treated, make it known that abuse and neglect are not acceptable, and possibly become involved in activities to assist them.

We do not expect to see perfect solutions to the problems we have articulated, given the circumstances in which people flee their homelands and the reception they receive elsewhere. Our concern is to limit, as much as possible, the damage to these children, offering a new life to those whose worlds have been shattered, letting them know that someone cares about them, giving them hope, and providing realistic ways for them to begin to reconstruct their lives.

Abbreviations Used in This Book

ARCWP. Aid to Refugee Children Without Parents. A nonprofit voluntary organization that has assisted Vietnamese unaccompanied minors in refugee camps. The coauthors founded this organization.

ACWP. Aid to Children Without Parents. The revised name of the organization listed above, which has extended its assistance to repatriated unaccompanied minors and other children at risk in Vietnam.

AVS. Agency for Volunteer Services. This agency provides legal aid and counseling for asylum seekers.

CADP. Center for Assistance to Displaced Persons. A Catholic-run nongovernmental organization in the Philippines that often disagreed with the UNHCR on humanitarian grounds and opposed the repatriation of Vietnamese asylum seekers.

CPA. Comprehensive Plan of Action. The international agreement, signed by 51 nations in 1989, intended to provide a uniform set of principles and procedures to evaluate the refugee status of asylum seekers from Vietnam and Laos.

DELISA. Department of Labor, War Invalids, and Social Affairs. The provincial agency in Vietnam that is involved with the reintegration of repatriated asylum seekers.

DPPU. Displaced Persons Protection Unit. A Thai armed unit assigned to protect refugees and asylum seekers on the border of Cambodia and Thailand.

ECIP. European Community International Program, also referred to as EC. An organization offering vocational training programs for repatriated adult Vietnamese asylum seekers, including aged-out minors. The aim was to help them reintegrate in Vietnam after residing for years in refugee camps in Hong Kong and Southeast Asia.

HO. Humanitarian Operation. An immigration program run by the United States that allows prisoners who spent at least three years in Vietnamese reeducation camps to move with their families to the United States.

ISS. International Social Service. The Hong Kong branch of this international voluntary organization worked successfully with the UNHCR in providing social and educational services to asylum seekers in detention centers.

KPNLF. Khmer Peoples National Liberation Front. Cambodian military faction that competed with the Khmer Rouge and affected refugees and asylum seekers on the border of Cambodia and Thailand.

MOLISA. Ministry of Labor, War Invalids, and Social Affairs. The national agency in Vietnam that is involved with the reintegration of repatriated asylum seekers.

NARV. Nordic Assistance to Repatriated Vietnamese. A nongovernmental organization consisting of a consortium of Scandinavian volunteer agencies under contract to UNHCR to assist in the reintegration of Vietnamese asylum seekers, including unaccompanied minors, who are repatriated to Vietnam.

NGO. Nongovernmental Organization. An organization, secular or religious, without formal government affiliation, that provides a variety of assistance services to people in need. Examples are NARV and ACWP.

ODP. Orderly Departure Program. An immigration program that allows Vietnamese to leave their homeland for countries such as the United States without resorting to dangerous escapes.

PFAC. Philippine First Asylum Camp, also known as Palawan First Asylum Camp or Palawan Camp. This camp, which afforded greater freedom than other camps in Hong Kong and Southeast Asia, housed Vietnamese asylum seekers who were being screened for refugee status and those who had been screened out.

UNHCR. The Office of the United Nations High Commissioner for Refugees. An organization that provides guidelines for the determination of refugee status and advocates for the protection of refugees, including unaccompanied minors.

Notes

Preface

1. The full details of a reference are given the first time that it is used in any chapter and in the references listed at the end of the book. Subsequent mention of a reference within a chapter is by author (or name of publication if no author is listed), date, and page number. James M. Freeman (1989), *Hearts of Sorrow: Vietnamese-American Lives* (Stanford: Stanford University Press).

2. James M. Freeman, Huu Nguyen, and Peggy Hartsell (1985), "The Tribal Lao Training Project," *Cultural Survival Quarterly* 9, no. 2: 10–12.

3. Lucia Ann McSpadden (1999), "Struggles to Secure Rights for Non-Citizens: Protection Endangered" (paper presented at the meetings of the American Anthropological Association, Chicago, November), 2. See also U.S. Committee for Refugees (1999), *World Refugee Survey 1999* (Washington, D.C.: U.S. Committee for Refugees), 3.

4. United Nations High Commissioner for Refugees (n.d.-a), "Basic Facts," available from World Wide Web:
(http://www.unhcr.ch/cgi-bin/texis/vtx/home?page=basics).

Chapter One

1. Philippe Agret (2001), "Vietnamese Boat People Saga Ends with Departure of Handful of Refugees," Agence France Presse via NewsEdge Corporation, dateline Bangkok, Thursday, February 8; reprint UNHCR Refugee NewsNet: Vietnam, available from World Wide Web:
(http://www.unhcr.ch/cgi-bin/texis/vtx/home?page=news).

2. The precise number who died is a matter of debate.

3. United Nations High Commissioner for Refugees (2001), *The State of the World's Refugees 2000: Fifty Years of Humanitarian Action* (New York: Oxford University Press); available from World Wide Web:
(http://www.unhcr.ch/pubs/sowr2000/sowr2000toc.htm). See Chapter 4, "Flight from Indochina," 79–103; statistics are on 85, 89, 94, 98, 99.

4. The final report on Vietnamese migrants published by the government of Hong Kong is [Hong Kong Government] (1997), "Vietnamese Migrants in Hong Kong: Special Administrative Region Fact Sheet no. 15" (n.p., July); the statistics are on page 2. Mona Laczo (2000) describes the situation of the Vietnamese in Hong Kong and Thailand in January 2000 in her article, "Holding on to Hope," *Diakonia*, no. 51 (January): 7. The repatriation of Vietnamese from Hong Kong in February 2000 is reported in *Cali Today* (2000), "Hong Kong truc xuat 148 nguoi Viet ti nan (Hong Kong Deports 148 Vietnamese Refugees)," no. 276 (February 18): 1. The announcement of the closing of the last camp in Hong Kong is found in *Thoi Bao* (San Jose, Calif.) (2000), "Hong Kong dong cua trai ty nan cuoi cung (Hong Kong Closes the Last Refugee Camp)," no. 2725, February 23. Regarding the Philippines, see Center for Assistance to Displaced Persons (1997b), *1997 Yearly Activity Report: The Remaining Boat People in the Philippines, Particularly the Viet Village, Puerta Princesa City, Palawan* (Manila: Center for Assistance to Displaced Persons); and Center for Assistance to Displaced Persons (1999), *Summary Report on the Remaining Vietnamese Nationals* (Manila: Center for Assistance to Displaced Persons).

5. *Refugees Daily* (2000), "Hong Kong: Vietnamese Protest as Camp Closes," Thursday, June 1; reprint UNHCR Refugee NewsNet: Vietnam, available from World Wide Web: (http://www.unhcr.ch/cgi-bin/texis/vtx/home?page=news).

6. See the discussion of this point by Ariste R. Zolberg, Astri Suhrke, and Sergio Aguayo (1989), *Escape from Violence: Conflict and the Refugee Crisis in the Developing World* (New York: Oxford University Press), 3–33.

7. Although the word "refugee" first appears in sixteenth century France, only in the twentieth century has the world community come to recognize, through international law, refugees as a unique category of human rights victims who need special protection and benefits. The literature on refugees in international law is vast. Our purpose in this section is not to summarize these studies but to call attention to the political underpinnings of the word "refugee." See Guy S. Goodwin-Gill (1983), *The Refugee in International Law* (New York: Clarendon Press), 1–65; Gil Loescher (1994), "The International Refugee Regime," *Journal of International Affairs* 47, no. 2 (winter): 351–377; Vitit Muntarbhorn (1992), *The Status of Refugees in Asia* (New York: Clarendon Press), 3–54; and Zolberg, Suhrke, and Aguayo (1989, 3–33).

8. On the establishment of the UNHCR, see Louise W. Holborn (1975), *Refugees: A Problem of Our Time: The Work of the United Nations High Commissioner for Refugees, 1951–1972*, 2 vols. (Metuchen, N.J.: The Scarecrow Press), especially 55–157; Goodwin-Gill 1983, 127–148; Yefime Zarjevski (1988), *A Future Preserved: International Assistance to Refugees* (Oxford: Pergamon Press), 1–17; Gil Loescher (1993),

Beyond Charity: International Cooperation and the Global Refugee Crisis (New York: Oxford University Press).

9. See Holborn (1975: 93–96) on the significance of the definition of a refugee. On pages 1,399–1,435, Holborn discusses the expanded functions of UNHCR through the early 1970s and the process by which this expansion occurred. She also describes the administrative organization of UNHCR and its relation with other United Nations organizations as well as with member states.

10. As pointed out by many authors, the definition of refugee has been revised and expanded over the years, and there remain areas that are unclear. "Persecution" is not defined in the 1951 Convention. Goodwin-Gill observes that while the core meaning of persecution seems readily to include the threat of deprivation of life or physical freedom, "in its broader sense, it remains very much a question of degree and proportion," that whether various "restrictions amount to persecution within the 1951 Convention will again turn on an assessment of a complex of factors" (1983: 38, 39). While the notion of "good offices" has been used to render assistance to those in a refugee-like situation who are not clearly within the UNHCR statute, economic migrants who claimed they were refugees or deserve special assistance and protection were not included. Muntarbhorn (1992: 44) notes that the reaction against economic migrants is particularly forceful. "Few states and international organizations dealing directly with refugees have espoused the cause of 'economic migrants' for fear of opening floodgates and exhausting their limited resources." On the concept of good offices, see Goodwin-Gill (1983: 7); Holborn (1975: 434–449); Muntarbhorn (1992: 42); Zarjevski (1988: 16–17, 165–167).

11. W. Courtland Robinson (1998), *Terms of Refuge: The Indochinese Exodus and the International Response* (New York: Zed), 24.

12. Linda Hitchcox (1990), *Vietnamese Refugees in Southeast Asian Camps* (London: Macmillan/St. Antony's), claims that UNHCR's view of Vietnamese economic migrants is politically motivated and influenced by countries of first asylum. Host governments distinguish between political and economic motives specifically to contain and impede the refugee movement, despite "considerable difficulties in distinguishing between economic and political reasons for leaving." These difficulties are not new; they have been there since the Indochinese exodus began. "The difference," says Hitchcox, "is that the movement of Vietnamese has lately been seen as burdensome for host countries." See Hitchcox (1990: 22).

13. A more detailed discussion of variable policies of resettlement for different Indochinese nationalities is found in Robinson (1998).

14. On the chaotic exit of the United States and the turmoil surrounding the escape of first-wave refugees, see David Butler (1985), *The Fall of Saigon* (New York: Simon

and Schuster); Larry Englemann (1990), *Tears Before the Rain* (New York: Oxford University Press); Stanley Karnow (1991), *Vietnam: A History,* rev. ed. (New York: Viking); Gail Paradise Kelly (1977), *From Vietnam to America* (Boulder, Colo.: Westview Press); William T. Liu, Maryanne Mamanna, and Alice Murata (1979), *Transition to Nowhere: Vietnamese Refugees in America* (Nashville, Tenn.: Charter House Publishers, Inc.); Frank Snepp (1978), *Decent Interval: An Insider's Account of Saigon's Indecent End Told by the CIA's Chief Strategy Analyst in Vietnam* (New York: Vintage).

15. On Vietnam's postwar political and economic reforms, see William Duiker (1995), *Vietnam: Revolution in Transition,* 2nd ed. (Boulder, Colo.: Westview Press). A refugee's critical account of the early years of these reforms is found in Nguyen Long with Harry Kendall (1981), *After Saigon Fell: Daily Life under the Vietnamese Communists* (Berkeley: University of California Press). On malnutrition, see [Socialist Republic of Vietnam] (1992), *National Report on Two Years' Implementation of the United Nations Convention on the Rights of the Child* (Hanoi: Committee for the Protection and Care of Children), 42.

16. For accounts of the boat people between 1975 and 1981, see Bruce Grant and Age Contributors (1979), *The Boat People: An 'Age' Investigation* (Harmondsworth, Middlesex: Penguin Books); and Barry Wain (1981), *The Refused: The Agony of the Indochinese Refugees* (New York: Simon and Schuster).

17. Coverage of the exodus of ethnic Chinese from Vietnam is found in K. Das and Guy Sacerdoti (1978), "The Economics of a Human Cargo" and "Digging in for a Long Stay," *Far Eastern Economic Review* 101, no. 45: 10–12; Peter Weintraub (1978), "The Exodus and the Agony," *Far Eastern Economic Review* 102, no. 51: 8–11; John K. Whitmore (1985), "Chinese from Southeast Asia," in *Refugees in the United States,* ed. David W. Haines (Westport, Conn.: Greenwood Press), 59–76; and Wain (1981: 15–35). The story of the voyage of fishing boat PK 504, which made the 5,000–mile voyage, is also found in Wain (1981). An ethnic Chinese refugee describes how be was coerced to leave Vietnam in Freeman (1989:409–410).

18. Freeman (1989: 339–40) tells the story of a man imprisoned for trying to escape from Vietnam. For estimates on the loss of life among people fleeing Vietnam, see Michael Richardson (1979), "How Many Died?" *Far Eastern Economic Review* 106, no. 43 (October 26): 34. See also Ruben Rumbaut (1995), "Vietnamese, Laotian, and Cambodian Americans," in *Asian Americans: Contemporary Issues and Trends,* ed. Pyong Gap Min (Thousand Oaks, Calif.: Sage Publications), 232–270; the figures are mentioned on p. 238.

19. The pirate attacks are described in K. Das (1978), "The Tragedy of the KG 0729," *Far Eastern Economic Review* 101, no. 45 (December 22): 13; Freeman (1989: 325–335); and Nhat Tien, Duong Phuc, and Vu Thanh Thuy (1981), *Pirates on the*

Gulf of Siam: Report from the Vietnamese Boat People Living in the Refugee Camp in Songkhla, Thailand (San Diego, Calif.: Boat People S.O.S. Committee). See also Grant and Age Contributors (1979) and Wain (1981).

20. See Freeman (1989: 320–335).

21. Life in the camps is described by Das and Sacerdoti (1978:10–11); Grant (1979: 75–76); and Freeman (1989: 319).

22. United Nations High Commissioner for Refugees (2001: 92, 93, 95–97).

23. The Philippines ratified the Convention Relating to the Status of Refugees in July 1981. On the principle of non-return, see Wain (1981: 31–32); and Muntarbhorn (1992: 31, 83, 163–191).

24. See Freeman (1989) and Wain (1981).

25. On the U.S. Refugee Act of 1980, see Edward M. Kennedy (1981), "Refugee Act of 1980," *International Migration Review* 15, no. 1 (spring): 141–156.

26. For further information on ODP, see James M. Freeman (1995), *Changing Identities: Vietnamese Americans 1975–1995* (Boston: Allyn and Bacon), 34–36; and Zolberg, Suhrke, and Aguayo (1989: 167). On delays in allowing people to emigrate, see also Mary Lee (1979), "Long Wait for the Promised Land," *Far Eastern Economic Review* 106, no. 45: 30.

27. Robinson (1998: 273). He quotes from United Nations High Commissioner for Refugees (1994b), "Resettlement in the 1990s: A Review of Policy and Practice: Evaluation Summary Prepared by the Inspection and Evaluation Service for the Formal Consultations on Resettlement, October 12–14," p. 1.

28. The Comprehensive Plan of Action is reprinted in Muntarbhorn (1992), Appendix III. Appendices I and II present the 1951 Convention Relating to the Status of Refugees and the 1967 Protocol Relating to the Status of Refugees; see also his discussion of the significance of the CPA on p. 50. Other documents focus specifically on unaccompanied minors. These include: United Nations High Commissioner for Refugees (1991a), "The Comprehensive Plan of Action: Guidelines for Implementation of the Special Procedures" (August 20); United Nations High Commissioner for Refugees (1991b), "Note on the Technical Meeting Between UNHCR and NGOs on Refugee Status Determination and Special Procedures Under the Comprehensive Plan of Action (Document 6)" (September 5); United Nations High Commissioner for Refugees (1991c), "Note on the Technical Meeting of Steering Committee of the International Conference on Indochinese Refugees, Jakarta, September 12–13"; and United Nations (1989), "Convention on the Rights of the Child," adopted November 20, 1989, G.A. res. 44/25, annex, 44 U.N. GAOR Supp. (No. 49) at 167, U.N. Doc. A/44/49 (1989), entered into force Sept. 2, 1990. Critical evaluations both of UNHCR guidelines for the treatment

of refugee children and more specifically of the impact of the CPA on unaccompanied minors seeking asylum include: United States Department of State (1991), "UNHCR Guidelines on Refugee Children: A Survey of their Implementation after Three Years," Bureau for Refugee Programs, Washington, D.C. (September); Carole McDonald (n.d.), "Unaccompanied Minors in Camps in South-East Asia," n.p.; Shepard C. Lowman (1991), "The Comprehensive Plan of Action: Trip Report," Refugees International, Washington, D.C. (April); Indochina Resource Action Center (1989), "Review of the Comprehensive Plan of Action and Recommendations for Effective Implementation" (paper submitted to the Steering Committee of the International Conference on Indochinese Refugees at their meeting in Geneva, October 16–17); Dawn Calabia (1991), "Checklist for UNHCR Consideration of Unaccompanied Minors," Migration and Refugee Services, U.S. Catholic Conference, Washington, D.C. (August 15). The most detailed critique of the CPA is Alan Nichols and Paul White (1993), *Refugee Dilemmas: Reviewing the Comprehensive Plan of Action for Vietnamese Asylum Seekers* (Manila: LAWASIA Human Rights Committee, Ateneo de Manila University), and much of our discussion in this section is drawn from their book.

29. See Goodwin-Gill (1983:11) for problems that arose regarding the right to return to Vietnam. Attorney Janelle M. Diller quotes three articles of the Criminal Code of the Socialist Republic of Vietnam that deal with illegal departure; see Janelle M. Diller (1988), *In Search of Asylum: Vietnamese Boat People in Hong Kong* (Washington, D.C.: Indochina Resource Action Center), 58. On the imprisonment of people attempting to flee Vietnam, see Freeman (1989: 339–340) and Wain (1981: 46).

30. United Nations High Commissioner for Refugees (2001: 82, 84–85, 88–89, 98).

31. See United Nations High Commissioner for Refugees (1993a), one-page statement distributed in Hong Kong to nongovernmental organizations and government agencies, including the U.S. Consulate.

32. Some of the improvements as well as economic challenges facing Vietnam are described in Mya Than and Joseph L. H. Tan, eds. (1993), *Vietnam's Dilemmas and Options* (Singapore: ASEAN Economic Research Unit, Institute of Southeast Asian Studies). See also Nicholas Nugent (1996), *Vietnam: The Second Revolution* (Brighton, U.K.: In Print).

33. Robinson (1998: 221).

34. See Center for Assistance to Displaced Persons and the Department of Social Welfare and Development, The Philippines (1996), "Memorandum of Understanding Made and Entered Into by the Department of Social Welfare and Development and the Center for Assistance to Displaced Persons, Inc." (reprinted in *ACWP Newsletter: Special Issue: The Philippines Miracle* 9 (summer-fall 1996):

7–11); *San Jose Mercury News* (1996b), "Philippines Decides Vietnamese Refugees Can Stay," July 14, section A, p. 16 (reprint from the *Los Angeles Times,* n.d.); Carolyn Jung (1996), "Viet Community Unites to Aid Refugees," *San Jose Mercury News,* August 15, section B, pp. 1, 4; Lily Dizon (1996), "Philippines Let Vietnamese Stay Permanently," *Los Angeles Times,* July 14, n.p.

35. See *San Jose Mercury News* (1996c), "Philippines Reportedly To Return Boat People," February 27, section A, p. 3; and Center for Assistance to Displaced Persons (1997a), "Viet Village Status Report," Center for Assistance to Displaced Persons, Manila (August 15).

36. In 2000, Hong Kong allowed about 1,400 Vietnamese to remain in Hong Kong. This is not comparable to the action of the Philippines. The Vietnamese in Hong Kong were children who had been born there or people classified as refugees who, because of drug-related problems or criminal records, were rejected for resettlement by third countries. Since they were refugees, Vietnam would not receive them back; they were the responsibility of UNHCR. Vietnam also refused to accept several hundred ethnic Chinese because Vietnam had no record of their residence there; resettlement countries where their families had gone would not take them. Hong Kong allowed these "stateless" people to apply for Hong Kong identification cards. Since 1979, Hong Kong had taken care of 210,000 boat people. Hong Kong requested that UNHCR reimburse them 150 million U.S. dollars for taking on this "heavy responsibility"; see *Thoi Bao* (San Jose, Calif.) (2000). As indicated in connection with Chapter 1, note 5, in June 2000 Hong Kong closed Pillar Point Camp and the inhabitants were allowed to remain in Hong Kong.

37. W. Courtland Robinson (1998: 282) claims that UNHCR was in favor of the Philippine solution. He writes, "It is no secret that UNHCR would like to see more countries in Asia follow the example of the Philippines." He quotes UNHCR official Francois Fouinat in a 1996 interview as saying, "We hope we have inculcated in these governments the norms and standards of status determination and the possibility of a normal presence for UNHCR." In light of the bitter conflicts between UNHCR and the Catholic-run Center for Assistance to Displaced Persons, which provided assistance for asylum seekers in Palawan and advocated for their protection and against their forcible repatriation, Robinson's conclusion is not credible to us. Neither is the UNHCR official's attempt to take credit for a solution they in fact had opposed.

38. Sister Pascale Le Thi Triu (2000), open letter (in Vietnamese), October 15.

39. United Nations High Commissioner for Refugees (2001: 94).

40. Ibid.

41. Robinson (1998: 214). Robinson's research was facilitated by UNHCR. While he is generally sympathetic to their position, he strongly criticizes Special Procedures.

CHAPTER TWO

1. On the Shek Kong riot, see *San Jose Mercury News* (1992), "18 Vietnamese Killed in Refugee Camp Riot," February 4, section A, p. 6; Ken McLaughlin, S. J. (1992), "Vietnamese Unsurprised by Riot: Hong Kong Deaths Laid to North-South Rivalry," *San Jose Mercury News,* February 5, section A, p. 5; Peter Johnson (1992), letter to the editor (by Director, Hong Kong Economic and Trade Office, San Francisco), *San Jose Mercury News,* February 28, section B, p. 6. Examples of a riot elsewhere are found in *San Jose Mercury News,* 1996a), "Boat People Riot in Malaysia as Deportation Nears," January 19, section A, p. 16. Kristin Huckshorn (1996) reports on other violence in "Detainees Report Beatings," *San Jose Mercury News,* February 16, section A, pp. 1, 10.

2. Laura A. Furcinitti (1993). "Humanity in Distress," *ARCWP Newsletter* 4, no. 4: 7–13. The incident is described on page 12.

3. See United Nations High Commissioner for Refugees (1988), "Guidelines on Refugee Children" (August); United Nations High Commissioner for Refugees (1991a), "The Comprehensive Plan of Action: Guidelines for Implementation of the Special Procedures" (August 20); United Nations High Commissioner for Refugees (1991b), "Note on the Technical Meeting Between UNHCR and NGOs on Refugee Status Determination and Special Procedures Under the Comprehensive Plan of Action" (Document 6)" (September 5); United Nations High Commissioner for Refugees (1994e), "Working with Unaccompanied Minors in the Community," Geneva; United Nations High Commissioner for Refugees (1994a), "Refugee Children: Guidelines on Protection and Care," Geneva; United Nations (1989), "Convention on the Rights of the Child," adopted November 20, 1989, G.A. res. 44/25, annex, 44 U.N. GAOR Supp. (No. 49) at 167, U.N. Doc. A/44/49 (1989), entered into force Sept. 2, 1990; and United Nations High Commissioner for Refugees (1990a), "Note on Unaccompanied Minors, Comprehensive Plan of Action." A general discussion of care and protection of unaccompanied minors is found in Everett M. Ressler, Neil Boothby, and Daniel J. Steinbeck (1988), *Unaccompanied Children: Care and Protection in Wars, Natural Disasters, and Refugee Movements* (New York: Oxford University Press).

4. John Chr. Knudsen (1992), *Chicken Wings: Refugee Stories from a Concrete Hell* (Bergen: Magnat Forlag), 27.

5. Heather Stroud (1999), *The Ghost Locust* (Hong Kong: Asia 2000 Limited).

6. Diana Bui (1990), *Hong Kong: The Other Story: The Situation of Vietnamese Women and Children in Hong Kong's Detention Centres* (Washington, D.C.: Indochina Resource Action Center), 12.

7. Linda Hitchcox (1990), *Vietnamese Refugees in Southeast Asian Camps* (London: Macmillan/St. Antony's), 115–122, 137–146.

8. Susan Comerford, Victoria Lee Armour-Hileman, and Sharon Rose Walker (1991), *Defenseless in Detention: Vietnamese Children Living Amidst Increasing Violence in Hong Kong* (Kowloon, Hong Kong: Refugee Concern Hong Kong), 139.

9. Ibid., 140.

10. Ibid., 71–100. Other reports critical of the treatment of detainees in Hong Kong and elsewhere include: Lawyers Committee for Human Rights (1989a), "Inhumane Deterrence: The Treatment of Vietnamese Boat People in Hong Kong," New York; Nguyen Dinh Huu and James M. Freeman (1992), "Disrupted Childhood: Unaccompanied Minors in Southeast Asian Refugee Camps: Summary of Fact-Finding Trip to Hong Kong, Philippines, Thailand, Malaysia, Singapore, Indonesia," Aid to Refugee Children Without Parents, Inc., San Jose, Calif.

11. Sister Carole McDonald RSM (1992), "Children *Still* Seeking Asylum," *The Mustard Seed* n.v.: 9–11; [Jesuit Brother] ([1990]), letter from Petaling Jaya, Malaysia, to Nguyen Dinh Huu.

12. Michael Bociurkiw (1993), "Terrorized in the Camp of Shame," *South China Morning Post,* June 6, Spectrum section, p. 4. Statistics on the numbers of asylum seekers in Galang about two months before we visited the camp are found in United Nations High Commissioner for Refugees (1991d), "Operations Profile in Respect of Refugees and Asylum Seekers in Indonesia" (September 30).

13. The Thai-Cambodian border camps are described in Amara Pongsapich and Noppawan Chongwatana (1988), "The Refugee Situation in Thailand," in *Indochinese Refugees: Asylum and Resettlement,* eds. Supang Chantavanich and E. Bruce Reynolds (Bangkok: Institute of Asian Studies, Chulalongkorn University), 12–47; and Eva Mysliwiec (1988), *Punishing the Poor: The International Isolation of Kampuchea* (Oxford: Oxfam); see Chapter 6, "The Thai-Kampuchean Border," pp. 93–112, especially, 106–107. The *Bangkok Post* (May 10, 1990) reports that Thai guards raped, beat, and degraded Vietnamese boat people in holding camps before sending them to detention camps. An Australian volunteer who worked at Site 2 between 1985 and 1986, and who visited the area again in 1988, was an eyewitness to numerous atrocities and abuses, especially to Khmer but also to Vietnamese asylum seekers in the camp. He describes them in his unpublished diaries, as well as in his interview with Freeman in Melbourne in January 1997.

14. See W. Courtland Robinson (1998), *Terms of Refuge: The Indochinese Exodus and the International Response* (New York: Zed), 95–96; Committee for Co-ordination of Services to Displaced Persons in Thailand (1983), *The CCSDPT Handbook: Refugee Services in Thailand* (Bangkok: CCSDPT), 9, 47. A more critical assessment of these events is found in James M. Freeman and Huu Dinh Nguyen (1992), "The Terror and Tragedy of Dong Rek," *San Jose Mercury News,* September 6, Perspective section, pp. 1, 3.

15. Lawyers Committee for Human Rights (1989b), "Refuge Denied: Problems in the Protection of Vietnamese and Cambodians in Thailand and the Admission of Indochinese into the United States," New York, 38–40, 92–94.

16. The mistreatment of detainees in Sikhiu is described in James M. Freeman (1989), *Hearts of Sorrow: Vietnamese-American Lives* (Stanford: Stanford University Press), 345–348. The information also comes from the Australian volunteer mentioned in Chapter 2, note 13. The *Bangkok Post* (May 10, 1990) reported claims of rapes and beatings in another camp. UNHCR had been denied full access to the camp. When informed of the situation, UNHCR immediately contacted the provincial governor. Six volunteer guards were accused, but they were not taken into custody, and they fled.

17. On Vietnam's post-war political and economic reforms, see William J. Duiker (1995), *Vietnam: Revolution in Transition,* 2nd ed. (Boulder, Colo.: Westview Press). A refugee's critical account of the early years of these reforms is found in Nguyen Long with Harry Kendall (1981), *After Saigon Fell: Daily Life under the Vietnamese Communists* (Berkeley: University of California Press).

18. A concise discussion of traditional Vietnamese family values is found in Neil L. Jamieson (1993), *Understanding Vietnam* (Berkeley: University of California Press), 15–30. For a brief discussion of continuity and change in the family in Vietnam, see James M. Freeman (1995), *Changing Identities: Vietnamese Americans 1975–1995* (Boston: Allyn and Bacon), 87–94.

Chapter Three

1. Linda Hitchcox (1990), *Vietnamese Refugees in Southeast Asian Camps* (London: Macmillan/St. Antony's), 113.

2. See James M. Freeman (1989), *Hearts of Sorrow: Vietnamese-American Lives* (Stanford: Stanford University Press), 19–20, on the *Tale of Kieu.* See Neil L. Jamieson (1993), *Understanding Vietnam* (Berkeley: University of California Press), Chapter 1, for a discussion of the concept of fate in Vietnam. See Huynh Sanh Thong, trans. (1983), *The Tale of Kieu: A Bilingual Edition of Truyen Kieu by Nguyen Du* (New Haven: Yale University Press).

3. See the discussion in Jamieson (1993), Chapter 1, on traditional values.

Chapter Four

1. United Nations High Commissioner for Refugees (1994a), "Refugee Children: Guidelines on Protection and Care," Geneva, 99–101; United Nations High Commissioner for Refugees (1994e), "Working with Unaccompanied Minors in the Community," Geneva, 23–54, 69–80; Jan Williamson and Audrey Moser (1988),

Unaccompanied Children in Emergencies: A Field Guide for Their Care and Protection (Geneva: International Social Service).

2. Margaret McCallin (1992), *Living in Detention: A Review of the Psychosocial Well-Being of Vietnamese Children in the Hong Kong Detention Centres* (Geneva: International Catholic Child Bureau), 2; see also page 15.

3. Ibid., 6–7.

4. Ibid., 17–20.

5. Ibid., 16.

6. Ibid., 2.

7. Guus van der Veer (1992), *Counseling and Therapy with Refugees: Psychological Problems of Victims of War, Torture, and Repression* (New York: John Wiley & Sons), 203–207.

8. Ibid., 218–222.

CHAPTER FIVE

1. See Janelle M. Diller (1988), *In Search of Asylum: Vietnamese Boat People in Hong Kong* (Washington, D.C.: Indochina Resource Action Center); Lawyers Committee for Human Rights (1989a), "Inhumane Deterrence: The Treatment of Vietnamese Boat People in Hong Kong," New York; Leonard Davis (1991), *Hong Kong and the Asylum-Seekers from Vietnam* (New York: St. Martin's Press), especially the chapter on screening, pp. 17–47; John Chr. Knudsen (1992), *Chicken Wings: Refugee Stories from a Concrete Hell* (Bergen: Magnat Forlag); Anne Wagley Gow (1991), "Protection of Vietnamese Asylum Seekers in Hong Kong: Detention, Screening and Repatriation" (working paper submitted to the United Nations Economic and Social Council, Commission on Human Rights), Human Rights Advocates, Berkeley, Calif.; and dozens of articles and editorials from the *South China Morning Post.*

2. See [Hong Kong Government] (1994a), "Arrivals and Departures: Monthly Statistical Report"; (1994b), "Executive Summary"; (1994c), "Hong Kong's Centers for Vietnamese Refugees and Migrants"; (1994d), "Status Determination Procedures"; (1994e), "Vietnamese Migrants in Hong Kong: Monthly Fact Sheet"; (1994f), "Vietnamese Migrants in Hong Kong: What the Hong Kong Government Has Done," all n.p., June.

3. See Vitit Muntarbhorn (1992), *The Status of Refugees in Asia* (New York: Clarendon Press), 52–54. On criticism of the Special Procedures for unaccompanied minors in Hong Kong, see Refugee Concern Hong Kong (1991a), "Position Paper on Unaccompanied Minors," January 8, 1991. Refugee Concern Hong Kong questioned how best interests can be served in the absence of clear guidelines for

recommendations of best interests, when cultural biases affected the interviews, when there was no appeals process, and when the Hong Kong government was strongly biased to send back the children. See also Maryanne Loughry and Ruth Esquillo (1994), *In Whose Best Interest?* (Bangkok: Jesuit Refugee Service). The UNHCR responses to the criticisms of their activities include United Nations High Commissioner for Refugees (1995a), "The Comprehensive Plan of Action: Information Bulletin," August; and United Nations High Commissioner for Refugees (1995b), "UNHCR Report on Alleged Corruption in the Refugee Status Determination in the Philippines," Washington, D.C., October.

4. See Diller (1988: 21–25, 31).

5. Ibid., 85–89.

6. Gow (1991: 24–29).

7. Quoted in Alan Nichols and Paul White (1993), *Refugee Dilemmas: Reviewing the Comprehensive Plan of Action for Vietnamese Asylum Seekers* (Manila: LAWA-SIA Human Rights Committee, Ateneo de Manila University), 54–55.

8. Gow (1991: 31).

9. Gow (1991:30–32). Mougne's quote is from Christine Mougne (1989), "Difficult Decisions," *Refugees* (UNHCR) (November): 37. On the case of Nguyen Ngoc Toan, see the following: *South China Morning Post* (1991), "Ruling in the 'Best Interests' of Boy," January 30, p. 6; Lindy Course (1991a), "Refugee Status Denied to Boy Despite Report," *South China Morning Post,* January 29, pp. 1, 4; Lindy Course (1991b), "Screening Out Boy 'Breach of Natural Justice,'" *South China Morning Post,* February 1, pp. 1–2; *South China Morning Post* (1990), "Viet Boy to Fight Status in 'Refugee' Test Case," December 11. See also Hong Kong Supreme Court (1991), "In the Supreme Court of Hong Kong High Court Miscellaneous Proceedings. In the matter of an application by Nguyen Ngoc Toan, a minor, by his next friend Nguyen Duyen Huu [*sic:* Nguyen Huu Duyen], and in the matter of Order 53 and an application for Judicial Review. Between Nguyen Ngoc Toan by his next friend Nguyen Duyen Huu [*sic:* Nguyen Huu Duyen], Applicant and Chan Leung Wai Ching, a Senior Immigration Officer, Respondant." M.P. No. 3759 of 1990, Coram J. Bokhary in Court; Date of Hearing: January 28–31, 1991; Date of delivery of Judgment: January 31, 1991.

10. See Hong Kong Supreme Court (1991), especially 4–5, 6, 12, 14.

11. The quote is from United Nations High Commissioner for Refugees (1995a: 6).

12. See Nichols and White (1993: 31).

13. See especially United Nations High Commissioner for Refugees (1995b). This 21–page document consists of a detailed point-by-point refutation of specific accusations made by a U.S. advocacy organization against Philippine officials and

UNHCR. UNHCR wrote that they found all of the accusations and claims to be baseless.

14. United Nations High Commissioner for Refugees (1995a: 6). UNHCR also presented their case in meetings with NGOs. See United Nations High Commissioner for Refugees (1992b), UNHCR Chairman of the CPA Steering Committee, Statement for the International Forum on the CPA, Washington, D.C., April 25.

15. See Rob Stewart (1994), "Corruption in Indonesia Discredits Screening," *Refugee Concern Newsmagazine,* no. 3 (September/October): 1–8; and Michael Bociurkiw (1993), "Terrorized in the Camp of Shame," *South China Morning Post,* June 6, Spectrum section, p. 4. The UNHCR response is contained in United Nations High Commissioner for Refugees (1995d), Rene van Rooyen, UNHCR Representative, open letter on alleged corruption, October 18. See also United Nations High Commissioner for Refugees (1995a) and United Nations High Commissioner for Refugees (1995b: 7).

16. See W. Courtland Robinson (1998), *Terms of Refuge: The Indochinese Exodus and the International Response* (New York: Zed), 207. He quotes from the U.S. General Accounting Office (1996), *Vietnamese Asylum Seekers: Refugee Screening Procedures Under the Comprehensive Plan of Action* (Washington, D.C.: General Accounting Office).

17. See *Philippine Star* (1991), "Immigration Officer to be Probed," October 28. The article refers to a complaint given to the Bureau of Immigration by UNHCR, concerning an immigration regulation officer's alleged extortion and sexual harassment of asylum seekers. The case was subsequently dropped for lack of evidence. As UNHCR writes, "it proved impossible for Philippine authorities to prosecute . . . due to the refusal of the asylum seekers to cooperate with the criminal investigation." See United Nations High Commissioner for Refugees (1995b: 5)

18. United Nations High Commissioner for Refugees (1995b: 13).

19. See United Nations High Commissioner for Refugees (1995b: 9–10, 16).

20. UNHCR responds that she "was known in the camp as a 'killer' interviewer since she was very particular about evaluating cases as credible. If she felt a person was not credible she would not hesitate to reject the case, even if strong elements were present." Her acceptance rate of 29 percent was much below the average in the Philippines of 43 percent. UNHCR neither accepted nor denied the allegation, since apparently there was insufficient supporting evidence, but they tilted their response in her favor by saying that it was possible that a corrupt Bureau of Immigration official would use her name, threatening to send a case to her unless a bribe was paid. In this way, she would be implicated. See United Nations High Commissioner for Refugees (1995b: 5).

21. He is referring to a 24–page pamphlet in English (22 pages in Vietnamese) distributed to asylum seekers in 1990: United Nations High Commissioner for Refugees (1990b), *Nhung dieu can biet cho nguoi lanh cu Viet Nam tai Trai PFAC (Information that Needs to be Known for Vietnamese Displaced Persons in PFAC)* (Manila: United Nations High Commissioner for Refugees). See footnote 32 in that publication for the reference to unaccompanied minors. According to UNHCR, "These pamphlets were distributed in the barracks during registration (within two weeks after arrival) and again before the prescreening." The major, however, had arrived and been prescreened before the pamphlet was written. See United Nations High Commissioner for Refugees (1995b: 10).

22. The major was interviewed twice, first in the Palawan First Asylum Camp, the Philippines, on December 26, 1991, and a second time in San Jose, California, on October 16, 1994. The text presented is based on quotations taken from these two interviews.

23. United Nations High Commissioner for Refugees (1995b: 10–11).

24. United Nations High Commissioner for Refugees (1992a), Senior Regional Social Services Officer, "Memo: Social Services Mission to the Philippines, 19–28 October, 1992," December 3. On resistance to repatriation, see Philip Shenon (1995a), "Boat People Prefer Death to Homeland," *New York Times,* March 6, 1995, section A, p. 1.

25. Center for Assistance to Displaced Persons (1997b), *1997 Yearly Activity Report: The Remaining Boat People in the Philippines, Particularly the Viet Village, Puerta Princesa City, Palawan* (Manila: Center for Assistance to Displaced Persons), 1.

26. The pamphlet distributed to unaccompanied minors is United Nations High Commissioner for Refugees (n.d.-b), *Tin tuc co ban cho tre em duoi tuoi vi thanh nien va nhung ca nhan thuoc dien nhan dao dac biet (Basic Information for Minors and Individuals Who Fall into Special Humanitarian Categories).*

CHAPTER SIX

1. The UNHCR advocacy of repatriation is seen in many publications and documents. UNHCR official Christine Mougne writes, "Inevitably there has been some fierce opposition to the idea of returning children to their parents in Viet Nam. Some of the opposition has come from the parents themselves. . . . Despite such protests, recommendations for family reunion in Viet Nam have now been made in well over a hundred cases." Christine Mougne (1990), "The Tide is Turning," *Refugees* (UNHCR) (December): 25. For a more general discussion of issues of repatriation and resettlement, see *Journal of International Affairs* 47, no. 2 (winter 1994), especially the articles by Dennis Gallagher (1994), "Durable Solutions in a New Political Era," 429–450; Charles B. Keely and Sharon Stanton Russell (1994),

"Responses of Industrial Countries to Asylum-Seekers," 399–417; and the interview in the same journal with Sadako Ogata (1994), the United Nations High Commissioner for Refugees, 419–428.

2. Nordic Assistance to Repatriated Vietnamese (n.d.), *Tro ve khong co nghia la tat ca da het ma do moi chi la bat dau (Returning Home is Not the End of Everything But is Only the Beginning)*.

3. Nguyen Dinh Bin (1992), "For a Good Solution to the Question of Unaccompanied Children," *Science Information Review* (The National Institute for Educational Science in Vietnam, Hanoi), no. 38: 19–21 (Vietnamese and English).

4. Christine Mougne (1993), "A Childhood Held in Suspense," *Science Information Review* (The National Institute for Educational Science in Vietnam, Hanoi), no. 38: 22–27 (Vietnamese and English).

5. Jon Liden (1993), "A Childhood Crushed in the Detention Centers," *Science Information Review* (The National Institute for Educational Science in Vietnam, Hanoi), no. 38: 28–32 (Vietnamese and English).

6. Nguyen Dinh Huu and James M. Freeman (1993), "Nowhere to Return: The Crisis of Repatriated Unaccompanied Minors without Parents: Summary Report of the ARCWP Fact-Finding Team on the Situation of Repatriated Unaccompanied Minors in Vietnam," Aid to Refugee Children Without Parents, Inc., San Jose, Calif., July, pp. 1–5.

7. Nguyen and Freeman (1993). See also Beryl Cook (1993), "Homeless Viet Children Spark Refugee Inquiry," *South China Morning Post,* August 30.

8. Nguyen Dinh Huu and James M. Freeman (1994), "Without a Trace: The Repatriation of Vietnamese Unaccompanied Minors, 1994: The 1994 Summary Report of the ARCWP Fact-Finding Team on the Situation of Repatriated Unaccompanied Minors in Vietnam," Aid To Refugee Children Without Parents, San Jose, Calif.; James M. Freeman and Nguyen Dinh Huu (1996), "Repatriated to Vietnam: Children Without Parents," *Practicing Anthropology* 18, no. 1: 28–32. For another assessment of repatriation, see Interaction (1995), "NGO Mission to Vietnam and First Asylum Countries in Southeast Asia, November 26–December 16, 1994," American Council for Voluntary International Action, January 12.

9. See United Nations High Commissioner for Refugees (1993a), "Operation Family Reunion," one-page statement distributed in Hong Kong to nongovernmental organizations and government agencies, including the U.S. Consulate.

10. Refugee Concern Hong Kong, under the direction of Hong Kong attorney Pam Baker, publicized the situation of Ngo Van Ha and many other asylum seekers in *Refugee Concern Newsmagazine*. Because of their efforts and those of others, Ngo Van Ha's case was then taken up by the *South China Morning Post* of Hong

Kong, which ran several articles on Ha, while at the same time covering the repatriation of other asylum seekers. Some of the coverage includes: Steve Ball (1994), "Viet Boy Tries to Kill Himself," January 17, pp. 1–2; Scott McKenzie (1994c), "Viet Protesters End Sit-in," January 19, p. 3; Ruth Mathewson (1994), "U.S. Politician Joins Protest at Return of Boy Refugee," January 23, p. 3; Scott McKenzie (1994a), "Hearing Over Orphan Viet's Right to Review," February 8, p. 3; Scott McKenzie (1994b), "U.S. Dream Comes True for Viet Orphan," February 24, p. 3; *South China Morning Post* (1994), "Rule Book Not Always Right," editorial, February 25, p. 18; Lindy Course and Scott McKenzie (1994), "Orphan Ha Wins Temporary Reprieve," January 25, pp. 1, 8; and letters to the editor by prominent Hong Kong residents, including Chair of the Hong Kong Family Law Association Sharon A. Ser (1994), "Vietnamese Child's Interests Must Come First," January 22, p. 18; longtime wealthy benefactor of refugees Anne Marden (1994), "Vietnamese Orphan's Case Crucial," February 23, p. 20; and Legislative Councillor Elsie Tu (1994), "Viet Boy's Case a Disgrace," February 3, p. 14.

11. The NARV Consultant in Can Tho expressed her concerns formally in Nordic Assistance to Repatriated Vietnamese (1993), NARV Consultant, Can Tho, letter to Head, UNHCR Working Group, Ho Chi Minh City, June 28.

12. Nordic Assistance to Repatriated Vietnamese (1994c), Consultant, Ho Chi Minh City, "Report on the Three Children of Binh Thuan Province."

13. See Nordic Assistance to Repatriated Vietnamese (1995a), Irene Mortensen, UNAM Programme Director, "Final Report: Achievements of the NARV Programme, October 1992–April 1995," and earlier monthly status reports, e.g., Nordic Assistance to Repatriated Vietnamese (1994a), Irene Mortensen, UNAM Programme Director, "Monthly Programme Report, UNAM Programme," December.

14. United Nations High Commissioner for Refugees (1995a), "The Comprehensive Plan of Action: Information Bulletin," August, pp. 10–11.

15. World Bank in Vietnam (1999a), *Vietnam: Attacking Poverty,* The World Bank in Vietnam, Hanoi, December 14–15; World Bank in Vietnam (1999b), *Vietnam: Preparing for Take-off?* The World Bank in Vietnam, Hanoi, December 14–15.

16. United Nations High Commissioner for Refugees (1994d), Durable Solutions Counselor, Thailand, Letter of Request, Case #13, United Nations High Commissioner for Refugees, n.p., November 29.

17. [Cousin of the Three Children of Binh Thuan Province] (1993), letter to Nguyen Dinh Huu concerning their situation, Sikhiu Camp, Thailand, August 26.

18. Nguyen Dinh Huu (1993), Executive Director, ARCWP, two letters to the Director, Regional Bureau for Asia and Oceania, UNHCR, October 7 and December 4.

19. United Nations High Commissioner for Refugees (1993c), UNHCR Director, Regional Bureau for Asia and Oceania, letter to Huu Dinh Nguyen, Aid to Refugee Children Without Parents, December 20.

20. United Nations High Commissioner for Refugees (1993b), UNHCR Repatriation Officer, "Report," October 15, 1993.

21. Nordic Assistance to Repatriated Vietnamese (1994b), NARV Social Worker, "Monitoring Report," May 24; Nordic Assistance to Repatriated Vietnamese (1994c).

22. Joint Voluntary Agency, Bangkok (1994), letter from the Chief of Operations to the Regional Director, International Rescue Committee, San Jose, Calif., February 16.

23. United Nations High Commissioner for Refugees (1994c), UNHCR Head of Desk, Regional Bureau for Asia and Oceania, letter to ARCWP, April 20.

24. Nordic Assistance to Repatriated Vietnamese (1995c), NARV Field Worker, letter to Nguyen Dinh Huu, January 19.

25. See Sharon Stephens (1995), "Children and the Politics of Culture in Late Capitalism," in *Children and the Politics of Culture,* ed. Sharon Stephens (Princeton, N.J.: Princeton University Press), 3–48; see also Robert Borofsky, ed. (1994), *Assessing Cultural Anthropology* (New York: McGraw Hill), especially the articles by Roger Keesing (1994), "Theories of Culture Revisited," 301–310; and Andrew P. Vayda (1994), "Actions, Variations, and Change: The Emerging Anti-Essentialist View in Anthropology," 320–329.

26. United Nations High Commissioner for Refugees (1995c), "Sixth Meeting of the Steering Committee of the International Conference on Indochinese Refugees, March 16, 1995"; *San Jose Mercury News* (1995a), "End of a Dream: U.N. Tells Boat People to Give Up Hope of Asylum: Decision Affects 50,000 Indochinese," March 17, section A, pp. 1, 26.; *San Jose Mercury News* (1995b), "Invitation to a Flood: U.S. Should Stick to International Agreement on Refugees" (editorial), May 24., section B, p. 8 (supporting the Steering Committee decision and criticizing a proposal by U.S. Rep. Christopher Smith to bypass it); Nordic Assistance to Repatriated Vietnamese (1994a).

27. Ruth Marshall (1995), "Final Act: Closing Down the CPA," *Refugees* 1: 9–14; the quotes are on pp. 10, 11. See also Philip Shenon (1995b), "U.N., U.S. Risk Bad-Guy Role by Forcing Boat People Back," *San Jose Mercury News,* April 8, section F, p. 4 (reprinted from *New York Times*).

28. Maryanne Loughry and Nguyen Xuan Nghia (1997), "The Reintegration of Unaccompanied Returnee Children (URC) in Thua Thien Hue Province" (unpublished paper for the Open University HCMC Women's Studies Department, Ho

Chi Minh City, December); quotes on pages 5, 29. For DELISA statistics on the number of returnees to Thua Thien Hue, see Department of Labor, War Invalids, and Social Affairs (1994), "Report on Returnee Receipt and Reintegration from 1989 to 1994," no. 243LTDBXH, Thua Thien Hue, April 9. The NARV report (based only on Hanoi sources, since the NARV offices had already closed) is found in Nordic Assistance to Repatriated Vietnamese (1995b), "Statistics on the Return of UNAMs [Unaccompanied Minors]," March 4.

29. Nguyen Thanh Ha (1994), "Life of a Repatriated Unaccompanied Minor," *ARCWP Newsletter* 7 (winter): 5–7.

30. Loughry and Nguyen (1997: 29).

31. Rachel Burr (2000), letter to James Freeman concerning repatriated unaccompanied minors, January 4.

CHAPTER SEVEN

1. Tran Minh Tung, M.D. (1980), *Indochinese Patients: Cultural Aspects of the Medical and Psychiatric Care of Indochinese Patients* (Washington, D.C.: Action for South East Asians, Inc.), 51–52.

2. William T. Liu, Maryanne Mamanna, and Alice Murata (1979), *Transition to Nowhere: Vietnamese Refugees in America* (Nashville, Tenn.: Charter House Publishers), 146–147.

3. Jim Dickey (1983), "Alone in a New Land," *San Jose News,* Wednesday, April 13.

4. Carol A. Mortland and Maura G. Egan (1987), "Vietnamese Youth in American Foster Care," *Social Work* (May–June): 240–245. The quote from the study by Walter and Cox is on page 241; see L. Walter and C. Cox (1979), "Resettlement in the United States of Unattached and Unaccompanied Indochinese Refugee Minors (1975–1978) by Lutheran Immigration and Refugee Services," *International Migration* 17: 139–171.

5. Mortland and Egan (1987: 243).

6. See Donald A. Ranard and Douglas A. Gilzow (1989), "The Amerasians," *America: Perspectives on Refugee Resettlement* (Refugee Service Center, Center for Applied Linguistics, Washington, D.C.), no. 4 (June): 3–4; Marilyn Lacey (1985), *In Our Father's Land: Vietnamese Amerasians in the United States* (Washington, D.C.: United States Catholic Conference), 6–16; Thomas A. Bass (1996), *Vietnamerica: The War Comes Home* (New York: Soho).

7. This youth's story is reported in Gail Fisher (1992), "Coming Home," *Los Angeles Times,* Thursday, November 26, section BB1 Orange County, Part Two, pp. 6–7. The writer uses American word order for the names of the children; we use the Vietnamese word order.

8. J. Kirk Felsman, Mark C. Johnson, Frederick T. L. Leuong, and Irene C. Felsman (1989), "Vietnamese Amerasians: Practical Implications of Current Research," Office of Refugee Resettlement, Family Support Administration, Department of Health and Human Services, Washington, D.C., 40–41.

9. See Anh Do (1992), "Abandoned Again," *Orange County Register,* June 9, pp. 1–2.

10. Felsman et al. (1989: 8).

11. Lacey (1985: 61–67).

12. See, for example, Nathan Caplan, John K. Whitmore, and Marcella H. Choy (1989), *The Boat People and Achievement in America: A Study of Family Life, Hard Work, and Cultural Values* (Ann Arbor: University of Michigan Press). See also their sequel, Nathan Caplan, Marcella H. Choy, and John K. Whitmore (1991), *Children of the Boat People: A Study of Educational Success* (Ann Arbor: University of Michigan Press). For a striking study of a Vietnamese parish in a suburb of New Orleans, see Min Zhou and Carl L. Bankston III (1994), "Social Capital and the Adaptation of the Second Generation: The Case of Vietnamese Youth in New Orleans," *International Migration Review* 28, no. 4 (winter): 821–845. See also their book (1998), *Growing Up American: How Vietnamese Children Adapt to Life in the United States* (New York: Russell Sage Foundation).

13. Not all Vietnamese are happy to be in America, particularly in the period of initial adjustments. In this chapter, Hoang and Hai expressed these views. See also James M. Freeman (1995), *Changing Identities: Vietnamese Americans 1975–1995* (Boston: Allyn and Bacon), 62–65.

Chapter Eight

1. Nancy Scheper-Hughes (1987), "The Cultural Politics of Child Survival," Introduction to *Child Survival: Anthropological Perspectives on the Treatment and Maltreatment of Children,* ed. Nancy Scheper-Hughes (Boston: D. Reidel Publishing Company), 19.

2. See especially Claire Monod Cassidy (1987), "World View, Conflict and Toddler Malnutrition: Change Agent Dilemmas," in *Child Survival: Anthropological Perspectives on the Treatment and Maltreatment of Children,* ed. Nancy Scheper-Hughes (Boston: D. Reidel Publishing Company), 293–324. Cassidy discusses the ways in which change agents cause or perpetuate conflict created more by their own "culture blocks" than those of their clients, and conflicts in the world views of different types of change agents.

3. Scheper-Hughes (1987: 20).

4. Scheper-Hughes (1987: 24). See also Scheper-Hughes and Howard F. Stein (1987), "Child Abuse and the Unconscious in American Popular Culture," in *Child Survival: Anthropological Perspectives on the Treatment and Maltreatment of Children,*

ed. Nancy Scheper-Hughes (Boston: D. Reidel Publishing Company), 339–358. This article calls attention to the lack of agreement on definitions of child abuse, neglect, child sexual exploitation, and the "best interests of the child." Scheper-Hughes and Stein claim that attention paid to individual child abusers in the United States and the rest of the world deflects attention away from "the complicity (and collective responsibility) in the implementation of local, national, and international policies that are placing our nation's and, indeed, the world's children at great risk" (341). Nancy Scheper-Hughes (1992) describes in detail the effects of extreme poverty on the treatment of children in *Death Without Weeping: The Violence of Everyday Life in Brazil* (Berkeley: University of California Press).

5. See Scheper-Hughes and Stein (1987: 352–353).

6. See Scheper-Hughes (1987: 10–11, 11–12).

7. See James M. Freeman (1989), *Hearts of Sorrow: Vietnamese-American Lives* (Stanford: Stanford University Press), 27–107; James M. Freeman (1995), *Changing Identities: Vietnamese Americans 1975–1995* (Boston: Allyn and Bacon), 88–92.

8. See Cassidy (1987: 299–300).

9. James M. Freeman and Huu Dinh Nguyen (1992), "The Terror and Tragedy of Dong Rek," *San Jose Mercury News,* September 6, Perspective section, pp. 1, 3; James M. Freeman and Huu Dinh Nguyen (1995), "Terror at Dong Rek," *Global Justice* 1, no. 3 (fall): 54–68.

10. United Nations High Commissioner for Refugees (1992c), Nguyen Dinh Huu et al., "UNHCR-Sponsored Fact-Finding Visit to Vietnam from 7–14 December, 1991."

11. United Nations High Commissioner for Refugees (1995e), UNHCR Chief of Mission, Hong Kong, letter to Nguyen Dinh Huu, July 11.

12. An example of the concerns of Vietnamese officials is seen in an article, *Vietnam Economic Times* (1997), "Tien vien tro cho Viet Nam bi lam dung va chi tieu sai lech (Foreign Aid for Vietnam Has Been Abused and Misused)," n.d.; reported in *Thoi Bao* (San Jose, Calif.), August 13.

CHAPTER NINE

1. See Lewis Aptekar (1988), *Street Children of Cali* (Durham, N.C.: Duke University Press); James Garbarino, Kathleen Kostelny, and Nancy Dubrow (1991), *No Place to Be a Child: Growing Up in a War Zone* (Lexington, Mass.: D.C. Heath and Company); Alex Kotlowitz (1991), *There are No Children Here: The Story of Two Boys Growing Up in the Other America* (New York: Doubleday); Jonathan Kozol (1995), *Amazing Grace: The Lives of Children and the Conscience of a Nation* (New York: Crown Books); Nancy Scheper-Hughes, ed. (1987), *Child Survival: Anthropological Perspectives on the Treatment and Maltreatment of Children* (Boston:

D. Reidel Publishing Company); and Sharon Stephens, ed. (1995), *Children and the Politics of Culture* (Princeton, N.J.: Princeton University Press). On child soldiers, see reports such as Neil Boothby, Abubacar Sultan, and Peter Upton (1991), "Children of Mozambique: The Cost of Survival," U.S. Committee for Refugees, Washington, D.C., November 1991; and Human Rights Watch/Africa and Human Rights Watch Children's Rights Project (1994), *The Lost Boys: Child Soldiers and Unaccompanied Minors in Southern Sudan* (New York: Human Rights Watch). An example of "social cleansing" of street youth is found in another Human Rights Watch Children's Rights Project publication, Human Rights Watch/Americas and Human Rights Watch Children's Rights Project (1994), *Generation Under Fire: Children and Violence in Colombia* (New York: Human Rights Watch). Human Rights Watch Children's Rights Project reports in another publication how guards physically abused children in confinement in Louisiana facilities. Discipline was administered in an arbitrary fashion. The children were improperly restrained by handcuffs. The guards often beat them with handcuffs, deprived them of sufficient food, and placed them in isolation cells for long periods of time. See Human Rights Watch Children's Rights Project (1995), *Children in Confinement in Louisiana* (New York: Human Rights Watch).

2. Garbarino, Kostelny, and Dubrow (1991: 150).

3. Ibid., 152–153, 154.

4. Nancy Scheper-Hughes (1987), "The Cultural Politics of Child Survival," Introduction to *Child Survival: Anthropological Perspectives on the Treatment and Maltreatment of Children,* ed. Nancy Scheper-Hughes (Boston: D. Reidel Publishing Company), 15, 16.

5. [Socialist Republic of Vietnam] (1992), *National Report on Two Years' Implementation of the United Nations Convention on the Rights of the Child* (Hanoi: Committee for the Protection and Care of Children), 4.

6. [Socialist Republic of Vietnam] (1992: 37). See also [Socialist Republic of Vietnam] (n.d.), "National Program of Action for Children 1991–2000: Summary."

7. Anuradha Vittachi (1989), *Stolen Childhood: In Search of the Rights of the Child* (Cambridge, U.K.: Polity Press), 1.

8. Vittachi (1989: 37).

9. See Scheper-Hughes (1987: 20–23).

10. Rachel Burr (1999), "A Discussion of the United Nations Convention on the Rights of the Child in the Context of Vietnam" (paper presented at the Annual meetings of the American Anthropological Association, Chicago, November).

11. D. Michael Hughes, "When Cultural Rights Conflict with the 'Best Interests of the Child': A View from Inside the Child Welfare System," in *Child Survival:*

Anthropological Perspectives on the Treatment and Maltreatment of Children, ed. Nancy Scheper-Hughes (Boston: D. Reidel Publishing Company), 377–387; quotes on pages 386–387.

12. James M. Freeman and Huu Dinh Nguyen (1992), "The Terror and Tragedy of Dong Rek," *San Jose Mercury News,* September 6, Perspective section, pp. 1, 3.

13. United Nations High Commissioner for Refugees (1993d), Robert Van Leeuwen, UNHCR Chief of Mission, Hong Kong, "Implementation of the Comprehensive Plan of Action in 1993/1994: Basic Framework for the Annual Review of Assistance Programs in Hong Kong," UNHCR, Kowloon, Hong Kong, March 15, pp. 1–2.

14. Don Handelman (1987), "Bureaucracy and the Maltreatment of the Child: Interpretive and Structural Implications," in *Child Survival: Anthropological Perspectives on the Treatment and Maltreatment of Children,* ed. Nancy Scheper-Hughes (Boston: D. Reidel Publishing Company), 359–376; quote on page 373.

15. Neil Boothby (1992), "Displaced Children: Psychological Theory and Practice from the Field," *Journal of Refugee Studies* 5, no. 2:119, 120.

References

Agret, Philippe. 2001. Vietnamese Boat People Saga Ends with Departure of Handful of Refugees. Agence France Presse via NewsEdge Corporation, dateline Bangkok, Thursday, February 8. Reprint UNHCR Refugee NewsNet: Vietnam, available from World Wide Web: (http://www.unhcr.ch/cgi-bin/texis/vtx/home?page=news).

Aptekar, Lewis. 1988. *Street Children of Cali.* Durham, N.C.: Duke University Press.

Ball, Steve. 1994. Viet Boy Tries to Kill Himself. *South China Morning Post,* January 17, pp. 1–2.

Bangkok Post. 1990. Article on abuse of Vietnamese boat people by Thai Guards. May 10, n.p.

Bass, Thomas A. 1996. *Vietnamerica: The War Comes Home.* New York: Soho.

Bociurkiw, Michael. 1993. Terrorized in the Camp of Shame. *South China Morning Post,* June 6, Spectrum section, p. 4.

Boothby, Neil. 1992. Displaced Children: Psychological Theory and Practice from the Field. *Journal of Refugee Studies* 5, no. 2: 106–122.

Boothby, Neil, Abubacar Sultan, and Peter Upton. 1991. Children of Mozambique: The Cost of Survival. U.S. Committee for Refugees, Washington, D.C., November.

Bui, Diana. 1990. *Hong Kong: The Other Story: The Situation of Women and Children in Hong Kong's Detention Centers.* Washington, D.C.: Indochina Resource Action Center.

Burr, Rachel. 1999. A Discussion of the United Nations Convention on the Rights of the Child in the Context of Vietnam. Paper presented at the Annual Meetings of the American Anthropological Association, Chicago, November.

———. 2000. Letter to James M. Freeman concerning repatriated unaccompanied minors, January 4.

Butler, David. 1985. *The Fall of Saigon.* New York: Simon and Schuster.

Calabia, Dawn. 1991. Checklist for UNHCR Consideration of Unaccompanied

Minors. Migration and Refugee Services, U.S. Catholic Conference, Washington, D.C., August 15.

Cali Today. 2000. Hong Kong truc xuat 148 nguoi Viet ti nan (Hong Kong Deports 148 Vietnamese Refugees). No. 276 (February 18): 1.

Caplan, Nathan, John K. Whitmore, and Marcella H. Choy. 1989. *The Boat People and Achievement in America: A Study of Family Life, Hard Work, and Cultural Values.* Ann Arbor: University of Michigan Press.

Caplan, Nathan, Marcella H. Choy, and John K. Whitmore. 1991. *Children of the Boat People: A Study of Educational Success.* Ann Arbor: University of Michigan Press.

Cassidy, Claire Monod. 1987. World View, Conflict and Toddler Malnutrition: Change Agent Dilemmas. In *Child Survival: Anthropological Perspectives on the Treatment and Maltreatment of Children,* ed. Nancy Scheper-Hughes, 293–324. Boston: D. Reidel Publishing Company.

Center for Assistance to Displaced Persons. 1997a. Viet Village Status Report. Center for Assistance to Displaced Persons, Manila, August 15.

———. 1997b. *1997 Yearly Activity Report: The Remaining Boat People in the Philippines, Particularly the Viet Village, Puerta Princesa City, Palawan.* Manila: Center for Assistance to Displaced Persons.

———. 1999. *Summary Report on the Remaining Vietnamese Nationals.* Manila: Center for Assistance to Displaced Persons.

Center for Assistance to Displaced Persons and the Department of Social Welfare and Development, The Philippines. 1996. Memorandum of Understanding Made and Entered Into by the Department of Social Welfare and Development and the Center for Assistance to Displaced Persons, Inc. Reprint *ACWP Newsletter: Special Issue: The Philippines Miracle* 9 (summer-fall 1996): 7–11.

Comerford, Susan, Victoria Lee Armour-Hileman, and Sharon Rose Walker. 1991. *Defenseless in Detention: Vietnamese Children Living Amidst Increasing Violence in Hong Kong.* Kowloon, Hong Kong: Refugee Concern Hong Kong.

Committee for Co-ordination of Services to Displaced Persons in Thailand. 1983. *The CCSDPT Handbook: Refugee Services in Thailand.* Bangkok: CCSDPT.

Cook, Beryl. 1993. Homeless Viet Children Spark Refugee Inquiry. *South China Morning Post,* August 30, n.p.

Course, Lindy. 1991a. Refugee Status Denied to Boy Despite Report. *South China Morning Post,* January 29, pp. 1, 4.

———. 1991b. Screening Out Boy "Breach of Natural Justice." *South China Morning Post,* February 1, pp. 1–2.

Course, Lindy, and Scott McKenzie. 1994. Orphan Ha Wins Temporary Reprieve. *South China Morning Post,* February 25, pp. 1, 8.

[Cousin of the Three Children of Binh Thuan Province]. 1993. Letter to Nguyen Dinh Huu concerning their situation, Sikhiu Camp, Thailand, August 26.

Das, K. 1978. The Tragedy of the KG 0729. *Far Eastern Economic Review* 101, no. 45 (December 22): 13.

Das, K., and Guy Sacerdoti. 1978. The Economics of a Human Cargo *and* Digging in for a Long Stay. *Far Eastern Economic Review* 101, no. 45: 10–12.

Davis, Leonard. 1991. *Hong Kong and the Asylum-Seekers from Vietnam.* New York: St. Martins Press.

Department of Labor, War Invalids, and Social Affairs. 1994. Report on Returnee Receipt and Reintegration from 1989 to 1994, no. 243LTDBXH. Thua Thien Hue, April 9.

Dickey, Jim. 1983. Alone in a New Land. *San Jose News,* Wednesday, April 13.

Diller, Janelle M. 1988. *In Search of Asylum: Vietnamese Boat People in Hong Kong.* Washington, D.C.: Indochina Resource Action Center.

Dizon, Lily. 1996. Philippines Let Vietnamese Stay Permanently. *Los Angeles Times,* July 14, n.p.

Do, Anh. 1992. Abandoned Again. *Orange County Register,* June 9, pp. 1–2.

Duiker, William J. 1995. *Vietnam: Revolution in Transition,* 2nd ed. Boulder, Colo.: Westview Press.

Englemann, Larry. 1990. *Tears Before the Rain.* New York: Oxford University Press.

Felsman, J. Kirk, Mark C. Johnson, Frederick T. Leuong, and Irene C. Felsman. 1989. Vietnamese Amerasians: Practical Implications of Current Research. Office of Refugee Resettlement, Family Support Administration, Department of Health and Human Services, Washington, D.C., December.

Fisher, Gail. 1992. Coming Home. *Los Angeles Times,* Thursday, November 26, section BB1 Orange County, Part Two, pp. 6–7.

Freeman, James M. 1989. *Hearts of Sorrow: Vietnamese-American Lives.* Stanford: Stanford University Press.

———. 1995. *Changing Identities: Vietnamese Americans 1975–1995.* Boston: Allyn and Bacon.

Freeman, James M., and Huu Dinh Nguyen. 1992. The Terror and Tragedy of Dong Rek. *San Jose Mercury News,* September 6, Perspective section, pp. 1, 3.

———. 1995. Terror at Dong Rek. *Global Justice* 1, no. 3 (fall): 54–68.

———. 1996. Repatriated to Vietnam: Children Without Parents. *Practicing Anthropology* 18, no. 1: 28–32.

Freeman, James M., Huu Nguyen, and Peggy Hartsell. 1985. The Tribal Lao Training Project. *Cultural Survival Quarterly* 9, no. 2: 10–12.

Furcinitti, Laura A. 1993. Humanity in Distress. *ARCWP Newsletter* 4, no. 4: 7–13.

Gallagher, Dennis. 1994. Durable Solutions in a New Political Era. *Journal of International Affairs* 47, no. 2 (winter): 429–450.

Garbarino, James, Kathleen Kostelny, and Nancy Dubrow. 1991. *No Place to Be a Child: Growing Up in a War Zone.* Lexington, Mass.: D.C. Heath and Company.

Goodwin-Gill, Guy S. 1983. *The Refugee in International Law*. Oxford: Clarendon Press.

Gow, Anne Wagley. 1991. Protection of Asylum Seekers in Hong Kong: Detention, Screening and Repatriation. Working paper submitted to the United Nations Economic and Social Council, Commission on Human Rights. Human Rights Advocates, Berkeley, Calif.

Grant, Bruce, and Age Contributors. 1979. *The Boat People: An 'Age' Investigation*. Harmondsworth, Middlesex: Penguin Books.

Handelman, Don. 1987. Bureaucracy and the Maltreatment of the Child: Interpretive and Structural Implications. In *Child Survival: Anthropological Perspectives on the Treatment and Maltreatment of Children*, ed. Nancy Scheper-Hughes, 359–376. Boston: D. Reidel Publishing Company.

Hitchcox, Linda. 1990. *Vietnamese Refugees in Southeast Asian Camps*. London: Macmillan/St. Antony's.

Holborn, Louise W. 1975. *Refugees: A Problem of Our Time: The Work of the United Nations High Commissioner for Refugees, 1951–1972*. 2 vols. Metuchen, N.J.: The Scarecrow Press.

[Hong Kong Government]. 1994a. Arrivals and Departures: Monthly Statistical Report. N.p., June.

———. 1994b. Executive Summary. N.p., June.

———. 1994c. Hong Kong's Centers for Vietnamese Refugees and Migrants. N.p., June.

———. 1994d. Status Determination Procedures. N.p., June.

———. 1994e. Vietnamese Migrants in Hong Kong: Monthly Fact Sheet. N.p., June.

———. 1994f. Vietnamese Migrants in Hong Kong: What the Hong Kong Government Has Done. N.p., June.

———. 1997. Vietnamese Migrants in Hong Kong: Special Administrative Region Fact Sheet no. 15. N.p., July.

Hong Kong Supreme Court. 1991. In the Supreme Court of Hong Kong High Court Miscellaneous Proceedings. In the matter of an application by Nguyen Ngoc Toan, a minor, by his next friend Nguyen Duyen Huu [*sic:* Nguyen Huu Duyen], and in the matter of Order 53 and an application for Judicial Review. Between Nguyen Ngoc Toan by his next friend Nguyen Duyen Huu [*sic:* Nguyen Huu Duyen], Applicant and Chan Leung Wai Ching, a Senior Immigration Officer, Respondent. M.P. No. 3759 of 1990, Coram J. Bokhary in Court; Date of Hearing: January 28–31, 1991; Date of delivery of Judgment: January 31, 1991.

Huckshorn, Kristin. 1996. Detainees Report Beatings. *San Jose Mercury News*, February 16, section A, pp. 1, 10.

Hughes, D. Michael. 1987. When Cultural Rights Conflict with the "Best Interests of the Child": A View from Inside the Child Welfare System. In *Child Survival: Anthropological Perspectives on the Treatment and Maltreatment of Children,* ed. Nancy Scheper-Hughes, 377–387. Boston: D. Reidel Publishing Company.

Human Rights Watch/Africa and Human Rights Watch Children's Rights Project. 1994. *The Lost Boys: Child Soldiers and Unaccompanied Minors in Southern Sudan.* New York: Human Rights Watch.

Human Rights Watch/Americas and Human Rights Watch Children's Rights Project. 1994. *Generation under Fire: Children and Violence in Colombia.* New York: Human Rights Watch.

Human Rights Watch Children's Rights Project. 1995. *Children in Confinement in Louisiana.* New York: Human Rights Watch.

Huynh Sanh Thong, trans. 1983. *The Tale of Kieu: A Bilingual Edition of Truyen Kieu by Nguyen Du.* New Haven: Yale University Press.

Indochina Resource Action Center. 1989. Review of the Comprehensive Plan of Action and Recommendations for Effective Implementations. Paper submitted to the Steering Committee of the International Conference on Indochinese Refugees at their meeting in Geneva, October 16–17.

Interaction. 1995. NGO Mission to Vietnam and First Asylum Countries in Southeast Asia, November 26–December 16, 1994. American Council for Voluntary International Action, n.p., January 12.

Jamieson, Neil L. 1993. *Understanding Vietnam.* Berkeley: University of California Press.

[Jesuit Brother]. [1990]. Letter from Petaling Jaya, Malaysia, to Nguyen Dinh Huu.

Johnson, Peter. 1992. Letter to the editor (by Director, Hong Kong Economic and Trade Office, San Francisco). *San Jose Mercury News,* February 28, section B, p. 6.

Joint Voluntary Agency, Bangkok. 1994. Letter from the Chief of Operations to the Regional Director, International Rescue Committee, San Jose, Calif., February 16.

Jung, Carolyn. 1996. Viet Community Unites to Aid Refugees. *San Jose Mercury News,* August 15, section B, pp. 1, 4.

Karnow, Stanley. 1991. *Vietnam: A History,* rev. ed. New York: Viking.

Keely, Charles B., and Sharon Stanton Russell. 1994. Responses of Industrial Countries to Asylum Seekers. *Journal of International Affairs* 47, no. 2 (winter): 399–417.

Keesing, Roger. 1994. Theories of Culture Revisited. In *Assessing Cultural Anthropology,* ed. Robert Borofsky, 301–310. New York: McGraw Hill.

Kelly, Gail Paradise. 1977. *From Vietnam to America.* Boulder, Colo.: Westview Press.

Kennedy, Edward M. 1981. Refugee Act of 1980. *International Migration Review* 15, no. 1 (spring): 141–156.

Knudsen, John Chr. 1992. *Chicken Wings: Refugee Stories from a Concrete Hell.* Bergen: Magnat Forlag.

Kotlowitz, Alex. 1991. *There are No Children Here: The Story of Two Boys Growing Up in the Other America.* New York: Doubleday.

Kozol, Jonathan. 1995. *Amazing Grace: The Lives of Children and the Conscience of a Nation.* New York: Crown Books.

Lacey, Marilyn. 1985. *In Our Father's Land: Vietnamese Amerasians in the United States.* Washington, D.C.: United States Catholic Conference.

Laczo, Mona. 2000. Holding on to Hope. *Diakonia,* no. 51 (January): 7.

Lawyers Committee for Human Rights. 1989a. Inhumane Deterrence: The Treatment of Vietnamese Boat People in Hong Kong. Lawyers Committee for Human Rights, New York.

———. 1989b. Refuge Denied: Problems in the Protection of Vietnamese and Cambodians in Thailand and the Admission of Indochinese Refugees into the United States. Lawyers Committee for Human Rights, New York.

Lee, Mary. 1979. Long Wait for the Promised Land. *Far Eastern Economic Review* 106, no. 45: 30.

Liden, Jon. 1993. A Childhood Crushed in the Detention Centers. *Science Information Review* (The National Institute for Educational Science in Vietnam, Hanoi), no. 38: 28–32. In Vietnamese and English.

Liu, William T., Maryanne Mamanna, and Alice Murata. 1979. *Transition to Nowhere: Vietnamese Refugees in America.* Nashville, Tenn.: Charter House Publishers.

Loescher, Gil. 1993. *Beyond Charity: International Cooperation and the Global Refugee Crisis.* New York: Oxford University Press.

———. 1994. The International Refugee Regime. *Journal of International Affairs* 47, no. 2 (winter): 351–377.

Loughry, Maryanne, and Ruth Esquillo. 1994. *In Whose Best Interest?* Bangkok: Jesuit Refugee Service.

Loughry, Maryanne, and Nguyen Xuan Nghia. 1997. The Reintegration of Unaccompanied Returnee Children (URC) in Thua Thien Hue Province. Unpublished paper for the Open University HCMC Women's Studies Department, Ho Chi Minh City, December.

Lowman, Shepard C. 1991. The Comprehensive Plan of Action: Trip Report. Refugees International, Washington, D.C., April.

Marden, Anne. 1994. Vietnamese Orphan's Case Crucial (letter to the editor). *South China Morning Post,* February 23, p. 20.

Marshall, Ruth. 1995. Final Act: Closing Down the CPA. *Refugees* 1: 9–14.

Mathewson, Ruth. 1994. U.S. Politician Joins Protest at Return of Boy Refugee. *South China Morning Post,* January 23, p. 3.

McCallin, Margaret. 1992. *Living in Detention: A Review of the Psychosocial Well-Being of Vietnamese Children in the Hong Kong Detention Centres.* Geneva: International Catholic Child Bureau.

McDonald, Carole, RSM. 1992. Children *Still* Seeking Asylum. *The Mustard Seed* n.v., n.d.: 9–11.

———. n.d. Unaccompanied Minors in Camps in South-East Asia. N.p.

McKenzie, Scott. 1994a. Hearing Over Orphan Viet's Right to Review. *South China Morning Post,* February 8, p. 3.

———. 1994b. U.S. Dream Comes True for Viet Orphan. *South China Morning Post,* February 24, p. 3.

———. 1994c. Viet Protesters End Sit-in. *South China Morning Post,* January 19, p. 3.

McLaughlin, Ken, S. J. 1992. Vietnamese Unsurprised by Riot: Hong Kong Deaths Laid to North-South Rivalry. *San Jose Mercury News,* February 5, section A, p. 5.

McSpadden, Lucia Ann. 1999. Struggles to Secure Rights for Non-Citizens: Protection Endangered. Paper presented at the Meetings of the American Anthropological Association, Chicago, November.

Mortland, Carol A. and Maura G. Egan. 1987. Vietnamese Youth in American Foster Care. *Social Work* n.v. (May–June): 240–245.

Mougne, Christine. 1989. Difficult Decisions. *Refugees* (United Nations High Commissioner for Refugees, n.p.) n.v. (November): 37.

———. 1990. The Tide is Turning. *Refugees* (United Nations High Commissioner for Refugees, n.p.) n.v. (December): 25.

———. 1993. A Childhood Held in Suspense. *Science Information Review* (The National Institute for Educational Science of Vietnam, Hanoi), no. 38:22–27. In Vietnamese and English.

Muntarbhorn, Vitit. 1992. *The Status of Refugees in Asia.* New York: Clarendon Press.

Mya Than and Joseph L. H. Tan, eds. 1993. *Vietnam's Dilemmas and Options.* Singapore: ASEAN Economic Research Unit, Institute of Southeast Asian Studies.

Mysliwiec, Eva. 1988. *Punishing the Poor: The International Isolation of Kampuchea.* Oxford: Oxfam.

Nguyen Dinh Bin. 1992. For a Good Solution to the Question of Unaccompanied Children. *Science Information Review* (The National Institute for Educational Science in Vietnam, Hanoi), no. 38: 19–21. In Vietnamese and English.

Nguyen Dinh Huu. 1993. Executive Director, ARCWP. Two letters to the Director, Regional Bureau for Asia and Oceania, UNHCR, October 7 and December 4.

Nguyen Dinh Huu and James M. Freeman. 1992. Disrupted Childhood: Unaccompanied Minors in Southeast Asian Refugee Camps: Summary of Fact-Finding Trip to Hong Kong, Philippines, Thailand, Malaysia, Singapore, Indonesia. Aid to Refugee Children Without Parents, Inc., San Jose, Calif., n.d.

―――. 1993. Nowhere to Return: The Crisis of Repatriated Unaccompanied Minors Without Parents: Summary Report of the ARCWP Fact-Finding Team on the Situation of Repatriated Unaccompanied Minors in Vietnam. Aid to Refugee Children Without Parents, Inc., San Jose, Calif., July.

―――. 1994. Without a Trace: The Repatriation of Vietnamese Unaccompanied Minors, 1994: The 1994 Summary Report of the ARCWP Fact-Finding Team on the Situation of Repatriated Unaccompanied Minors in Vietnam. Aid to Refugee Children Without Parents, Inc., San Jose, Calif., n.d.

Nguyen Long with Harry Kendall. 1981. *After Saigon Fell: Daily Life under the Vietnamese Communists.* Berkeley: University of California Press.

Nguyen Thanh Ha. 1994. Life of a Repatriated Unaccompanied Minor. *ARCWP Newsletter* 7 (winter): 5–7.

Nhat Tien, Duong Phuc, and Vu Thanh Thuy. 1981. *Pirates on the Gulf of Siam: Report from the Vietnamese Boat People Living in the Refugee Camp in Songkhla, Thailand.* San Diego, Calif.: Boat People S.O.S. Committee.

Nichols, Alan, and Paul White. 1993. *Refugee Dilemmas: Reviewing the Comprehensive Plan of Action for Vietnamese Asylum Seekers.* Manila: LAWASIA Human Rights Committee, Ateneo de Manila University.

Nordic Assistance to Repatriated Vietnamese. 1993. NARV Consultant, Can Tho. Letter to Head, UNHCR Working Group, Ho Chi Minh City, June 28.

―――. 1994a. Irene Mortensen, UNAM Programme Director. Monthly Programme Report, UNAM Programme. Nordic Assistance to Repatriated Vietnamese, n.p., December.

―――. 1994b. NARV Social Worker. Monitoring Report. Nordic Assistance to Repatriated Vietnamese, n.p., May 24.

―――. 1994c. Consultant, Ho Chi Minh City. Report on the Three Children of Binh Thuan Province. Nordic Assistance to Repatriated Vietnamese, n.p., n.d.

―――. 1995a. Irene Mortensen, UNAM Programme Director. Final Report: Achievements of the NARV Programme, October 1992–April 1995. Nordic Assistance to Repatriated Vietnamese, n.p., n.d.

―――. 1995b. Statistics on the Return of UNAMs [Unaccompanied Minors]. Nordic Assistance to Repatriated Vietnamese, n.p., March 4.

―――. 1995c. NARV Field Worker. Letter to Nguyen Dinh Huu, January 19.

―――. n.d. *Tro ve khong co nghia la tat ca da het ma do moi chi la bat dau (Returning Home is Not the End of Everything But is Only the Beginning).* Nordic Assistance to Repatriated Vietnamese, n.p.

Nugent, Nicholas. 1996. *Vietnam: The Second Revolution.* Brighton, U.K.: In Print.

Ogata, Sadako. 1994. Interview with Sadako Ogata, the United Nations High Commissioner for Refugees. *Journal of International Affairs* 47, no. 2 (winter): 419–428.

Pascale Le Thi Triu, Sister. 2000. Open letter, October 15. In Vietnamese.

Philippine Star. 1991. Immigration Officer to be Probed. October 28.

Pongsapich, Amara, and Noppawan Chongwatana. 1988. The Refugee Situation in Thailand. In *Indochinese Refugees: Asylum and Resettlement,* eds. Supang Chantavanich and E. Bruce Reynolds, 12–47. Bangkok: Institute of Asian Studies, Chulalongkorn University.

Ranard, Donald A., and Douglas A. Gilzow. 1989. The Amerasians. *America: Perspectives on Refugee Resettlement* (Refugee Service Center, Center for Applied Linguistics, Washington, D.C.), no. 4 (June): 3–4.

Refugee Concern Hong Kong. 1991a. Position Paper on Unaccompanied Minors. Refugee Concern Hong Kong, Hong Kong, January 8.

Refugees Daily. 2000. Hong Kong: Vietnamese Protest as Camp Closes. Thursday, June 1. Reprint UNHCR Refugee NewsNet: Vietnam, available from World Wide Web: (http://www.unhcr.ch/cgi-bin/texis/vtx/home?page=news).

Ressler, Everett M., Neil Boothby, and Daniel J. Steinbock. 1988. *Unaccompanied Children: Care and Protection in Wars, Natural Disasters, and Refugee Movements.* New York: Oxford University Press.

Richardson, Michael. 1979. How Many Died? *Far Eastern Economic Review* 106, no. 43 (October 26): 34.

Robinson, W. Courtland. 1998. *Terms of Refuge: The Indochinese Exodus and the International Response.* New York: Zed.

Rumbaut, Ruben. 1995. Vietnamese, Laotian, and Cambodian Americans. In *Asian Americans: Contemporary Issues and Trends,* ed. Pyong Gap Min, 232–270. Thousand Oaks, Calif.: Sage Publications.

San Jose Mercury News. 1992. 18 Vietnamese Killed in Refugee Camp Riot. February 4, section A, p. 6.

———. 1995a. End of a Dream: U.N. Tells Boat People to Give Up Hope of Asylum: Decision Affects 50,000 Indochinese. March 17, section A, pp. 1, 26.

———. 1995b. Invitation to a Flood: U.S. Should Stick to International Agreement on Refugees (editorial). May 24, section B, p. 8.

———. 1996a. Boat People Riot in Malaysia as Deportation Nears. January 19, section A, p. 16.

———. 1996b. Philippines Decides Vietnamese Refugees Can Stay. July 14, section A, p. 16. Reprint from the *Los Angeles Times,* n.d.

———. 1996c. Philippines Reportedly To Return Boat People. February 27, section A, p. 3.

Scheper-Hughes, Nancy. 1987. The Cultural Politics of Child Survival. Introduction to *Child Survival: Anthropological Perspectives on the Treatment and Maltreatment of Children,* ed. Nancy Scheper-Hughes. Boston: D. Reidel Publishing Company.

———. 1992. *Death Without Weeping: The Violence of Everyday Life in Brazil.* Berkeley: University of California Press.

Scheper-Hughes, Nancy, ed. 1987. *Child Survival: Anthropological Perspectives on the Treatment and Maltreatment of Children.* Boston: D. Reidel Publishing Company.

Scheper-Hughes, Nancy, and Howard F. Stein. 1987. Child Abuse and the Unconscious in American Popular Culture. In *Child Survival: Anthropological Perspectives on the Treatment and Maltreatment of Children,* ed. Nancy Scheper-Hughes, 339–358. Boston: D. Reidel Publishing Company.

Ser, Sharon A. 1994. Vietnamese Child's Interests Must Come First (letter to the editor). *South China Morning Post,* January 22, p. 18.

Shenon, Philip. 1995a. Boat People Prefer Death to Homeland. *New York Times,* March 6, 1995, section A, p. 1.

———. 1995b. U.N., U.S. Risk Bad-Guy Role by Forcing Boat People Back. *San Jose Mercury News,* April 8, section F, p. 4. Reprinted from *New York Times,* n.d.

Snepp, Frank. 1978. *Decent Interval: An Insider's Account of Saigon's Indecent End Told by the CIA's Chief Strategy Analyst in Vietnam.* New York: Vintage.

[Socialist Republic of Vietnam]. 1992. *National Report on Two Years' Implementation of the United Nations Convention on the Rights of the Child.* Hanoi: Committee for the Protection and Care of Children.

———. n.d. National Program of Action for Children 1991–2000: Summary. N.p.

South China Morning Post. 1990. Viet Boy to Fight Status in "Refugee" Test Case. December 11.

———. 1991. Ruling in the "Best Interests" of Boy. January 30, p. 6.

———. 1994. Rule Book Not Always Right (editorial). February 25, p. 18.

Stephens, Sharon. 1995. Children and the Politics of Culture in Late Capitalism. In *Children and the Politics of Culture,* ed. Sharon Stephens, 3–48. Princeton, N.J.: Princeton University Press.

Stephens, Sharon, ed. 1995. *Children and the Politics of Culture.* Princeton, N.J.: Princeton University Press.

Stewart, Rob. 1994. Corruption in Indonesia Discredits Screening. *Refugee Concern Newsmagazine,* no. 3 (September/October): 1–8.

Stroud, Heather. 1999. *The Ghost Locust.* Hong Kong: Asia 2000 Ltd.

Thoi Bao (San Jose, Calif.). 2000. Hong Kong dong cua trai ty nan cuoi cung (Hong Kong Closes the Last Refugee Camp). No. 2725, February 23.

Tran Minh Tung, M.D. 1980. *Indochinese Patients: Cultural Aspects of the Medical and Psychiatric Care of Indochinese Patients.* Washington, D.C.: Action for South East Asians, Inc.

Tu, Elsie. 1994. Viet Boy's Case a Disgrace (letter to the editor). *South China Morning Post,* February 3, p. 14.

United Nations. 1989. Convention on the Rights of the Child, adopted November 20, 1989. G.A. res. 44/25, annex, 44 U.N. GAOR Supp. (No. 49) at 167, U.N. Doc. A/44/49 (1989), entered into force Sept. 2, 1990.

United Nations High Commissioner for Refugees. 1988. Guidelines on Refugee Children. United Nations High Commissioner for Refugees, n.p., August.

———. 1990a. Note on Unaccompanied Minors, Comprehensive Plan of Action. United Nations High Commissioner for Refugees, n.p., n.d.

———. 1990b. *Nhung dieu can biet cho nguoi lanh cu Viet Nam tai Trai PFAC (Information that Needs to be Known for Vietnamese Displaced Persons in PFAC)*. Manila: United Nations High Commissioner for Refugees, Branch Office.

———. 1991a. The Comprehensive Plan of Action: Guidelines for Implementation of the Special Procedures. United Nations High Commissioner for Refugees, n.p., August 20.

———. 1991b. Note on the Technical Meeting Between UNHCR and NGOs on Refugee Status Determination and Special Procedures Under the Comprehensive Plan of Action (Document 6). United Nations High Commissioner for Refugees, n.p., September 5.

———. 1991c. Note on the Technical Meeting of Steering Committee of the International Conference on Indochinese Refugees, Jakarta, September 12–13. United Nations High Commissioner for Refugees, n.p., n.d.

———. 1991d. Operations Profile in Respect of Refugees and Asylum Seekers in Indonesia. United Nations High Commissioner for Refugees, n.p., September 30.

———. 1992a. Senior Regional Social Services Officer. Memo: Social Services Mission to the Philippines, 19–28 October, 1992. United Nations High Commissioner for Refugees, n.p., December 3.

———. 1992b. UNHCR Chairman of the CPA Steering Committee. Statement for the International Forum on the CPA, Washington D.C., April 25.

———. 1992c. Nguyen Dinh Huu et al. UNHCR-Sponsored Fact-Finding Visit to Vietnam from 7–14 December, 1991. United Nations High Commissioner for Refugees, n.p., n.d.

———. [1993a]. Operation Family Reunion. One-page statement distributed in Hong Kong to nongovernmental organizations and government agencies, including the U.S. Consulate. United Nations High Commissioner for Refugees, Hong Kong, n.d.

———. 1993b. UNHCR Repatriation Officer. Report. United Nations High Commissioner for Refugees, n.p., October 15.

———. 1993c. UNHCR Director, Regional Bureau for Asia and Oceania. Letter to Huu Dinh Nguyen, Aid to Refugee Children Without Parents, December 20.

———. 1993d. Robert Van Leeuwen, UNHCR Chief of Mission, Hong Kong. Implementation of the Comprehensive Plan of Action in 1993/1994: Basic Framework for the Annual Review of Assistance Programs in Hong Kong. United Nations High Commissioner for Refugees, Kowloon, Hong Kong, March 15.

———. 1994a. Refugee Children: Guidelines on Protection and Care. United Nations High Commissioner for Refugees, Geneva, n.d.

———. 1994b. Resettlement in the 1990s: A Review of Policy and Practice: Evaluation Summary Prepared by the Inspection and Evaluation Service for the Formal Consultations on Resettlement, October 12–14. United Nations High Commissioner for Refugees, n.p., n.d.

———. 1994c. UNHCR Head of Desk, Regional Bureau for Asia and Oceania. Letter to ARCWP, April 20.

———. 1994d. Durable Solutions Counselor, Thailand. Letter of Request, Case #13. United Nations High Commissioner for Refugees, n.p., November 29.

———. 1994e. Working with Unaccompanied Minors in the Community. United Nations High Commissioner for Refugees, Geneva, n.d.

———. 1995a. The Comprehensive Plan of Action: Information Bulletin. United Nations High Commissioner for Refugees, n.p., August.

———. 1995b. UNHCR Report on Alleged Corruption in the Refugee Status Determination in the Philippines. United Nations High Commissioner for Refugees, Washington, D.C., October.

———. 1995c. Sixth Meeting of the Steering Committee of the International Conference on Indochinese Refugees, Geneva, March 16. United Nations High Commissioner for Refugees, n.p., n.d.

———. 1995d. Rene van Rooyen, UNHCR Representative. Open letter on alleged corruption. United Nations High Commissioner for Refugees, n.p., October 18.

———. 1995e. UNHCR Chief of Mission, Hong Kong. Letter to Nguyen Dinh Huu, July 11, 1995.

———. 2001. The State of the World's Refugees 2000: Fifty Years of Humanitarian Action. New York: Oxford University Press. Available from World Wide Web: (http://www.unhcr.ch/pubs/sowr2000/sowr2000toc.htm).

———. n.d.-a. Basic Facts. Available from World Wide Web: (http://www.unhcr.ch/cgi-bin/texis/vtx/home?page=basics).

———. n.d.-b. Tin tuc co ban cho tre em duoi tuoi vi thanh nien va nhung ca nhan thuoc dien nhan dao dac biet (Basic Information for Minors and Individuals Who Fall into Special Humanitarian Categories). United Nations High Commissioner for Refugees, n.p.

United States Department of State. 1991. UNHCR Guidelines on Refugee Children: A Survey of their Implementation After Three Years. Bureau for Refugee Programs, Washington, D.C., September.

U.S. Committee for Refugees. 1999. World Refugee Survey 1999. Washington, D.C.: U.S. Committee for Refugees.

van der Veer, Guus. 1992. Counseling and Therapy with Refugees: Psychological Problems of Victims of War, Torture, and Repression. New York: John Wiley & Sons.

Vayda, Andrew P. 1994. Actions, Variations, and Change: The Emerging Anti-Essentialist View in Anthropology. In *Assessing Cultural Anthropology,* ed. Robert Borofsky, 320–329. New York: McGraw Hill.

Vietnam Economic Times. 1997. Tien vien tro cho Viet Nam bi lam dung va chi tieu sai lech (Foreign Aid for Vietnam Has Been Abused and Misused). N.v., n.d. Reported in *Thoi Bao* (San Jose, Calif.), August 13, n.p.

Vittachi, Anuradha. 1989. *Stolen Childhood: In Search of the Rights of the Child.* Cambridge, U.K.: Polity Press.

Wain, Barry. 1981. *The Refused: The Agony of the Indochinese Refugees.* New York: Simon and Schuster.

Walter, L. and C. Cox. 1979. Resettlement in the United States of Unattached and Unaccompanied Indochinese Refugee Minors (1975–1978) by Lutheran Immigration and Refugee Services. *International Migration* 17: 139–171. Cited in Mortland and Egan 1987.

Weintraub, Peter. 1978. The Exodus and the Agony. *Far Eastern Economic Review* 102, no. 51: 8–11.

Whitmore, John. 1985. Chinese from Southeast Asia. In *Refugees in the United States,* ed. David W. Haines, 59–76. Westport, Conn.: Greenwood Press.

Williamson, Jan, and Audrey Moser. 1988. *Unaccompanied Children in Emergencies: A Field Guide for Their Care and Protection.* Geneva: International Social Service.

World Bank in Vietnam. 1999a. *Vietnam: Attacking Poverty.* Hanoi: The World Bank in Vietnam.

———. 1999b. *Vietnam: Preparing for Take-off?* Hanoi: The World Bank in Vietnam.

Zarjevski, Yefime. 1988. *A Future Preserved: International Assistance to Refugees.* Oxford: Pergamon Press.

Zhou, Min and Carl L. Bankston III. 1994. Social Capital and the Adaptation of the Second Generation: The Case of Vietnamese Youth in New Orleans. *International Migration Review* 28, no. 4 (winter): 821–845.

———. 1998. *Growing Up American: How Vietnamese Children Adapt to Life in the United States.* New York: Russell Sage Foundation.

Zolberg, Ariste R., Astri Suhrke, and Sergio Aguayo. 1989. *Escape from Violence: Conflict and the Refugee Crisis in the Developing World.* New York: Oxford University Press.

INTERVIEWS

Government and Agency Officials

Center for Assistance to Displaced Persons, the Philippines
Director, December 23, 1991
Staff, December 28, 1991

Community and Family Services International
Program Coordinator and Former Member of the Special Committee
for Unaccompanied Minors, December 20, 1991
Program Coordinator, June 10, 1993

Hong Kong Government
Chairman, Refugee Status Review Board, December 18, 1991
Refugees Coordinator, December 1, 1995
Deputy Head, Shek Kong Detention Centre, December 16, 1991

International Social Service, Hong Kong Branch
Director and staff, December 19, 1991; June 7, 1993; August 9, 1994

Jesuit Refugee Service
Director, Palawan Office, the Philippines, December 26, 1991
Director, Aranyaprathet Office, Thailand, for Site 2, January 3, 1992

Joint Voluntary Agency/U.S. Refugee Program
Director, Hong Kong Office, December 17, 1991; June 10, 1993

Nordic Assistance to Repatriated Vietnamese
Resident Representative and Programme Director, Hanoi, June 15, 1993;
August 15, 1994
Consultant, Can Tho, July 7, 1993
Consultant, Ho Chi Minh City, August 30, 1994
Staff, Ho Chi Minh City, July 3, 1993; August 30, 1994
Team Leader, Haiphong, August 19, 1994
Regional Manager and staff, Thua Thien Hue, August 22, 24, 1994

Red Crescent Society, Malaysia
Refugee Director, January 7, 1992

Refugee Concern Hong Kong
Director, June 10, 1993; August 11, 1994

Save the Children Fund, Hong Kong
Representative, June 10, 1993

Singapore Government
Camp Administrator, Hawkins Road Camp, January 8, 1992

Socialist Republic of Vietnam
Ambassador, Assistant Foreign Minister, and Director General, Institute for
International Relations, Hanoi, June 17, 1993; August 17, 1994
Deputy Director, Department of International Relations and Director,

Programmes of Protection for Displaced Children, Ministry of Labor, War Invalids, and Social Affairs (MOLISA), Hanoi, June 18, 1993; August 18, 1994

Professor and Director, Institute of Sociology, Hanoi, June 17, 1993

Programme Coordinator, People's Aid Coordination Committee (PACCOM), Hanoi, June 18, 1993; September 25, 2000.

Director, Committee for Protection and Care of Children, Hanoi, June 17, 1993

Vice-Chairman, People's Committee, Thua Thien Hue Province, August 23, 1994

Director, Department of Labor, War Invalids, and Social Affairs of Thua Thien Hue Province, August 23, 1994

Deputy Director and staff, Department of Labor, War Invalids, and Social Affairs of Phan Thiet, Binh Thuan Province, August 31, 1994

United Nations High Commissioner for Refugees (UNHCR)

HONG KONG

Deputy Head of Mission and staff, December 18, 1991

Assistant Field Officer, Chi Ma Wan Detention Centre, December 19, 1991

Head of Mission and staff, June 7, 1993

Deputy Head of Mission and staff, August 10, 1994

THAILAND

Deputy Head of Mission and staff, Bangkok, December 28, 1991

Durable Solutions Officer, Sikhiu Camp, December 30, 1991

Screening Officer, Sikhiu Camp, December 30, 1991

Field Officer, Phanat Nikhom Camp, January 4, 1992

SINGAPORE

Representative, January 8, 1992

MALAYSIA

Deputy Head of Mission, Kuala Lumpur, January 6, 1992

Associate Field Officer, Sungei Besi Camp, January 7, 1992

INDONESIA

Durable Solutions Officer for Galang Camp, Tanjung Pinang, January 9, 1992

The Philippines

Field Officer, Philippine First Asylum Camp, Palawan, December 24, 1991

Assistant Field Officer, Philippine First Asylum Camp, Palawan, December 24, 26, 1991

VIETNAM

Representative in Vietnam, Hanoi, December 7, 1991; June 18, 1993

Head of Working Group and staff, Ho Chi Minh City, July 6, 1993

United States Consulate General, Hong Kong
  Refugee Officer, December 18, 1991; June 7, 1993
  Chief of Immigration, November 30, 1995

Unaccompanied Minors and Other Children in Camps

Phanat Nikhom Camp, Thailand, October 20, 1987; October 20, 1988;
  October 25, 1989; January 4, 1992
Ban Thad Camp, Site 2, Thailand, October 13, 1988
Section 5 Camp, Site 2, Thailand, October 13, 1988
Platform Camp, Site 2, Thailand, October 13, 1988
Pulau Bidong Camp, Malaysia, October 27–29, 1989
Sungei Besi Camp, Malaysia, November 1, 1989; January 7, 1992
Palawan First Asylum Camp, the Philippines, November 6–10, 1990;
  December 22–29, 1991
Shek Kong Detention Center, Hong Kong, December 16, 20, 1991
Pillar Point Transit Camp, Hong Kong, December 17, 1991
Whitehead Detention Center, Hong Kong, December 17, 1991; June 8, 1993
Chi Ma Wan Detention Center, Hong Kong, December 19, 1991
Sikhiu Camp, Thailand, December 30, 1991
Section 19 Camp, Site 2, Thailand, January 1, 1992
Galang Camp, Indonesia, January 10, 1992
Hawkins Road Camp, Singapore, January 12, 1992
Tai A Chau Detention Center, Hong Kong, June 12, 1993
High Island Detention Center, Hong Kong, August 12, 1994
Viet Village, Palawan, the Philippines, December 1–4, 1996; June 1–3, 1998

Unaccompanied Minors in Vietnam

Hanoi, December 9, 1991
Haiphong, June 19, 1993; August 19, 1994
Thua Thien Hue, June 25, 1993; August 24, 1994; March 22–23, 1999;
  September 16–19, 2000
Ho Chi Minh City, July 3, 1993; August 30, 1994
Kien Giang Province, July 7, 1993
Binh Thuan Province, August 31, 1994; December 17, 1995

Unaccompanied Minors or Aged-Out Minors in the United States

San Jose, California, January 24, 1993; June 6, 1995; June 9, 1995;
  June 20, 1997; October 21, 1999; April 8, 2002

Adult Refugees in the United States
Milpitas, California: Mrs. Hue, May 15, 1992
San Jose, California: The Major, October 16, 1994 (previously interviewed in Palawan
First Asylum Camp, the Philippines, December 26, 1991)

ESTABLISHING AND MONITORING THE PROJECT OF AID
TO CHILDREN WITHOUT PARENTS IN THUA THIEN HUE, VIETNAM
June 6–July 9, 1993
August 7–September 4, 1994
March 25–April 3, 1995
November 27–December 24, 1995
November 30–December 24, 1996
June 4–July 10, 1998
March 13–April 3, 1999
September 10–28, 2000

INDEX

Included in this index are the names of some public figures who were directly involved in the care and protection of unaccompanied minors. All other commentators and critics are mentioned in the notes and references.